Climate change, environmental impact and the limited natural resources urge scientific research and novel technical solutions. The monograph series Green Energy and Technology serves as a publishing platform for scientific and technological approaches to "green"—i.e. environmentally friendly and sustainable—technologies. While a focus lies on energy and power supply, it also covers "green" solutions in industrial engineering and engineering design. Green Energy and Technology addresses researchers, advanced students, technical consultants as well as decision makers in industries and politics. Hence, the level of presentation spans from instructional to highly technical.

Indexed in Scopus.

More information about this series at http://www.springer.com/series/8059

Pablo del Río · Christoph P. Kiefer ·
Javier Carrillo-Hermosilla ·
Totti Könnölä

The Circular Economy

Economic, Managerial and Policy Implications

Springer

Pablo del Río
Institute of Public Goods and Policies
Consejo Superior de Investigaciones
Científicas
Madrid, Spain

Javier Carrillo-Hermosilla
Department of Economics and Business
Management
University of Alcalá
Madrid, Spain

Christoph P. Kiefer
Fraunhofer Institute for Systems
and Innovation Research
Karlsruhe, Germany

Totti Könnölä
Insight Foresight Institute
Madrid, Spain

ISSN 1865-3529 ISSN 1865-3537 (electronic)
Green Energy and Technology
ISBN 978-3-030-74794-7 ISBN 978-3-030-74792-3 (eBook)
https://doi.org/10.1007/978-3-030-74792-3

This Springer imprint is published by the registered company Springer Nature Switzerland AG
The registered company address is: Gewerbestrasse 11, 6330 Cham, Switzerland

Foreword

It is a pleasure and an honour to write the foreword for *The Circular Economy: Economic, Managerial and Policy Implications*. The community of sustainability researchers has been waiting a long time for book like this one. Perhaps the reason it took so long to produce one was because writing it demanded a team of authors capable of covering the broad landscape of the circular economy. We got that team with this book.

Over the last two decades, I have been fortunate to know, and professionally work with, three-fourths of the writing team. I first met Pablo del Rio at an International Society of Ecological Economics Conference in Santiago, Chile, after which we began a periodic, but long-lasting professional association. Shortly after meeting Pablo, I met Javier Carrillo and Totti Könnölä in 2000 when I took a faculty position at IE Business School in Madrid, Spain. Over the years, I have done research and published with all three of these authors and I continue to follow their research closely. While they reliably produce insightful and opportune works, this book is especially suited to our times.

The Circular Economy: Economic, Managerial and Policy Implications is coming out at the right moment to fill a void in the available literature about the circular economy. Unlike existing circular economy texts, this book provides a scholarly "big picture" overview of the circular economy while also convincingly situating a circular economy within the wider space of sustainable development and related fields. As such, *The Circular Economy: Economic, Managerial and Policy Implications* can serve as a valuable introduction for scholars seeking to orient themselves in the wider world of circular economy, while also encouraging other sustainability experts in other subfields to discover the intersections of their discipline with the circular economy.

As I noted, the team of researchers that has been assembled to write this book is uniquely suited to tackle the complexities of the issue. The circular economy is an expansive topic. It has important linkages to established academic concepts like sustainable development, industrial ecology, economic transformation and technological innovation. It also has important practical implications for the professional worlds of both corporate management and public policy.

Tackling this breadth and complexity is most likely beyond the ken of any single researcher alone. That is why this research team is so effective. The authors hail from public research institutions like the Spanish National Research Council (CSIC, Spain), but also from academia like the University of Alcala and even the world of consulting like the Insight Foresight Institute. Integrating across these sectors and disciplines is important for any book trying to comprehensively cover the circular economy.

As I read *The Circular Economy: Economic, Managerial and Policy Implications*, I realized it was leaving nothing out. The book initially positioned circular economy within the broader landscape of sustainability research, drawing connections to the broadest fields of sustainable development down to niche subfields like regenerative design and the product–service economy. The book also makes persuasive the importance of innovation. It connects to the authors' previous work in the area of eco-innovation, illustrating the need for creativity in both technological and organizational design. It becomes clear to readers that the circular economy is truly a junction, or as the authors put it a crossroads, for many sustainability concepts.

I immediately recognized this book would make an excellent university textbook for courses teaching sustainability and the circular economy. It provides a comprehensive introduction to the aspects of circular economy and clarifies existing definitions and taxonomies used in circular economy work. For undergraduate and graduate students, this book is a concise way to understand both the strengths and weaknesses of the circular economy as an academic concept and it is practical application in the worlds of business and government.

For those interested in seeing circular economy applications in the real world, the book provides a useful guide to understanding the drivers and barriers to broader adoption. The use of contemporary case studies to both explore and illustrate these drivers and barriers is especially effective. Again the multisectoral nature of this writing team brings a valuable plurality of perspectives on these cases. For many readers, the exposition of the case studies alone, and their subsequent analysis, would make this book valuable. However, it goes on to provide a comprehensive overview of both the managerial implications of circular economy for corporations and the policy implications for the public sector.

I wish I would have had access to a book like this when I first began exploring circular economy ideas back in the late 1990s. If I had *The Circular Economy: Economic, Managerial and Policy Implications* , I would have wasted much less time and gone down far fewer dead ends. For students and scholars of sustainable development and those interested in the circular economy, you have picked up the right book.

Dr. Gregory C. Unruh
Guest Sustainability Editor
MIT Sloan Management Review
Arison Group Endowed Professor
George Mason University
Fairfax, USA

Contents

Chapter 1
Introduction

More than a decade ago, three of us joined forces to write a book on the role of innovation in environmental protection. The title of that book "Eco-Innovation: When Sustainability and Competitiveness Shake Hands" [2] captured our conviction to explore win-win solutions for a wider impact. Continuing our journey with this new book, we realize that the world has changed quite a bit in a decade. Today, we find that the environment and innovation are both pertinent centrepieces of the highest policy and business agendas. Among all efforts to link competitiveness and sustainability, the concept of circular economy (CE) is probably the one with the highest momentum.

The CE draws a desirable future end state of an economic system that is fully circular and sustainable. Circular means that all resources, components and products do not leave production and consumption processes as waste but are maintained as valuable inputs in subsequent processes, thus retaining value by "circulating" continuously through the economy and mitigating the environmental impacts of production and consumption activities. Input and output restrictions within both ends of production and consumption systems guide materials to be continuously reused and re-circled with positive economic value [1]. With this rhetoric of redesigning the economy, rather than downplaying it, the concept has attracted the interest of decision-makers from both business and policy.

The CE has emerged with strength in the last decade to tackle not only environmental degradation but also increasing pressures on resource availability and prices [7]. The policy relevance of the concept is indisputable. Many national and supranational policy bodies have taken up on the fundamentals of CE in their industrial and environmental strategies and policies. It is an attractive concept for policy-makers, as it promises to contribute to environmental sustainability, but also brings about economic and social benefits. Hence, it is not surprising that many policy-makers are committed to it. In 2015, the European Commission finalized the European Circular Economy Action Plan [COM [4] 614 final], which is an extensive plan for transitioning to a CE in Europe. Recently, the European Commission has adopted a new Circular Economy Action Plan, which includes

P. del Río et al., *The Circular Economy*, Green Energy and Technology,
https://doi.org/10.1007/978-3-030-74792-3_1

legislative and non-legislative measures to promote circular initiatives along the entire life cycle of products (see [5]). The same momentum is also visible at the national level across the globe. China, for instance, has been a pioneer in this regard, adopting a Circular Economy Plan already in 2008. Similarly, many other countries have elaborated or are elaborating such plans, such as Germany, Spain, Italy and the UK.

While the CE is the subject of an increasing list of publications, in-depth analyses of the concept at the micro-level (the firm) and an updated literature review of the CE at this level are missing. This book tries to cover this gap. Special attention is given to actors at the micro-level (firms and other organizations). We assess also the drivers and barriers for circular practices of firms and their implications for business leaders and public policy-makers. Furthermore, we propose a policy framework with instruments that encourage the uptake of CE practices. Therefore, this book aims to provide an in-depth perspective of the micro-level of the CE, contextualizing it in the broader discussions on sustainability and other CE levels (macro and meso) and providing insight on the CE practices that can be developed and adopted by firms as well as the drivers and barriers to those practices.

Based on our background, as a result of working decades on the topic, and a thorough review of the state of the art, the book takes a look at the CE from a fresh angle. Besides having a focus on theory, the chapters are designed for policy-makers and business leaders that wish to apply the CE practices and contribute to societal transitions towards ecological, social and economic sustainability. The approach is based on concepts from different disciplinary traditions in economics and management, which are integrated for the analysis of the CE. Consequently, this is not only a "management" book, although it provides insights for managers since it focuses on the drivers for and barriers to the development and adoption of CE practices at the micro-level and identifies appropriate policies (both at the firm and government levels) to encourage them.

With this purpose, the book provides multiple perspectives on the CE. First, it addresses both the economic and environmental benefits of the CE. This can be understood as a direct answer to society's call for sustainability, apart from the academic imperative to consider all aspects of a phenomenon under study. Second, it theoretically roots CE in sustainable development, industrial ecology, eco-innovation and the product–service economy, among others, and addresses the interconnection of those other concepts and approaches to the CE, widening the existing scope in previous books. However, despite being comprehensive, this book is focused on the micro-level and on how firms can contribute to the CE through new products, services, processes or business models (i.e. eco-innovations), and what competitive advantage and other benefits they can generate therewith.

At a micro-level, the CE focuses on individual actors, particularly companies [9, 10]. Examples include: eco-design and cleaner production strategies; resource efficiency initiatives; labelling systems; and sustainable production and consumption methods [3]. At this level, companies focus on improving their processes and developing eco-innovations [8].

The micro-level is the level that has received less attention in studies of the CE. de Jesus et al. [3] argue that it represents the smallest corpus in the CE literature. Similarly, Lieder and Rashid [6] observe that the literature on micro-level contributions to sustainability and the CE is extremely thin and that most analyses on the CE have addressed issues of resource use and environmental impacts, neglecting the economic aspects pertinent to business actors. Also in this context, we offer novel contributions with the explicit focus on the assessment of the drivers for and barriers to the CE at the micro-level, and their managerial and public policy implications. In other words, this bottom-up analysis could contribute to a better design of the top-down policies for the transition to the CE, facilitating a mutual fit between both the micro- and the macro-levels of decision-making.

This book has three thematic parts, which are interrelated in a sequential manner. The first part of the book provides a broad view of the topic, contextualizing it in the wider discussion on sustainability and other concepts and approaches. It assumes that the CE is a construct of several components and it is instrumental in facilitating a transition towards sustainability. Thus, the first part of the book relates the CE concept to other concepts (e.g. sustainable development and eco-innovation) and provides an analysis of the CE in the broader context of sustainability transitions (Chap. 2). It digs deeper into the CE concept, providing a review of definitions, taxonomies and classifications (Chap. 3).

The aforementioned discussion is instrumental for the second part of the book, which focuses exclusively on the micro-level of the CE. Chapter 4 explains how the CE is made operative at this level, i.e. what CE practices exist at this level. The drivers and barriers to those practices are theoretically discussed in Chap. 5. The ten case studies in Chap. 6 illustrate the CE practices that can be developed or adopted by firms as well as the drivers and barriers to those practices.

The third part of the book focuses on the managerial and public policy implications of the analysis performed in the second part. Therefore, Chap. 7 discusses the measures company managers and governments can take to move towards the CE by either activating the drivers or mitigating the barriers to the CE at the micro-level. Chapter 8 concludes the book.

References

1. Andersen MS (2007) An introductory note on the environmental economics of the circular economy. Sustain Sci 2:133–140. https://doi.org/10.1007/s11625-006-0013-6
2. Carrillo-Hermosilla J, del Río P, Könnölä T (2009) Eco-innovation: when sustainability and competitiveness shake hands. Palgrave Macmillan, Hampshire
3. de Jesus A, Antunes P, Santos R, Mendonça S (2018) Eco-innovation in the transition to a circular economy: an analytical literature review. J Clean Prod 172:2999–3018. https://doi.org/10.1016/j.jclepro.2017.11.111
4. European Commission (2015) Closing the loop—an EU action plan for the circular economy. Retrieved from Brussels: https://ec.europa.eu/environment/circular-economy/index_en.htm

5. European Commission (2020) A new circular economy plan for a cleaner and more competitive Europe. Retrieved from Brussels, Belgium: https://eur-lex.europa.eu/legal-content/EN/TXT/?qid=1583933814386&uri=COM:2020:98:FIN
6. Lieder M, Rashid A (2016) Towards circular economy implementation: a comprehensive review in context of manufacturing industry. J Clean Prod 115:36–51. https://doi.org/10.1016/j.jclepro.2015.12.042
7. Milios L (2017) Advancing to a circular economy: three essential ingredients for a comprehensive policy mix. Sustain Sci. https://doi.org/10.1007/s11625-017-0502-9
8. Prieto-Sandoval V, Jaca C, Ormazabal M (2018) Towards a consensus on the circular economy. J Clean Prod 179:605–615. https://doi.org/10.1016/j.jclepro.2017.12.224
9. Yuan Z, Bi J, Moriguichi Y (2006) The circular economy: a new development strategy in China. J Ind Ecol 10:4–8
10. Zhu Q, Geng Y, Lai KH (2010) Circular economy practices among Chinese manufacturers varying in environmental-oriented supply chain cooperation and the performance implications. J Environ Manage 91(6):1324–1331. https://doi.org/10.1016/j.jenvman.2010.02.013

Chapter 2
At the Crossroad: The Circular Economy Within the Broader Picture

Although the CE has emerged as an important concept in current debates about sustainability and also in policy-making at the public sector and company levels, it has certainly not emerged from scrap. On the contrary, it builds on several previous approaches and, in turn, overlaps, contributes and interacts with them.[1]

The aim of this chapter is to discuss the antecedents to the CE and its interrelationships with other approaches. This will allow us to contextualize the concept of CE, understand its different definitions (Chap. 3) and go deeper into what it means and how it is made operative, particularly at the micro-level (Chap. 4).

2.1 Sustainable Development

Sustainable development (SD) is a widespread concept used both in academia and policy-making worldwide. It has become a main goal all around the world. It draws an ideal end state of the world with an appropriate balance between the economic, social and environmental dimensions.

At an academic level, many definitions of the concept have been proposed from different disciplines. However, the concept of SD has also been criticized as vague, too general and even useless. Naudé [104, p. 52] argues that SD is "a theoretical dream" and not an "implementable reality". Engelman [42, p. 3] argues that "we live today in an age of 'sustain bubble', a cacophonous profusion of uses of the word 'sustainable' to mean anything from environmentally better to cool".

Despite the many definitions of SD, the most commonly cited is the one from the World Commission on Environment and Development [18], also known as

[1]This is also believed to be the case by other authors. For example, Franco ([48], p. 834) argues that the origins of the CE can be traced back to environmental economics, general systems theory, industrial ecology, as well as to models of regenerative design, performance economy, cradle-to-cradle design, biomimicry and the blue economy.

P. del Río et al., *The Circular Economy*, Green Energy and Technology,
https://doi.org/10.1007/978-3-030-74792-3_2

Brundtland report, as "development that meets the needs of the present without compromising the ability of future generations to meet their own needs". However, this is a general, but not an operative definition which, based on it, could allow us to say whether a given country or region is in a transition process towards sustainability or the extent to which a given development path is "sustainable".

It is a widely shared view that sustainability is made up of three dimensions: economic, social and environmental. In fact, Geissdoerfer et al. [52, p. 766] define it as the "balanced integration of economic performance, social inclusiveness and environmental resilience, to the benefit of current and future generations". It can be argued that the social and economic dimensions are conditioned by the environment that provides the basic means for life.

A sustainability transition, understood as a process which leads to improvements in those three dimensions, has been deemed desirable [79]. Scholars have recently and increasingly devoted research efforts to sustainability transitions from different perspectives and based on different theoretical frameworks [59]. They share the common diagnosis that such a transition is a highly complex issue due to the need for (systemic) change at different levels, lock-in conditions and triple externality problems [93, 139].[2]

Sustainability is more than reaching an ideal end goal. It is also the process to get there what matters. In this context, it is useful to make a first distinction between *substantive* and *procedural sustainability* as conceptual frameworks to assess sustainable development at different levels (macro, meso or micro) [32]. However, it should be taken into account that the procedural and the substantive approaches are not isolated from each other and are related to some extent.

Procedural sustainability views sustainability as a participatory approach which considers the views and interests of all stakeholders [120]. This calls for a wide social participation process in the implementation of SD [32]. Thus, the analysis of the sustainability of a given activity or project should focus not only on their objective impact but, also, on how this impact is perceived by the population, how the benefits are distributed among the different actors and how this perception and distribution affect the acceptance of the project and, thus, its feasibility [32, pp. 1329–1334].

Substantive sustainability refers to the dimensions that make it up as well as how these dimensions are measured. In this context, three complementary and traditional sustainability approaches can be identified: the triangular approach, the sustainability as capital approach and the material balance approach.[3]

---

[2]Three main market failures to clean technologies in the form of externalities have been considered in the literature: an environmental externality, an innovation externality (spillover effects in innovation) and a diffusion externality (which refers to initial investors not capturing the benefits of learning investments) [33].

[3]For in-depth details of these approaches, see, respectively, Munasinghe and Shearer [102] and Neumayer [105] (constant-capital approach), Turner [134] (triangular approach) and Hinterberger et al. [64] (materials balance approach).

(1) *The triangular approach.* The triangular approach takes into account the three dimensions of SD (economic, social and environmental) and tries to assess the sustainability of a given development proposal according to them. Therefore, a sustainable policy must tackle the three dimensions of sustainability (measured with dimension-specific indicators), with the aim to increase the standard of living of the citizens [101, 102, 123]:

- *Environmental.* This dimension refers to the reduction of local pollution and the exploitation of the natural resources in the territory and the maintenance of the resilience (ability to adapt to change), integrity and stability of the ecosystem.
- *Economic.* This dimension refers to the increase of per capita income and improvements in the standard of living of the population.
- *Social.* This dimension includes the achievement of peace and social cohesion, stability, social participation, inclusion, respect for cultural identity and institutional development. Increasing the quantity and quality of jobs (more permanent and "high-quality" jobs), higher levels of regional cohesion and lower poverty levels would improve the social dimension of sustainability.

A main issue is how different dimensions conflict against each other. SD implies that the objectives of these three dimensions should be maximized at the same time; i.e. the issue is not to maximize a particular dimension, but all of them combined, taking into account the possible *trade-offs* between them. Thus, those trade-offs need to be identified and balanced.

(2) *The constant-capital approach.* It is defined in terms of "allowing future generations to have the same opportunities as we have had" [123, p. 3], and thus it is also called the "sustainability as opportunity" approach. Following Atkinson [3], the essence of sustainability is the recognition of the effects of the current production and consumption activities on future generations. This approach aims to address the problem of costs transferred across generations, and the necessary condition to sustainability is to compensate those costs so that future generations can have a level of potential per capita welfare which is at least the one we enjoy today.

A relevant definition of SD based on this approach is the one by Neumayer [105, p. 9] for whom "development is sustainable if it does not reduce the capacity to provide non-decreasing per capita utility (welfare) over time". Thus, what needs to be maintained for sustainability is the capacity to provide welfare. This capacity is identified with the maintenance of the stocks of capital over time (constant-capital rule). Capital is defined as the stock which can generate the current and future flows of services and goods. Thus, SD is defined as the maximum development which can be achieved without exhausting the capital assets of a country (or other territorial unit) which are their resource base [134, p. 3].

In principle, there are several types of capital:

- *Manufactured capital*. This refers to the definition of capital in the financial and economic accounts, e.g. machines, buildings and roads.
- *Human capital*. This is defined by the OECD Centre for Educational Research and Innovation [109, p. 9] as the knowledge, technical skills, competences and other attributes embedded in individuals which are relevant for economic activities. Turner [134], Serageldin [123] and Pearce et al. [111] argue that human capital is the set of knowledge and skills incorporated in the human brain. Investments in education and health, for example, contribute to higher levels of human capital stocks.
- *Natural capital*. These are natural assets which lead to the flow of ecological goods and services with an economic value over time. The environment provides natural resources to the economy, it absorbs pollutants and directly provides environmental services.
- *Cultural and social capital*. Cultural capital would refer to the cultural assets embedded in individuals, whereas social capital would be defined in terms of networks, norms and trust and the way in which all these elements allow individuals and institutions to be more effective in the achievement of common goals [122].

The maintenance of capital assets over time may allow future generations to generate the same level of welfare as the current generation. However, there is substantial disagreement among different schools of thought on the types of the stocks of capital that need to be maintained over time in order to ensure sustainability. There are four versions of sustainability as constant capital, depending on the degree of substitutability between different types of capital and, thus, on what needs to be maintained, i.e. whether it is total capital which needs to be maintained, or also any of its components, and particularly natural capital: very weak sustainability, weak sustainability, strong sustainability and very strong sustainability (see Turner [134] for an in-depth discussion). According to the very weak sustainability rule, it is total capital which needs to be maintained [126]. The weak sustainability rule, proposed by the so-called London school (David Pearce, Kerry Turner and Anil Markandya, among others), takes into account that the substitutability among the different components of capital is not perfect. Thus, the maintenance of a minimum physical level of natural capital (the so-called critical natural capital) is justified [105, 134]. On the other hand, many authors and several approaches could be included under the strong sustainability rule (see [26]). They share the idea that sustainability requires the maintenance of the value of the total capital stock as well as natural capital over time (i.e., not only critical natural capital). Finally, the very strong sustainability approach argues that not only a given level of overall natural capital has to be maintained over time, but also each of the components of natural capital separately [134].

(3) *The materials balance approach*. Some authors have stressed that it is not the degree of saving and investment in an economy which determines its degree of sustainability but, rather, the material inputs of the economic activity [64].

> The materials balance approach has its roots in the work of Ayres and Kneese [7], which led to the analysis of industrial metabolism, e.g. the physical volume of matter and energy which flows through the economy. For this approach, an economic system is environmentally sustainable if it is physically in a stationary state. There are several approaches which use these general ideas, including the analysis of industrial metabolism in the context of industrial ecology (see Sect. 2.3) and the material input per unit of service (MIPS) approach [64].

In the international diplomacy, there have been some ambitious initiatives to implement SD globally. First, in 1992, the United Nations Conference on Environment and Development (UNCED, also known as the "Rio Earth Summit") adopted Agenda 21, a programme of action for sustainable development [68]. Second, the UN Millennium Summit in 2000 adopted the Millennium Declaration, which developed into the Millennium Development Goals (MDGs). The MDGs have become commonly accepted as a framework for measuring progress in development. Third, in 2002, the World Summit on Sustainable Development in Johannesburg adopted two main documents: the Johannesburg Plan of Implementation and the Johannesburg Declaration on Sustainable Development [68].

In 2015, all the United Nations Member States adopted the 17 Sustainable Development Goals (SDGs), which comprise a global agenda to end poverty, protect the planet and ensure all people enjoy peace and prosperity [70]. The SDGs include 169 targets that countries should reach by 2030. Unlike previous development goals, which were rather guidelines, all countries agreed to attempt to achieve the SDGs domestically and to use them to guide their bilateral and multilateral interactions with other countries [69].

The SDGs are organized in 17 categories: 1. No Poverty; 2. Zero Hunger; 3. Good Health and Well-Being; 4. Quality Education; 5. Gender Equality; 6. Clean Water and Sanitation; 7. Affordable and Clean Energy; 8. Decent Work and Economic Growth; 9. Industry, Innovation and Infrastructure; 10. Reduced Inequalities; 11. Sustainable Cities & Communities; 12. Responsible Consumption & Production; 13. Climate Action; 14. Life Below Water; 15. Life on Land; 16. Peace and Justice Strong Institutions; and 17. Partnerships for the Goals. Box 2.1 provides a brief description of those goals.

Box 2.1. The 17 SDGs

Goal 1: End poverty in all its forms everywhere.
Goal 2: End hunger, achieve food security and improved nutrition, and promote sustainable agriculture.
Goal 3: Ensure healthy lives and promote well-being for all at all ages.
Goal 4: Ensure inclusive and equitable quality education and promote lifelong learning opportunities for all.
Goal 5: Achieve gender equality and empower all women and girls.

Goal 6: Ensure availability and sustainable management of water and sanitation for all.
Goal 7: Ensure access to affordable, reliable, sustainable and modern energy for all.
Goal 8: Promote sustained, inclusive and sustainable economic growth, full and productive employment and decent work for all.
Goal 9: Build resilient infrastructure, promote inclusive and sustainable industrialization, and foster innovation.
Goal 10: Reduce income inequality within and among countries.
Goal 11: Make cities and human settlements inclusive, safe, resilient and sustainable.
Goal 12: Ensure sustainable consumption and production patterns.
Goal 13: Take urgent action to combat climate change and its impacts by regulating emissions and promoting developments in renewable energy.
Goal 14: Conserve and sustainably use the oceans, seas and marine resources for sustainable development.
Goal 15: Protect, restore and promote sustainable use of terrestrial ecosystems, sustainably manage forests, combat desertification, and halt and reverse land degradation and halt biodiversity loss.
Goal 16: Promote peaceful and inclusive societies for sustainable development, provide access to justice for all and build effective, accountable and inclusive institutions at all levels.
Goal 17: Strengthen the means of implementation and revitalize the global partnership for sustainable development.

Source United Nations [135].

A priori, it could be expected that the CE would be directly related to two SDGs (9 and 12), although potentially related to many others (6, 7, 8, 11, 13, 14 and 15). Schroeder et al. [121] analyse the extent to which CE practices are relevant for the implementation of the SDGs. The authors find that the strongest relationships exist between CE practices and the following SDGs: 6, 7, 8, 12 and 15. The paper also explores synergies and potential trade-offs that can be created through CE practices among several of the SDG targets [121, p. 75].

2.2 Eco-innovation

The term eco-innovation has been used in environmental management and policy, in diverse contexts and with different underlying connotations [21]. The definitions of eco-innovation seem to be quite general, and thus, many kinds of innovation can be defined as eco-innovations (see Box 2.2). And, in parallel, many similar concepts coexist, such as green or environmental innovation.

Eco-innovations can be considered as a subset of innovations. The Oslo Manual by the OECD [108, p. 1] defines innovation as "a new or improved product or process (or a combination thereof) that differs significantly from the unit's previous products or processes and that has been made available to potential users (product) or brought into use by the unit (process)" and distinguishes between innovation as an outcome (an innovation) and the activities by which innovations come about (innovation activities). As such, it subsumes product, process, organizational and marketing innovations.

Defining eco-innovation is not trivial, although several attempts have been made in the literature. In general, these definitions emphasize that eco-innovations are innovations which reduce the environmental impact caused by production and consumption activities, whether the main motivation for their development or deployment is environmental or not. As stressed by OECD [106], eco-innovation may be environmentally motivated, but may also occur as a side effect of other goals, such as reducing production costs. Kemp and Foxon [72] call the first category "environmentally motivated innovations", whereas the second is called "environmentally beneficial normal innovations".

The crucial distinctive feature between eco-innovations and other conventional innovations is, therefore, the better environmental performance of the former, which incorporate a reduction of the natural resources used as well as of the harmful substances released [67]. Definitions based on the actual environmental impact of eco-innovations rather than on their environmental protection intentionality have the drawback that it may be difficult to identify whether an innovation reduces the environmental impact of products and production.

However, a definition that focuses on the intention of the innovators also has its cons. As the industry moves on from end-of-pipe solutions to integrated technologies and product innovations, the environmental motivation of the innovation may become entangled with other motivations. It may also be difficult to establish a clear relationship between the dedicated environmental activities of firms and the environmental performance of the industry.

Therefore, it is certainly difficult to verify an environmental motivation or an environmental result, although the former may be more challenging. Of course, there might be technologies which are specifically designed to reduce the environmental impact of production and consumption activities, in addition to technologies that produce environmental gains as an unintended side effect [20].

As stressed in Carrillo-Hermosilla et al. [20] and [21], the concept of eco-innovation draws on an evolutionary perspective (see, e.g., [38]) indicating that innovation arises through a systemic process that refers to the mutual links and dynamic interactions between different actors and factors influencing the innovation process [31]. With this background, innovation relates to a systemic technological and social change process which consists of the invention of an idea for change and its application in practice.

Eco-innovations may contribute to the renovation of the whole innovation system, taking into account social, ecological and economic aspects. The long-term survival of the economic system depends on its ability to create and maintain sustainable economic processes, which do not involve short-term value creation at the expense of long-term wealth (see Sect. 2.1). Eco-innovations play a crucial role in this context.

Box 2.2. Definitions of eco-innovation

"Eco-innovation is any form of innovation aiming at significant and demonstrable progress towards the goal of sustainable development, through reducing impacts on the environment or achieving a more efficient and responsible use of natural resources, including energy" [45].

"Environmental innovation is an innovation that serves to prevent or reduce anthropogenic burdens on the environment, clean up damage already caused or diagnose and monitor environmental problems" [138].

"Eco-innovation is the creation of novel and competitively priced goods, processes, systems, services, and procedures designed to satisfy human needs and provide a better quality of life for all, with a life-cycle minimal use of natural resources (materials including energy, and surface area) per unit output, and a minimal release of toxic substances" [44].

"Eco-innovation is the process of developing new products, processes or services which provide customer and business value but significantly decrease environmental impact" [51].

"[Eco-innovation is] innovation which is able to attract green rents on the market" [2].

"Sustainable innovation as a process where sustainability considerations (environmental, social, financial) are integrated into company systems from idea generation through to research and development (R&D) and commercialisation. This applies to products, services and technologies, as well as new business and organisation models" [23].

"Environmental innovations are new and modified processes, equipment, products, techniques and management systems that avoid or reduce harmful environmental impacts" [9, 71].

"Eco-innovations are innovation processes toward sustainable development". They are "measures of relevant actors (firms, private households), which: (i) develop new ideas, behaviour, products and processes, apply or introduce them, and (ii) contribute to a reduction of environmental burdens or to ecologically specified sustainability targets" [118].

"In a broad sense, environmental innovations can be defined as innovations that consist of new or modified processes, practices, systems and products which benefit the environment and so contribute to environmental sustainability" [110].

"Eco-innovations are all measures of relevant actors (...) which develop new ideas, behaviour, products and processes, apply or introduce them and which contribute to a reduction of environmental burdens or to ecologically specified sustainability targets" [81].
"Eco-innovation is generally the same as other types of innovation but with two important distinctions: (1) Eco-innovation represents innovation that results in a reduction of environmental impact, whether such an effect is intended or not; (2) The scope of eco-innovation may go beyond the conventional organisational boundaries of the innovating organisation and involve broader social arrangements that trigger changes in existing socio-cultural norms and institutional structures" [106, 107].
Eco-innovation is "the production, assimilation or exploitation of a novelty in products, production processes, services or in management and business methods, which aims, throughout its lifecycle, to prevent or substantially reduce environmental risk, pollution and other negative impacts of resource use (including energy)" [46].
Eco-innovation is the "production, assimilation or exploitation of a good, service, production process, organizational structure, or management or business method that is novel to the firm or user and which results, throughout its lifecycle, in a reduction of environmental risk, pollution and the negative impacts of resources use (including energy use) compared with relevant alternatives" [73].
"Eco-innovation is the introduction of any new or significantly improved product (good or service), process, organisational change or marketing solution that reduces the use of natural resources (including materials, energy, water and land) and decreases the release of harmful substances across the whole life-cycle" [39].
Eco-innovation is "... all forms of innovation—technological and non-technological—that creates business opportunities and benefits the environment by preventing or reducing their impact, or by optimising the use of resources" [47].

Source Adapted and updated from Carrillo-Hermosilla et al. [21].

Furthermore, innovation refers to the change in the way a product is manufactured or a service is provided. Therefore, the level of change is deemed a relevant initial dimension to characterize eco-innovation. A main distinction between the radical and incremental changes which are brought about by eco-innovation can be made [20]:

- Incremental changes are gradual and continuous competence-enhancing modifications that preserve existing production systems and sustain the existing networks, creating value-added in the existing system in which innovations are rooted.

- Radical changes also create value added but, in contrast, are competence-destroying, discontinuous changes that seek the replacement of existing components or entire systems and the creation of new networks.

To reach the current and demanding environmental sustainability goals such as mitigating climate change, the economy and society at large should develop and adopt innovations which do not (only) follow an incremental path along existing trajectories, hence the need for radical technological change or even system innovation (e.g. [133]). More systemic changes generally embody higher potential benefits than small modifications [106]. More integrated sustainable manufacturing initiatives which follow higher-level circular practices, such as closed-loop production (see Chaps. 3 and 4), can potentially yield higher environmental improvements in the medium to long term, compared to simple, small and gradual modifications in processes and products.

Fundamentally, just like any innovation, different dimensions of change in the case of eco-innovations can be identified which together explain factors of success or failure. Eco-innovation is most commonly related to technological change in production processes and products. This has been addressed in many engineering-oriented studies and books. Furthermore, eco-innovation can be considered a change in the behaviour of individual users or organizations, which has been addressed in both the management and policy-related literature. Eco-innovation has also been studied as a strategic perspective to renew the business.

In practice, those dimensions are often intertwined. Hence when addressed together, they form a more comprehensive understanding of the analysis of eco-innovation. For instance, in the search of a holistic approach in the management of eco-innovation, in our earlier book [20] we provided a dashboard, a combination of the different aspects of eco-innovation related to design, the product–service business model, the user and governance which we called "dimensions":

- Design dimension: (i) Adding components: development of additional components to improve environmental quality, for example, "end-of-pipe" technologies; (ii) change of subsystems: improvement of a subsystem to reduce negative impacts on the environment, for example, eco-efficient solutions and optimization of subsystems; (iii) change of the system: redesign of systems to make them compatible with ecosystems, for example, eco-effective solutions.
- User dimension: (i) Development: innovation initiated and/or developed by users; (ii) acceptance: changes in the behaviour, practices and processes of users for the application of the innovation.
- Product–service dimension: (i) Changes in the product–service supplied, changes in the product–service provided and changes in the perception of the relationship with the client; (ii) changes in the value chain and relationships and changes in the value chain and relationships that allow the supply of the product–service.

- Governance dimension: Innovation in environmental governance refers to all innovative and applied solutions, at both the institutional and organizational levels, to resolve conflicts related to environmental resources, in both the public and private sectors.

Ultimately, the success of eco-innovations in providing new business opportunities and contributing to a transformation towards a sustainable society depends on the interplay of different dimensions and the engagement of key stakeholders in the innovation process.

2.3 Industrial Ecology

The CE has its more direct origins in industrial ecology (IE), a discipline born in the 1980s with prominent authors including Thomas E. Graedel, Braden Allenby, Robert U. Ayres, John Ehrenfeld, Robert Frosch and Robert Socolow, among others [1, 5, 41, 49, 58].[4] IE has recurrently used the biological analogy and the concept of industrial metabolism to suggest that the economic systems should close material cycles as done by natural ecosystems.

Two approaches in the IE can be distinguished: the analytical and the prescriptive dimensions. The first one aims to analyse the material and energy flows in the industrial system as well as their effects on the environment. It is defined by White [141] as the "study of the flows of materials and energy in industrial and consumer activities, of the effects of these flows on the environment, and of the influences of economic, political, regulatory, and social factors on the flow, use, and transformation of resources".

The prescriptive dimension is particularly relevant for this book, given the emphasis of the CE on "closing cycles", which was initially proposed and analysed by the IE. This dimension aims to identify and suggest the adoption of technological innovations which reduce the environmental impact of production systems, proposing changes in firms and in the relationships between them. The IE proposes changes in production and consumption processes in line with the biological analogy (see also Sect. 2.5.5 below). The philosophy behind IE consists of transferring to economic systems the environmental efficiency shown by natural ecosystems, in which closing of loops in general and recycling in particular is an intrinsic part of the system. As put by Graedel and Allenby [58, p. 9], "the concept requires that an industrial system be viewed not in isolation from its surrounding systems, but in concert with them. It is a systems view in which one seeks to optimize the total materials cycle from virgin material, to finished material, to component, to product, to obsolete product, and to ultimate disposal".

[4]As mentioned by Ghisellini et al. [55, p. 25] "so far the promotion of the concept of CE in China and worldwide seems mainly based on the industrial ecology theoretical framework and pillars".

Therefore, the IE proposes that industrial processes mimic natural ecosystems, which are characterized by the closure of material and energy cycles and for which everything is input for everything else. Material wastes should not reach the environment immediately, but should be reintroduced in the economic system as resources (through reuse and recycling), and residual energy (heat) should be used as much as possible.

Industrial ecologists view the current industrial system as basically "open" in the sense that only a small fraction of production is the result of recycled inputs. Therefore, the economic system, which uses energy and material resources inefficiently, should behave in the same manner as in biological cycles, encouraging the closing of material cycles through technological and other changes. Ayres [6] argues that this closing of cycles is a necessary condition for a sustainable industrial economy and that either material cycles or product cycles could be closed (through refurbishing, remanufacturing, reuse, etc.). In a similar manner, Tibbs [130, p. 7] considered that the global natural ecosystem has certain features which should be imitated by the industry: (1) the absence of wastes as a consequence of the "constructive absorption" of the residues of one part of the system by other part; (2) the efficient flow and transformation of materials and energy; (3) a dynamic system which is regulated by information; and (4) a system which allows the independent activity of each individual, but intertwines the activity patterns of all the species in a cooperative manner. However, some authors are somehow critical of this biological analogy. For example, Ehrenfeld [40, p. 73] argues that "the classical ecosystem analogy omits aspects of human social and cultural life central to sustainability".

The IE envisages a transition from a linear to a circular economy. For example, Richards et al. [119, p. 6] hypothetically considers that industrial ecosystems should evolve from the currently dominant "first type of industrial ecosystems" which are those whose resource flows follow a unidirectional and lineal trajectory to others in which the industrial system recycles its wastes. The aim would be to shift to an industrial ecosystem in which a total closing of the material flows is achieved, with the residues from one process being reused as raw materials in other processes.

Similarly, Ayres [4] argued that industry should change the way in which it deals with materials, energy inputs and wastes, and this change should be based on an understanding of the internal processes of the industrial ecosystem (i.e. the flow of materials). Therefore, he analysed, in the context of the so-called industrial metabolism, the flows of industrial materials which are significant from an environmental point of view as well as the discharge of wastes which are associated with them. His analysis suggested that the economic system should be based on a reduction of raw material extraction and wastes and an important increase of the recycling and reuse of materials.

The aforementioned two dimensions of IE (analytical and prescriptive) are not isolated from each other. The latter is influenced by the former. IE supports the implementation of an industrial sustainability strategy based on the analysis of flows of materials, products, processes and services, which has been very influential in the CE approach:

- Regarding the flows of materials and changes in processes, the aim is to minimize the use of physical resources as raw materials. This would lead to the multiple closing of material cycles in the economy and the use of energy resources in a cascading manner between the different processes (e.g. the residual heat from a process is used as energy input in another process). The reductions of energy and materials at the source and the greater recycling of wastes can be achieved with clean technologies, eco-design (more efficient process design) and the better use of materials.
- Regarding products and services, the IE already proposed that the aim would be to end up with products which have a lower environmental impact throughout the whole product value chain by designing them in a way which extends their life and facilitates recycling, reuse or repair, based on a life cycle analysis. In addition, emphasis was made on the provision of the service to the consumer rather than the provision of the product itself, which leads to a reduction of the quantity of materials being used (the product–service economy; see Sect. 2.4).

IE prescribes the development or adoption by the firm of eco-innovations which reduce the environmental impact. In this context, as mentioned in Sect. 2.2, eco-innovations represent opportunities to recycle wastes, allowing the closing of materials and energy, and leading to a network of firms in which the wastes of one firm are the production input for another (whether materials or energy). The use of one firm (B) of the wastes from another firm (A) would lead to a double environmental saving. It would avoid the disposal of the high-entropy wastes on the environment and the firm which uses those wastes would not have to buy raw materials for its production processes. When the interrelationships are between several firms which are closely located, an eco-industrial park can be created. This is an integrated industrial complex in which the material or energy by-products are used as raw materials in the same industrial complex rather than being discarded.

As argued by Chertow [24] and Lieder and Rashid [86], IE operates at three levels, namely factory level, inter-firm level and regional or global level. "On factory level attention is put on cleaner production through e.g. environmental protection or reduction of waste and emissions. On inter-firm level collaboration and synergies are emphasized that are enabled through geographic proximity, thus leading to industrial symbiosis and developments of eco-industrial parks" [86, p. 44]. The insights from the IE already suggested the need to contextualize the behaviour of the firm, considering it as an actor which is embedded in a network of relationships with other actors from which it receives stimulus for change, including suppliers, customers, public administrations and other firms.

2.4 The Product–Service Economy

Arguably, Stahel [127] was the first to propose the concept of a service society as a way to achieve sustainable development. According to this author, a functional economy "optimises the use (or function) of goods and services and thus, the management of existing wealth (goods, knowledge, and nature). The economic objective of the functional economy is to create the highest possible use-value for the longest possible time while consuming as few material resources and energy as possible" [127], as cited in [100, p. 238]. Later on, Goedkoop et al. [57, p. 18] defined a product–service system (PSS) as "a marketable set of products and services capable of jointly fulfilling a users' need". For Mont [100, p. 239] a PSS was "a system of products, services, supporting networks and infrastructure that is designed to be: competitive, satisfy customer needs and have a lower environmental impact than traditional business models".

The PSS refers to different alternatives to have a functional economy. For example, Williams [142] categorizes different types of deliverables of the PSS:

- Product-oriented services: They include concepts that focus on selling the product as well as supporting services needed during the stage of product use. This includes offering advice and consultancy (for instance, advising on the most efficient use of the product).
- Use-oriented services: They cover the approaches that focus on leasing the product. The provider retains ownership of a product and is responsible for maintenance and repair. In this case, the user pays a regular fee and has unlimited and individual access.
- Product renting or sharing: It refers to the provider retaining ownership of the product and its maintenance and repair. Hence, the user pays a regular fee but does not have unlimited and individual access. In this case, the same product can be used simultaneously by many users.
- Result-oriented services: This is a concept according to which the customer pays per service unit. The customer buys the output of a product only according to the level of use or functional result. The provider and consumer may also agree on an end result without specifying how the result is delivered.

The concept of PSS has received increasing attention in different research fields [15], while only a few studies focus on sustainability as the main topic [84]. Notwithstanding, the potential for PSS to improve environmental performance is often conveyed. According to Tukker [132], use-oriented and result-oriented business models could have the greatest environmental potential. PSSs are often outlined as potential enablers of new business models for the CE [14, 113]. The shift to PSSs and the development of more sustainable business models may provide the bases for a company to better contribute to the CE [103]. Bressanelli et al. [17] provide a summary of the literature findings regarding the relations among the different servitization business models and the CE value drivers, as well as the main drawback of each servitized business model type.[5]

However, it has been stressed in the past that limited knowledge is available on the choices to develop circular PSS solutions [60]. Thus, the field of PSS research is still in need of further development [65]. Following Mont [100], there are three

[5]Servitization refers to the use or the function of a product being sold instead of the product itself.

main uncertainties regarding the applicability and feasibility of PSSs: the readiness of companies to adopt them, the readiness of consumers to accept them and their environmental implications.

With respect to the readiness of companies, Henry et al. [62] questioned whether incumbents can fully embrace the more "radical" business model approaches to the CE, such as PSSs, while start-ups, as new market entrants, could have in contrast a higher capacity to adopt more disruptive circular business models. Shifting to PSS requires modifications in the levels of information exchange between stakeholders, as well as in the nature of relationships between the stakeholders [88, 143], and particularly close collaboration between producers and consumers [89]. With respect to the readiness of consumers, acceptance of the PSS model by customers is challenging, as argued by Vermunt et al. [140], since owning products is still culturally preferred, due to cultural and reputational values [85, 94, 100].

Regarding PSS and their environmental implications, the idea that they are more sustainable than traditional business models remains somewhat controversial. It is acknowledged that PSSs can be innovative and sustainable solutions, but the systems have to be designed with that purpose [63]. PSS may contribute to a CE, but this is not automatically so; it is determined by the chosen PSS business model and strategy applied throughout the entire life cycle [95]. According to Doni et al. [37], there is no clear evidence of the effects of servitization on performance or sustainability, particularly in a circular economy. Kjaer et al. [80] postulate that a PSS is not a guarantee for achieving a CE and that CE strategies do not necessarily lead to decoupling economic growth from resource consumption in absolute terms. Linder and Williander [87] underline the larger risk for manufacturers in business models based on PSS for the CE (compared to other CE alternatives, such as recycling, remanufacturing or reuse). The reason is that, in business models based on PSS for the CE manufacturer, the manufacturer retains ownership of the products even if the service is not successful in the market.

However, despite its environmental potential, the implementation of the PSS business model has not been well studied and understood [8, 117]. There is a need for strategic tools and methodologies that can provide companies with business-wide guidance for the implementation of PSS [98]. Geum and Park [54] or Manzini and Vezzoli [92] investigate how sustainability could be embedded into PSS development, and several methods and tools have been developed to assist companies to develop sustainable PSS business models, such as Matzen and McAloone [96] or Yang et al. [145, 144].

Carrillo-Hermosilla et al. [20] considered two crucial product–service dimensions: firstly, the change in the product–service deliverable and, secondly, the change in the value network processes. The change in the product–service deliverable consists of identifiable changes in the product–service delivered and changes in the perception of the customer relationship. The change in the product–service process consists of changes in the value networks (value chain and other relations) and processes which enable the delivery of the product–service.

Both dimensions deal with the changes in the earning logic of the company and the added value delivered to the customer. The product–service dimensions can play a crucial role in the process of redefining the purpose of product lines or even the corporate mission and of converting existing business practice towards sustainability. Ultimately, the exploration of the product–service dimensions of existing practices may lead to the identification of new customers and business partners. Firms can identify new opportunities by revisiting what they offer to their customers and how well they meet customer needs with what they offer.

The product–service dimensions of eco-innovation also address how the added value to the customer is generated [20]. This calls for a particular consideration of the overall business strategy and logic, including the convergence of supply chains. In doing so, the focus on management and operations moves from short-sighted local optimization to the entire supply chain during the production, consumption, customer service and post-disposal of products. This stresses the relevance of a supply chain and value network perspective in eco-innovation. It can be argued that the search for environmentally superior solutions, and their successful implementation, requires a broader view of innovation that goes beyond internal management systems and the factory gates of any single company. No single company, or government for that matter, can define and implement comprehensive environmental solutions alone. There is an increasing need to have business capabilities to orchestrate interactions between different actors in the value chains and networks.

2.5 Other Concepts and Approaches Related to the Circular Economy

The circular economy is not the only concept proposing circular ideas for economic activities. Many other concepts exist without, thus far, a clear differentiation. While all related concepts agree that circularity specifically stands in contrast to the linear economy based on a "take–make–dispose" sequence, they all have additional aspects that can help develop proactively new solutions and improve the existing practices towards more circular ways.

2.5.1 Regenerative Design

Regenerative design is based on systems theory, and as its name suggests, it focuses on the design stage of solutions. The concept has contributed to the CE, especially by expanding the discussion on not only reducing the environmental impact of economic activities but also developing approaches on how to recover and improve it.

Regenerative design aims at creating resilient and equitable systems that integrate the needs of society with the integrity of nature. The "regenerative" adjective stands for the possibility of renewing and revitalizing used energy and materials [25] and becoming completely waste-free.

The origins of the approach can be related to the history of agriculture. For instance, the term permaculture [50] was originally referred to "permanent agriculture", but was expanded to stand also for "permanent culture", as it was understood that social aspects were integral to a truly sustainable system, in which consumption focuses on services instead of goods. The concept of regenerative design was developed by Lyle, an architect, who aimed at creating a framework for a community that can function with the locally available renewable resources without destroying them, while reducing unnecessary transportation efforts [90].

Designers using systems thinking applied permaculture design principles and community development processes to design human and ecological systems. The development of regenerative design has contributed to and been influenced by other circular approaches mentioned in this chapter. For instance, Lyle (who coined the term) used to work with William McDonough, one of the promoters of the cradle-to-cradle concept (see Sect. 2.5.4).

Designers use the resilient models observed in systems ecology in their design process and recognize that ecosystems are resilient largely because they operate in closed-loop systems. Using this model, the regenerative design seeks feedback at every stage of the design process. Regeneration, in contrast to the emphasis on "doing less harm", carries the positive message of considering the act of building as one that can give back more than it receives, which would lead to the building of social and natural capital over time [25].

2.5.2 The Natural Step

Following the publication of the Brundtland Report in 1987 (see Sect. 2.1), the Swedish scientist Karl-Henrik Robèrt developed the Natural Step Framework, setting out the system conditions for the sustainability of human activities on earth. The framework was refined with about 50 scientists to reach consensus on what was later on labelled "the Framework for Strategic Sustainable Development" (FSSD) (originally the Natural Step Framework) [129]. This was first published in 1991 under the title "From the Big Bang to Sustainable Societies" [43]. The framework has contributed to the CE discussion by clarifying the importance of the design and, especially, the consideration of the materials used. It has also guided the introduction of circular thinking in organizations.

Robèrt's four system conditions are derived from a scientific understanding of universal laws and the aspects of our socio-ecological system, including the laws of gravity, the laws of thermodynamics and a multitude of social studies. There are four system conditions specified for sustainability. According to the Natural Step [129]:

"In the sustainable society, nature is not subject to systematically increasing …

1. … concentrations of substances extracted from the earth's crust.
2. … concentrations of substances produced by society.
3. … degradation by physical means.
   and, in that society,
4. … human needs are met worldwide".

Based on this approach, a non-profit organization ("the Natural Step") was founded in Sweden in 1989. The Natural Step has pioneered a "Backcasting from Principles" approach meant to advance society towards greater sustainability with numerous applications and tools to plan and design sustainable businesses. The approach has been implemented by business and other organizations around the world. Implementing sustainability is done through a four-step process [128]:

- Awareness building and understanding: Organizations are aligned with a common understanding of sustainability.
- Baseline mapping: Organizations assess their material and energy flows and the impact of the organization on society. This step uses the four system conditions.
- Create a vision and strategic plan: A long-term vision of the organization in a sustainable society is created. A strategy is enabled from a point of view of having achieved sustainability and looking backwards. This step uses back-casting and identifies step-by-step solutions to bring the organization from the current condition to a sustainable condition.
- Down to action: Organizations implement actions. Backcasting is used to continually assess decisions to ensure they meet the vision created above.

2.5.3 The Biosphere Rules

The Biosphere Rules were coined by Gregory C. Unruh. They emerged from a research programme established through a 2005 partnership between the renowned eco-designer William McDonough and the Center for Eco-Intelligent Management at the IE Business School. The principles were first published in 2008 [136]. The Biosphere Rules make up a framework for implementing closed-loop production processes. They imitate circular processes in nature but interpreted for—and translated to—industrial production systems. Thus, the rules can provide actionable guidance on how to address circularity in companies and how to design scalable circular systems.

The five principles that constitute the Biosphere Rules are:

- Materials parsimony: Minimize the types of materials used in products with a focus on materials that are life-friendly and economically recyclable.
- Value cycle: Recover and reincarnate materials from end-of-use goods into new value-added products.

- Power autonomy: Maximize the power autonomy of products and processes so that they can function on renewable energy.
- Sustainable product platforms: Leverage value cycles as product platforms for profitable scale, scope and knowledge economies.
- Function over form: Fulfil customers' functional needs in ways that sustain the value cycle.

Implementing the rules in a firm requires commitment and investment. Notwithstanding, the rules were designed in a modular fashion that allows for their stepwise implementation. A firm can take action to assess its inputs and move towards greater materials parsimony without having to implement all the other rules at the same time. Other rules can also be implemented gradually, which eases the disruptions to business [137].

2.5.4 Cradle-to-Cradle (C2C)

C2C is a concept originally developed by McDonough and Braungart [97] and related to the circular economy (CE) school of thought [55]. It can be argued that CE borrows from C2C by differentiating between biological and technical loops [13]. C2C operationalizes the CE with a product design concept rooted in the circulation of "healthy" materials to allow their recycling with lower risks [61].

The fundamental elements of C2C design are based on three principles that drive these systems in nature [97]:

- *Waste equals food*: This means designing materials and products to be used over and over in either technical or biological systems, collecting and recovering their value, and leaving a beneficial legacy for human or ecological health.
- *Use renewable energy*: The quality of energy matters. Energy from renewable sources is paramount to effective design.
- *Celebrate diversity*: Nature is the most inspiring source of ecological design.

Within this concept, the systemic approach to environmental design leads to two alternative design perspectives [16]: (1) closed cycles, which refer to the design of the uptake of the products back to industrial production processes at the end of their useful life to manufacture products of equal or more value, and (2) open cycles, which refer to the design of products that are biodegradable and become nutrients to new cycles within the ecosystem.

According to the first perspective, the product materials, such as minerals or plastics, do not need to be minimized because they are used again and are not thrown to a landfill as waste. The industry can make considerable savings by recovering valuable materials from used products and avoiding environmental sanctions. According to the second perspective, products made of natural, safely biodegradable materials can be returned to nature to feed ecosystems instead of harming them. Thus, at the end of its useful lifetime, the "disposal" of the product can become easy and even valuable [20]. Following McDonough and Braungart [97], these two approaches need to be applied intelligently, taking into consideration the impacts during the whole lifetime and life cycles of products.

C2C has been formalized into what can be considered the first comprehensive product certification standard, beyond many other specialized standards addressing aspects of the CE [61]. This certification programme evaluates products across five categories: material health, material reutilization, renewable energy, water stewardship and social fairness [27].

Although the concept has generally received a positive response since its inception, C2C has also been questioned in the literature. Skene [124] reflected on how the economy of nature is based on an open system, not a closed system (see also Sect. 2.7), Ceschin and Gaziulusoy [22] argued that C2C design is technically not very well justified, Toxopeus et al. [131] discussed the discrepancies between the theory and day-to-day practice of applying C2C, and Bjørn and Hauschild [12] highlighted that many cradle-to-cradle products may not perform well in a life cycle assessment (LCA).

2.5.5 *Biomimicry*

Together with cradle-to-cradle, biomimicry is regarded as an important sustainable design strategy in the implementation of the CE [114]. As explained in Sect. 2.3, the CE has its origins in industrial ecology, which consists of transferring to industrial processes the environmental efficiency shown by natural ecosystems, mimicking their closure of material and energy cycles. The term *biomimicry*, which comes from the Greek *bios* (life) and *mimesis* (imitation), had only been used in the fields of sciences and robotics until the innovation consultant Janine M. Benyus, who was also a writer on natural sciences, popularized it in her book *Biomimicry: Innovation Inspired by Nature* (*2002*). Benyus [10] discussed how nature's solutions to sustain life on earth have been the creative jumping-off points for individuals seeking solutions, developing or simply revitalizing processes or products [28]. Benyus [10] identified a set of ten nature-inspired strategies that should be applied when designing an artefact, named the "Ten Commandments of a Mature Ecosystem":

- Use waste as a resource.
- Diversify and cooperate to fully use the habitat.
- Gather and use energy efficiently.
- Optimize rather than maximize.
- Use materials sparingly.
- Do not foul their nests.
- Do not draw down resources.
- Remain in balance with biosphere.
- Run on information.
- Shop locally.

Janine Benyus, together with Bryony Schwan, founded the Biomimicry Institute in 2006.[6] Its purpose is to naturalize biomimicry in culture by promoting the transfer of ideas, designs and strategies from biology to sustainable human systems design. Their current definition of biomimicry reads as follows [11]:

> "Biomimicry offers an empathetic, interconnected understanding of how life works and ultimately where we fit in. It is a practice that learns from and mimics the strategies used by species alive today. The goal is to create products, processes, and policies—new ways of living—that solve our greatest design challenges sustainably and in solidarity with all life on earth".

They propose three essential elements when translating nature's strategies into design [11]:

- *Emulate*: learning from and then replicating nature's forms, processes and ecosystems to create more regenerative designs.
- *Ethos*: understanding how life works and creating designs that continuously support and generate conditions which are conducive to life.
- *(Re)Connect*: spending time in nature to understand how life works, so that we may have a better ethos to emulate biological strategies in our designs.

2.6 Where Is the CE Positioned at the Crossroads?[7]

The relationship of the CE concept with other concepts and approaches is a complex one. Three types of relationships can be distinguished. On the one hand, the CE has its roots in different approaches (especially the industrial ecology and the performance economy). On the other hand, the CE is deemed instrumental in achieving sustainable development. Finally, a substantial degree of overlap between eco-innovation and the CE exists.

(i) *CE is rooted in other approaches: industrial ecology and the product–service (performance) economy.*

Industrial ecology, which stresses the closing of flows of materials and energy, is at the core of CE. The "value retention" dimension of the CE was implicitly covered in industrial ecology. As mentioned before, industrial ecology stresses that the outputs of the production processes can be an input for other processes, mimicking what occurs in nature. This is also suggested by the biomimicry design strategy.

---

[6]http://biomimicry.org/.

[7]Preliminary ideas in this and the next section were presented in two workshops held in the University of Castilla-La Mancha in 2019 [34, 35]. The authors are grateful to the organizers and participants in these workshops for their useful comments as well as to the University of Castilla-La Mancha for covering the travel expenses of Pablo del Río and Christoph Kiefer to the first workshop.

On the other hand, a key component of the CE is the change from a "buy–sale products" philosophy to a "share, hire and exchange services" one. This directly contributes to the dematerialization of the economy. This product–service economy aspect, which is another element of the CE, represents an option to close the aforementioned cycles.

(ii) *CE is an instrument in the transition to sustainable development.*

Arguably, the criticism on the concept of SD being too vague and general contributed to the emergence of other concepts (such as "green economy", "green growth" and "CE"). They led to an operationalization of some aspects of the SD, but then capture often only a partial picture of the economic, social and environmental dimensions included in the SD. As observed by Kirchherr and Piscicelli [76, p. 2] "while sometimes presented as substitutes, it is noted that many of these terms usually do not cover all aspects of sustainable development; for instance, "green economy" largely, albeit not entirely, neglects the social pillar of sustainable development".

We believe that the CE cannot be and should not be a goal in itself, but be instrumental in achieving the end goal: greater welfare levels for humankind, which includes economic, environmental and social aspects, as captured by the concept of sustainable development (see Sect. 2.1). Therefore, this one is a more encompassing term and, thus, should include circularity practices.

Several authors have attested to this instrumental relationship of the CE towards sustainability. For example, Korhonen et al. [82] highlight that the CE helps realizing all three dimensions of sustainable development by addressing environmental, economic and social aspects. For Horbach and Rammer [66] and Millar et al. [99], the CE approach is a key element in greening the economy and is therefore in the centre of the sustainability policy debate. The definition of CE by Kirchherr et al. [78] captures this instrumental relationship. These authors define it as "an economic system that is based on business models which replace the 'end-of-life' concept with reducing, alternatively reusing, recycling and recovering materials in production/distribution and consumption processes, thus operating at the micro level (…), meso level (…) and macro level (…), with the aim to accomplish sustainable development, which implies creating environmental quality, economic prosperity and social equity, to the benefit of current and future generations" [78, pp. 224–225].

Although other authors also consider the CE as a promising concept for the pursuit of global sustainability [77, 114, 125], the link of CE and sustainable development has been, and still is, the subject of investigation [74]. Indeed, several authors suggest that the relationship between both concepts has not been sufficiently defined and that further research efforts should be devoted to relate them. For example, Millar et al. [99, p. 11] argue that "the conceptual relationship between the two notions remains ambiguous", with inconsistencies on how the CE can serve as a tool for SD. More fundamentally, Millar et al. [99, p. 17] state that there is "an absence of Circular Economy definitions that explicitly address Sustainable

Development which is allowing the concept to develop in a multitude of diverging conceptual directions that do not contemplate Sustainable Development" and that "there is a lack of coherence as to the scientific ability of the Circular Economy to achieve Sustainable Development" [99, p. 17]. Kirchherr et al. [77] note that, although much of the current enthusiasm regarding the CE is fuelled by its alleged benefits for sustainable development, this link is weak. According to these authors, the definitions of the CE show few explicit linkages of the CE concept to sustainable development [78]. Korhonen et al. [83] state that the theoretical connection of the CE and sustainability is not that clear. Similarly, Geissdoerfer et al. [52, p. 758] also argue that the "conceptual relationship between the Circular Economy and sustainability is not clear".

While both concepts share a global perspective on private and public agency for development, they also diverge. The CE aims at closing loops and establishing a fully closed system. Sustainability, on the other hand, has less clear-cut aims and embraces much broader and often context-dependent goals that include being beneficial to the economy, society and the environment in general [52].

Some authors claim that CE is a "precondition" [115] or an "important element" [91] for sustainable development. Yet, there is no agreement on how this is precisely so, as some see the CE as key for the environmental dimension of sustainable development, yet others for the economic dimension [52]. Much less is known about the relationship between the CE and the social dimension of sustainable development [52, 103] (see Sect. 2.7).

(iii) *Relationship with eco-innovation: CE as a subset of all possible eco-innovations.*

It is commonly shared in the literature that the transition to a CE is highly influenced by the composition and innovation intensity of the economy, by the evolution of new green markets and by the environmental and industrial policy settings [19, p. 1]. Ghisellini et al. [55, p. 25] state that "at micro level the transition towards CE implies the adoption of cleaner production and eco-design". As the concept of the CE builds on fundamental changes in products, services and also the general functioning of the economic system, it indeed makes sense to connect it with the innovation literature, specifically with the eco-innovation concept, which is still valid and useful. As observed by Horbach and Rammer [66], CE innovation activities are linked to the concept of eco-innovation.

Indeed, after analysing the most relevant scientific and policy literature on the subject, we reached the conclusion that eco-innovation continues to be a relevant and promising research field, possibly with a greater scope than the CE. In fact, there seems to be an observable tendency towards eco-innovations as a central transition mechanism towards the CE, an innovative approach is in fact needed for each aspect of the CE concept [125]. All strategic EU documents on the CE and other reports on the CE see innovation at the heart of any transition to a CE.

However, even if it is easy to imagine that eco-innovation (EI) and the CE are related, and that achieving the CE without EI is unlikely, their mutual connections have not been the focus of much research, although there are some exceptions. Several authors stress the relevance of EIs as a relevant factor in the transition towards a CE (see [74]). However, the way in which EI is to drive the pro-CE transition has been an insufficiently addressed issue [29], although the relationship between EI and CE has been explicitly addressed by several authors at a theoretical level [29, 30, 53, 125].

As argued in Kiefer et al. [74], some confusion remains on the relationships between CE and EI. For some authors, the CE overlaps with or even includes EI. For example, Smol et al. [125, p. 672] argue that the "planned EU transition to a CE is fostering eco-innovation development at the macro-, meso- and micro-levels. So, it is advisable to look at eco-innovation through the prism of the CE perspective".

For others, the CE is a subcategory of the EI. For example, Ghisetti and Montresor [56] claim that CE practices represent a particular case of environmental innovation, with similar enablers and barriers. Demirel and Danisman [36, p. 1908] argue that "pro-CE eco-innovations (or circular eco-innovations) is a term used to refer to EI that target recirculation of resources in loops of reuse, recycling, and renewal".

We agree more with this second interpretation. For us, and in line with Cainelli et al. [19] and Horbach and Rammer [66], CE innovations (CEIs) are a subset of all the possible innovations which reduce the environmental impact of production and consumption activities with respect to existing processes, products and business models.

Indeed, the CE can be regarded as made up of several eco-innovations. For example, if recycling is one CE practice (i.e. one of the "Rs" in the CE framework, see Chaps. 3 and 4), then innovations on recycling will be needed. Given the broad definition of EI provided above (Sect. 2.2), any CE practice or "R" in the CE framework is really also an eco-innovation. But, in contrast, not all EIs lead to circularity. For example, an end-of pipe (EOP) technology such as the catalytic converters in cars is a non-circular EI.[8] It may be argued that EOP eco-innovations are not compatible with sustainable development in the long term, since systemic changes are required. However, the sustainability transition literature argues that all EIs may be needed across different time frames, although systemic and radical changes are crucial in this context (Kiefer et al. 2019). In short, there may be acute local environmental problems which require that some urgent measures are taken, and EOP may be the only alternative available in the short term to do so. Nevertheless, it should be taken into account that this EOP may lead to a lock-in in less optimal technologies from a sustainability perspective. The CE is about value retention, which leads to environmental benefits. EI is directly about reduction of environmental impacts from consumption and production activities. Therefore, EI is a broader concept than the CE, and EIs can in fact be classified in two groups: non-circular and circular. Obviously, only the latter belong to the CE.

[8]As argued by Horbach and Rammer [66, p. 2] "eco-innovation, however, covers a broader set of activities aiming at reducing the environmental impact of firms, including end-of-pipe technologies to reduce air pollution or noise emissions".

On the other hand, if, compared to EI, the CE misses part of the picture on the innovations which can contribute to sustainable development, then the former is a more useful instrumental concept to steer a transition towards sustainable development. The EI allows establishing more links, and stronger ones, with the different dimensions of sustainability than the CE. In other words, it has a more direct relationship with the dimensions of sustainable development and its motors of change than the CE.

If the CE is a goal, then it is not comprehensive enough. Unlike "sustainable development", it lacks the social dimension and does not fully address the environmental dimension and its economic base is not too strong. If it is considered as an instrument (with respect to the goal of sustainability), then it is also imperfect with respect to other concepts, and particularly EI, since the latter provides more useful points for policy intervention.

We argue that the end goal for (world) society as a whole is to improve its welfare, which is a multilayered concept made up of several dimensions: economic, social and environmental. "Sustainable development" clearly grasps such multidimensional approach, although the concept has often been criticized as "too generic". However, the pre-eminence of this concept in public debates still remains, as observed by the fact that the so-called Sustainable Development Goals (SDGs) remain a crucial end goal at the world level (see Sect. 2.1).

If "sustainable development" is the end goal, then the immediate question is: what do we need in order to achieve it? The literature has an answer to this question: interrelated and simultaneous changes in technologies, institutions, behaviours (both by firms and consumers) and infrastructures.

From a public policy perspective, instruments should be implemented in order to steer those changes. How those instruments link with crucial concepts at this level is a critical issue. And this is where the CE and EI are relevant. We argue that, since CE is included in the broader concept of EI, the latter represents a more relevant point of intervention for policy-making, i.e. in order to steer the economy towards sustainable development. And this is so because EI connects better with at least two of the aforementioned dimensions (economic and environmental) than the CE, which is too focused on the idea of "closing cycles", an idea which nevertheless is already captured by the EI concept.

Regarding the environmental dimension, the link of EI with environmental protection is more direct than in the CE. This link is in the term and definition of EI itself, which includes an explicit connection to environmental protection. EI considers the environmental problem area in a more holistic manner than the CE. Those problems will entail closing cycles in many (maybe even most) cases but, as mentioned above, adopting other measures (e.g. EOP technologies) could be required in other cases to urgently address acute environmental protection issues that need an immediate solution.

Regarding the economic dimension, despite having the term "Economy" in it, "the economy part of the circular economy tends to be overlooked" [146, p. 600] (see also Sect. 2.7). This is in sharp contrast to the EI, which has been nurtured from insights from different economic and managerial disciplines, such as

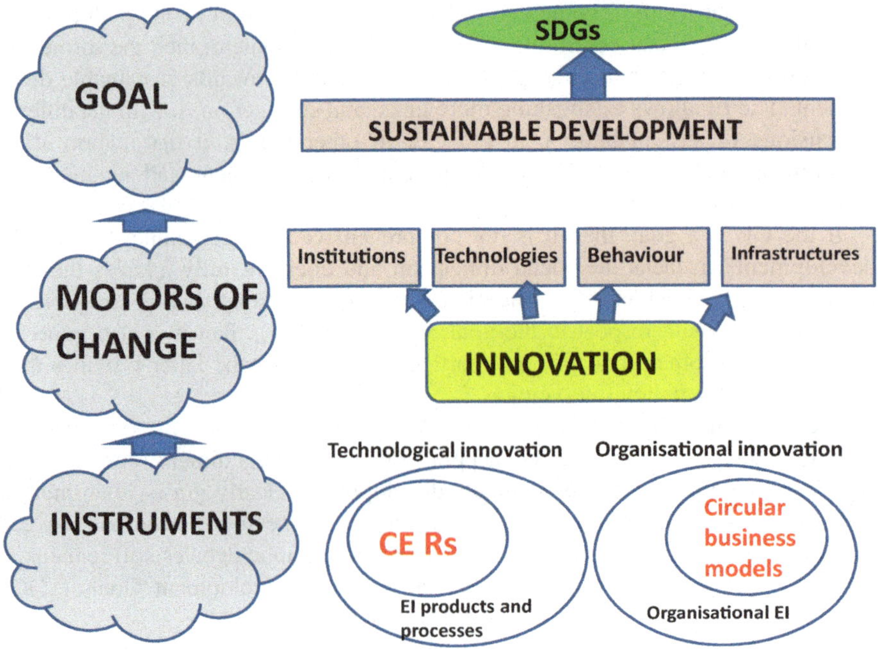

Fig. 2.1 Our view on the relationship between concepts. *Source* Own elaboration

innovation economics, environmental economics, evolutionary economics and the theory of industrial organization.

Finally, the social dimension has not been explicitly and systematically considered neither in the CE nor in the EI concepts, and only generic allusions to the need to address this dimension are mentioned in the respective literatures.

To sum up, in addition to being broader, more comprehensive and holistic, the EI is a more appropriate intermediate approach that the CE to implement policies which aim at a transition to sustainable development in its three dimensions and contribute to the SDGs since the former includes the latter. Figure 2.1 summarizes our view on the relationships between the aforementioned concepts

2.7 Criticisms of the Concept of the Circular Economy

Several authors have praised the CE for several reasons, i.e. for being "simple", "logical", "systemic and interorganizational", "visionary" of a future industrial paradigm, "provocative" or even "noble" since it aims to address economic and environmental challenges. The concept has certainly become very popular among policy-makers, capturing the attention of governments and the business community (see Box 2.3 for examples of literal statements on the positive features of the concept and its contribution).

Box 2.3. Statements on the positive features of the CE and its contribution

"The CE concept is of great interest to both scholars and practitioners because it is viewed as an operationalization for businesses to implement the much-discussed concept of sustainable development" [78, p. 221].

"CE is important for its power to attract both the business community and policy-making community to sustainability work" [82, p. 37].

"It makes common sense, that if you extract a resource from nature and work hard for it to become a product or a service that has an economic value, you use this value many times, not only once. This makes perfect business sense" [82, p. 45].

"As an approach CE has already demonstrated that it has unique power and value in attracting a diversity of sectors and a variety of organizational types to get involved in the work. The logic of turning from linear and wasteful to cyclical, restorative, reproductive and smart physical flow structures is appealing and positively provocative crossing sectoral, organizational, administrative and national boundaries and borders in its message" [83, p. 551].

However, the concept has also received some criticisms. Some of these have focused on its *lack of novelty*, having either been proposed long ago or being a reformulated version of other approaches. Regarding the former, Reike et al. [116, p. 246] argue that "the concept—in its dominant framing—is not as new as frequently claimed" and that "looking at the theoretical underpinnings of CE, these are arguably far from new" [116, p. 247]. Up to our knowledge, the concept appeared 3 decades ago as a chapter in the book by Pearce and Turner [112] on environmental economics. On the other hand, most of the ideas proposed by the CE were already in the approaches mentioned in the previous sections of this chapter and, notably, in industrial ecology and the product–service economy. For example, Ghisellini et al. [55, p. 24] observe that "the CE concept shows to be rooted in very diverse theoretical backgrounds". Korhonen et al. [82, p. 45] argue that "there is quite little that is truly new in the CE concept in terms of sustainability science research" whereas, for Lieder and Rashid [86, p. 37], "the concept of circularity, especially in terms of closed material loops, is not a concept of novelty originating from recent developments, but has been emerging now and then throughout the history".

A more fundamental line of criticism refers to the *robustness of the concept and its scientific content*. Some authors have criticized its vagueness, blurriness and being diffuse in its meaning. For Reike et al. [116, p. 259], "a shared understanding of the concept has yet to be established". "Different author(-groups) assign different attributes and meanings which implies that divergent conceptualizations of this key CE principle dominate the literature" [116, p. 247]. Similarly, Kirchherr et al. [78,

p. 221] note that it means "many different things to different people". It is often argued that the concept is not "scientifically sound" or that its scientific construction is weak. For Korhonen et al. [82], the scientific and research content of the CE concept is superficial, unorganized and largely unexplored and lacks critical analysis. "CE seems to be a collection of vague and separate ideas from several fields and semiscientific concepts" [82, p. 37]. According to Korhonen et al. [83], there have been more contributions to the CE at the level of metrics, indicators and measures than at the level of norms, values, visions of the world and concepts. "The basic assumptions concerning the values, societal structures, cultures, underlying world-views and the paradigmatic potential of CE remain largely unexplored" [83, p. 551]. These authors argue that the CE can be termed an "essentially contested concept". Blomsma and Brennan [13, p. 610] claim that "theoretical or paradigmatic clarity regarding the concept of CE has yet to emerge". For Reike et al. [116, p. 259], "definitions, degrees of circularity, its normative character, the relation to other sustainability concepts—and to sustainability itself as a concept—all of this is still far from being clear".

Apart from this general criticism on the scientific soundness and robustness of the concept, some authors have criticized *specific aspects*. For example, Skene [124], who assessed the thermodynamic and ecological foundations upon which these principles are apparently rooted, questioned the biological basis claimed for the principles underpinning the circular economy. He observes that the natural world operates in a very different way from that portrayed in the circular economy literature, arguing that "the economy of nature is based on an open system, not a closed system, that nature operates using short cycles, not extended lifetimes, that nature is sub-optimal, not optimal and that nature is eco-inefficient, not eco-efficient" [124, p. 479].[9] He concludes that "the circular economy works against both the laws of thermodynamics and the underpinning principles of nature. Given this, it is highly unlikely that this concept will pave the way to a sustainable future" [124, p. 488]. Millar et al. [99, p. 14] argues that "closed material loops are practically and theoretically impossible (…) a completely close-loop system is impossible to be achieved". Korhonen et al. [82] showed that there are severe physical (thermodynamic) and governance and managerial limitations and challenges in the practical application of the concept [82, p. 41].

Finally, some authors have been critical on the *usefulness* of the concept. This would mainly relate to the aforementioned issue of goals and instruments and, in particular, its relationship with sustainable development (see Sect. 2.6 above and Geissdoerfer et al. [52]). Although the CE is regarded to have potential in the light of all the three dimensions of sustainable development (economic, environmental and social) [82, p. 45], it is criticized that the CE puts too much emphasis on one of

[9]For example, the author argues that "the circular economy is based on the idea of a closed loop, where materials and energy cycle through the system, rather than a linear economy, where waste is continually generated, creating problems of waste management and resource depletion. This is thought to reflect how the natural world operates. However, in reality, nature's economy does not operate like this" [124, p. 482].

the dimensions of sustainable development to the neglect of others, suggesting that the contribution of the CE to sustainability would be unbalanced.

Interestingly, whereas some argue that the economic dimension is prioritized, others believe that it is the environmental dimension which is given too much attention. Regarding those who believe that the economic dimension has been prominent, Ghisellini et al. [55, p. 27] argue that "so far, (the) environmental and social dimensions of sustainability have attracted less interest compared to the economic sphere and need the right recognition". Similarly, Kirchherr et al. [78, p. 221] argue that "the main aim of the circular economy is considered to be economic prosperity, followed by environmental quality; its impact on social equity and future generations is barely mentioned". Murray et al. [103, p. 22] also argue that the literature on the CE is silent on the social dimension.

In contrast, other authors believe that the environmental dimension is prominent and that the economic dimension of the CE is overlooked [146]. For example, Lieder and Rashid [86, p. 46] find that "analyses and discussions about CE and towards CE development are to largest extent done from a resource scarcity and environmental impact perspective leaving economic benefits of industrial actors in general and specifically on individual level missing (…)". The research carried out by Geissdoerfer et al. [52, p. 765] also shows that "most authors focus on the environmental performance improvements of the Circular Economy rather than taking a holistic view on all three dimensions of sustainability (…) most authors conceptually simplify the Circular Economy to resource input, waste and emission output (…). This more limited focus comprises a narrow coverage of social well-being by most Circular Economy authors".

References

1. Allenby BR, Richards DJ (1994) Greening of industrial ecosystems. National Academy Press, Washington
2. Andersen MM (2002) Organising interfirm learning. In: de Bruijn T, Tukker A (eds) Partnership and leadership: building alliances for a sustainable future. Kluwer Academic Publishers, Amsterdam, pp 103–119
3. Atkinson G (1996) Desarrollo sustentable: teoría, medición y políticas. Información Comercial Española, ICE: Revista de economía 751:15–26
4. Ayres RU (1989) Industrial metabolism. In: Ausubel JH, Sladovich HE (eds) Technology and environment. National Academy Press, Washington
5. Ayres RU, Ayres LV (1997) Industrial ecology. Towards closing the materials cycle. Edward Elgar Publishing, Cheltenham
6. Ayres RU (1993) Industrial metabolism. In: Jackson T (ed) Clean production strategies. Lewis Publishers, Boca Raton, Florida
7. Ayres RU, Kneese AV (1969) Production, consumption, and externalities. Am Econ Rev 59 (3):282–297
8. Baines TS, Lightfoot HW, Evans S, Neely A, Greenough R, Peppard J, Tiwari A (2007) State-of-the-art in product-service systems. Proc Inst Mech Eng Part B: J Eng Manuf 221:1543–1552. https://doi.org/10.1243/09544054jem858

9. Bartolomeo M, Kemp R, Rennings K, Zwick T (2003) Employment impacts of cleaner production: theory, methodology and results. In: Employment impacts of cleaner production. Springer, Singapore, pp 3–53
10. Benyus J (1997) Biomimicry: innovation inspired by nature. Harper Collins, New York
11. Biomimicry Institute (2020) Biomimicry. Retrieved from https://biomimicry.org/
12. Bjørn A, Hauschild MZ (2013) Absolute versus relative environmental sustainability: what can the cradle-to-cradle and eco-efficiency concepts learn from each other? J Ind Ecol 17 (2):321–332
13. Blomsma F, Brennan G (2017) The emergence of circular economy: a new framing around prolonging resource productivity. J Ind Ecol 21(3):603–614
14. Bocken NM, De Pauw I, Bakker C, Van Der Grinten B (2016) Product design and business model strategies for a circular economy. J Ind Prod Eng 33(5):308–320
15. Boehm M, Thomas O (2013) Looking beyond the rim of one's teacup: a multidisciplinary literature review of product-service systems in information systems, business management, and engineering & design. J Clean Prod 51:245–260
16. Braungart M, McDonough W, Bollinger A (2007) Cradle-to-cradle design: creating healthy emissions—a strategy for eco-effective product and system design. J Clean Prod 15:1337–1348. https://doi.org/10.1016/j.jclepro.2006.08.003
17. Bressanelli G, Adrodegari F, Perona M, Saccani N (2018) Exploring how usage-focused business models enable circular economy through digital technologies. Sustainability 10 (3):639
18. Brundtland GH (1987) Report of the World Commission on environment and development: Our common future. Retrieved from New York: https://sustainabledevelopment.un.org/content/documents/5987our-common-future.pdf
19. Cainelli G, D'Amato A, Mazzanti M (2020) Resource efficient eco-innovations for a circular economy: evidence from EU firms. Res Policy 49(1):1–11. https://doi.org/10.1016/j.respol.2019.103827
20. Carrillo-Hermosilla J, del Río P, Könnölä T (2009) Eco-innovation: when sustainability and competitiveness shake hands. Palgrave Macmillan, Hampshire
21. Carrillo-Hermosilla J, Del Río P, Könnölä T (2010) Diversity of eco-innovations: reflections from selected case studies. J Clean Prod 18:1073–1083. https://doi.org/10.1016/j.jclepro.2010.02.014
22. Ceschin F, Gaziulusoy I (2016) Evolution of design for sustainability: from product design to design for system innovations and transitions. Des Stud 47:118–163
23. Charter M, Clark T (2007) Sustainable innovation: key conclusions from sustainable innovation conferences 2003–2006 organised by The Centre for Sustainable Design
24. Chertow MR (2000) Industrial symbiosis: literature and taxonomy. Annu Rev Energy Env 25(1):313–337
25. Cole RJ (2012) Regenerative design and development: current theory and practice. Build Res Inf 40(1):1–6
26. Costanza R (1994) Three general policies to achieve sustainability. Investing in natural capital: the ecological economics approach to sustainability, pp 392–407
27. Cradle to Cradle Products Innovation Institute (2020) Get certified. Retrieved from https://www.c2ccertified.org/get-certified. Retrieved on 15 Dec 2020
28. Cramer MD (1997) Book review of Biomimicry: innovation inspired by nature. Library J 122(11)
29. de Jesus A, Antunes P, Santos R, Mendonça S (2018) Eco-innovation in the transition to a circular economy: an analytical literature review. J Clean Prod 172:2999–3018. https://doi.org/10.1016/j.jclepro.2017.11.111
30. de Jesus A, Antunes P, Santos R, Mendonça S (2019) Eco-innovation pathways to a circular economy: envisioning priorities through a Delphi approach. J Clean Prod 228:1494–1513. https://doi.org/10.1016/j.jclepro.2019.04.049
31. del Río P (2005) Analysing the factors influencing clean technology adoption: a study of the Spanish pulp and paper industry. Bus Strategy Environ 14:20–37

32. del Río P, Burguillo M (2008) Assessing the impact of renewable energy deployment on local sustainability: towards a theoretical framework. Renew Sustain Energy Rev 12 (5):1325–1344. https://doi.org/10.1016/j.rser.2007.03.004
33. del Río P (2011) Climate Change Policies and new Technologies. In: Cerdá E, Labandeira X (eds) Climate change policies: global challenges and future prospects. Edward Elgar, Cheltenham, UK, pp 49–68
34. del Río P, Kiefer CP (2019) Relating the concepts of eco-innovation and circular economy in firms. 2019 Spring Workshop, Facultad de Derecho y Ciencias Sociales, Universidad de Castilla La Mancha (UCLM), Ciudad Real. 23 May 2019
35. del Río P (2020) "Economía circular: desafíos para la Ciencia y las políticas públicas". IV Seminario de Derecho Tributario Global "Opciones fiscales de apoyo a la economía circular en tiempos de pandemia". Universidad de Castilla La Mancha. Dember 1st 2020
36. Demirel P, Danisman GO (2019) Eco-innovation and firm growth in the circular economy: evidence from European small- and medium-sized enterprises. Bus Strategy Environ. https://doi.org/10.1002/bse.2336
37. Doni F, Corvino A, Martini SB (2019) Servitization and sustainability actions. Evidence from European manufacturing companies. J Environ Manage 234:367–378
38. Dosi G, Freeman C, Nelson R, Silverberg G, Soete L (1988) Technical change and economic theory, vol 988
39. EIO (2010) Methodological report. Eco-innovation observatory. Funded by the European Commission, DG Environment, Brussels. Retrieved from https://www.eco-innovation.eu/index.php/reports/methodological-report
40. Ehrenfeld J (2007) Would industrial ecology exist without sustainability in the background? J Ind Ecol 11(1):73–84
41. Ehrenfeld J (1995) Industrial ecology: a estrategic framework for product policy and other sustainable practices. Stockholm
42. Engelman R (2013) Beyond sustainababble. State of the world 2013: is sustainability still possible?. Island Press/Center for Resource Economics, Washington, DC, pp 3–16
43. Eriksson K, Robèrt K (1991) From the big bang to sustainable societies. Rev Oncol 4(2):5–14
44. Europa INNOVA (2006) Thematic workshop, lead markets and innovation, June 2006. Munich, Germany
45. European Commission (2007) Competitiveness and innovation framework programme (2007 to 2013), European Union, Brussels
46. European Commission (2008) Call for proposals under the eco-innovation 2008 programme. DG Environment. Retrieved from http://ec.europa.eu/environment/etap/ecoinnovation/library_en.htm
47. European Commission (2018) Eco-innovation the key to Europe's future competitiveness. Available at: http://ec.europa.eu/environment/pubs/pdf/factsheets/ecoinnovation/en.pdf
48. Franco MA (2017) Circular economy at the micro level: a dynamic view of incumbents' struggles and challenges in the textile industry. J Clean Prod 168:833–845. https://doi.org/10.1016/j.jclepro.2017.09.056
49. Frosch RA, Gallopoulos NE (1989) Strategies for manufacturing. Sci Am 161(3):144–153
50. Fukuoka M (1978) The one-straw revolution—an introduction to natural farming
51. Fussler C, James P (1996) A breakthrough discipline for innovation and sustainability. Pitman Publishing, London, UK
52. Geissdoerfer M, Savaget P, Bocken NMP, Hultink EJ (2017) The circular economy—a new sustainability paradigm? J Clean Prod 143:757–768. https://doi.org/10.1016/j.jclepro.2016.12.048
53. Gente V, Pattanaro G (2019) The place of eco-innovation in the current sustainability debate. Waste Manag 88:96–101. https://doi.org/10.1016/j.wasman.2019.03.026
54. Geum Y, Park Y (2011) Designing the sustainable product-service integration: a product-service blueprint approach. J Clean Prod 19(14):1601–1614

55. Ghisellini P, Cialani C, Ulgiati S (2016) A review on circular economy: the expected transition to a balanced interplay of environmental and economic systems. J Clean Prod 114:11–32. https://doi.org/10.1016/j.jclepro.2015.09.007
56. Ghisetti C, Montresor S (2020) On the adoption of circular economy practices by small and medium-size enterprises (SMEs): does "financing-as-usual" still matter? J Evol Econ 30 (2):559–586. https://doi.org/10.1007/s00191-019-00651-w
57. Goedkoop M, van Halen JG, Te Riele H, Rommens PJM (1999) Product service systems: ecological and economic basics
58. Graedel TE, Allenby BA (1995) Industrial ecology. Prentice Hall, New Jersey
59. Grubb M, McDowall W, Drummond P (2017) On order and complexity in innovations systems: conceptual frameworks for policy mixes in sustainability transitions. Energy Res Soc Sci 33:21–34. https://doi.org/10.1016/j.erss.2017.09.016
60. Guzzo D, Trevisan AH, Echeveste M, Costa JMH (2019) Circular innovation framework: verifying conceptual to practical decisions in sustainability-oriented product-service system cases. Sustainability 11(12):3248
61. Hansen EG, Schmitt JC (2020) Orchestrating cradle-to-cradle innovation across the value chain: overcoming barriers through innovation communities, collaboration mechanisms, and intermediation. J Ind Ecol
62. Henry M, Bauwens T, Hekkert M, Kirchherr J (2020) A typology of circular start-ups: an Analysis of 128 circular business models. J Clean Prod 245
63. Hernandez RJ (2019) Sustainable product-service systems and circular economies. Sustainability 11(19):5383
64. Hinterberger F, Luks F, Schmidt-Bleek F (1997) Material flows vs. natural capital': what makes an economy sustainable? Ecol Econ 23(1):1–14
65. Hobson K, Lynch N, Lilley D, Smalley G (2018) Systems of practice and the circular economy: transforming mobile phone product service systems. Environ Innov Societal Transitions 26:147–157
66. Horbach J, Rammer C (2019) Circular economy innovations, growth and employment at the firm level: empirical evidence from Germany. J Ind Ecol. https://doi.org/10.1111/jiec.12977
67. Horbach J, Reif C (2018) New developments in eco-innovation research. Springer, Singapore
68. IISD (2005) Earth negotiations bulletin, vol 5, no 212. Monday, 28 February 2005. https://enb.iisd.org/vol05/enb05212e.html
69. IISD (2020a) IISD's own work on the sustainable development goals. https://sustainable-development-goals.iisd.org/
70. IISD (2020b) Sustainable development goals. http://sdg.iisd.org/
71. Kemp R, Arundel A (1998) Survey indicators for environmental innovation. IDEA report, Oslo
72. Kemp R, Foxon T (2007) Typology of eco-innovation. Deliverable 2. EU FP6 funded project 044513: 24., Maastricht
73. Kemp R, Pearson P (2007) Final report MEI project about measuring eco-innovation, Maastricht
74. Kiefer CP, Río P, Carrillo-Hermosilla J (2021) On the contribution of eco-innovation features to a circular economy: a microlevel quantitative approach. Bus Strategy Environ 1–17:1–17. https://doi.org/10.1002/bse.2688
75. Kiefer CP, Carrillo-Hermosilla J, del Río P (2019) Building a taxonomy of eco-innovation types in firms. A quantitative perspective. Resour Conserv Recycl 145, 339–348. https://doi.org/10.1016/j.resconrec.2019.02.021
76. Kirchherr J, Piscicelli L (2019) Towards an education for the circular economy (ECE): five teaching principles and a case study. Resour Conserv Recycl 150:150. https://doi.org/10.1016/j.resconrec.2019.104406
77. Kirchherr J, Piscicelli L, Bour R, Kostense-Smit E, Muller J, Huibrechtse-Truijens A, Hekkert M (2018) Barriers to the circular economy: evidence from the European Union (EU). Ecol Econ 150:264–272. https://doi.org/10.1016/j.ecolecon.2018.04.028

78. Kirchherr J, Reike D, Hekkert M (2017) Conceptualizing the circular economy: an analysis of 114 definitions. Resour Conserv Recycl 127:221–232. https://doi.org/10.1016/j.resconrec.2017.09.005
79. Kitzing L, Fitch-Roy O, Islam M, Mitchell C (2018) An evolving risk perspective for policy instrument choice in sustainability transitions. Environ Innov Societal Transitions. https://doi.org/10.1016/j.eist.2018.12.002
80. Kjaer LL, Pigosso DC, Niero M, Bech NM, McAloone TC (2019) Product/service-systems for a circular economy: the route to decoupling economic growth from resource consumption? J Ind Ecol 23(1):22–35
81. Klemmer P, Lehr U (1999) Environmental innovation: incentives and barriers: German Ministry of Research and Technology (BMBF). Analytica-Verlag, Berlin
82. Korhonen J, Honkasalo A, Seppälä J (2018) Circular economy: the concept and its limitations. Ecol Econ 143:37–46. https://doi.org/10.1016/j.ecolecon.2017.06.041
83. Korhonen J, Nuur C, Feldmann A, Birkie SE (2018) Circular economy as an essentially contested concept. J Clean Prod 175:544–552. https://doi.org/10.1016/j.jclepro.2017.12.111
84. Kristensen HS, Remmen A (2019) A framework for sustainable value propositions in product-service systems. J Clean Prod 223:25–35
85. Lewandowski M (2016) Designing the business models for circular economy—towards the conceptual framework. Sustainability 8(1). https://doi.org/10.3390/su8010043
86. Lieder M, Rashid A (2016) Towards circular economy implementation: a comprehensive review in context of manufacturing industry. J Clean Prod 115:36–51. https://doi.org/10.1016/j.jclepro.2015.12.042
87. Linder M, Williander M (2017) Circular business model innovation: inherent uncertainties. Bus Strategy Environ 26(2):182–196
88. Lockett H, Johnson M, Evans S, Bastl M (2011) Product service systems and supply network relationships: an exploratory case study. J Manuf Technol Manage
89. Lozano R (2013) Are companies planning their organisational changes for corporate sustainability? An analysis of three case studies on resistance to change and their strategies to overcome it. Corp Soc Responsib Environ Manag 20(5):275–295
90. Lyle JT (1994) Strategies for regenerative design. Regenerative design for sustainable development
91. Läpple F (2007) Abfall-und Kreislaufwirtschaftlicher Transformationsprozess in Deutschland und in China: Analyse-Vergleich-Übertragbarkeit
92. Manzini E, Vezzoli C (2003) A strategic design approach to develop sustainable product service systems: examples taken from the 'environmentally friendly innovation' Italian prize. J Clean Prod 11(8):851–857
93. Markard J, Raven R, Truffer B (2012) Sustainability transitions: an emerging field of research and its prospects. Res Policy 41:955–967
94. Masi D, Day S, Godsell J (2017) Supply chain configurations in the circular economy: a systematic literature review. Sustainability 9(9). https://doi.org/10.3390/su9091602
95. Matschewsky J (2019) Unintended circularity?—assessing a product-service system for its potential contribution to a circular economy. Sustainability 11(10):2725
96. Matzen D, McAloone TC (2006) A tool for conceptualising in PSS development. In: Paper presented at the DFX 2006. Proceedings of the 17th Symposium on Design for X, Neukirchen/Erlangen, Germany, 12, 13.10. 2006
97. McDonough W, Braungart M (2002) Cradle to cradle: remaking the way we make things. North Point Press, New York, NY
98. Mendoza JMF, Sharmina M, Gallego-Schmid A, Heyes G, Azapagic A (2017) Integrating backcasting and eco-design for the circular economy: the BECE framework. J Ind Ecol 21 (3):526–544
99. Millar N, McLaughlin E, Börger T (2019) The circular economy: swings and roundabouts? Ecol Econ 158:11–19. https://doi.org/10.1016/j.ecolecon.2018.12.012
100. Mont O (2002) Clarifying the concept of product–service system. J Clean Prod 10:237–245. https://doi.org/10.1016/s0959-6526(01)00039-7

101. Munasinghe M (1993) Environmental economics and sustainable development. The World Bank
102. Munasinghe M, Shearer W (1995) Defining and measuring sustainability: the biogeophysical foundations
103. Murray A, Skene K, Haynes K (2017) The circular economy: an interdisciplinary exploration of the concept and application in a global context. J Bus Ethics 140:369–380. https://doi.org/10.1007/s10551-015-2693-2
104. Naudé M (2011) Sustainable development in companies: theoretical dream or implementable reality. Corp Ownership Control 8(4):352–364
105. Neumayer E (1999) Weak versus strong sustainability. Exploring the limits of two opposing paradigms. Edward Elgar, Cheltenham, UK
106. OECD (2009a) Sustainable manufacturing and eco-innovation. Framewok, practices and measurement. Synthesis report, Paris
107. OECD (2009b) Sustainable manufacturing and eco-innovation: towards a green economy. Policy Brief, June
108. OECD (2018) Oslo manual 2018 guidelines for collecting, reporting and using data on innovation. Retrieved from http://oe.cd/oslomanua
109. OECD Centre for Educational Research and Innovation (1998) Human capital investment: an international comparison. OECD, Paris, France
110. Oltra V, Saint Jean M (2009) Sectoral systems of environmental innovation: an application to the French automotive industry. Technol Forecast Soc Chang 76:567–583
111. Pearce D, Atkinson G, Moran K, Young C (1997) Measuring sustainable development. Edward Elgar, Cheltenham, UK
112. Pearce DW, Turner RK (1990) Economics of natural resources and the environment. JHU press
113. Pieroni MPP, McAloone TC, Pigosso DCA (2019) Business model innovation for circular economy and sustainability: a review of approaches. J Clean Prod 215:198–216. https://doi.org/10.1016/j.jclepro.2019.01.036
114. Prieto-Sandoval V, Jaca C, Ormazabal M (2018) Towards a consensus on the circular economy. J Clean Prod 179:605–615. https://doi.org/10.1016/j.jclepro.2017.12.224
115. Rashid A, Asif FM, Krajnik P, Nicolescu CM (2013) Resource conservative manufacturing: an essential change in business and technology paradigm for sustainable manufacturing. J Clean Prod 57:166–177
116. Reike D, Vermeulen WJV, Witjes S (2018) The circular economy: new or refurbished as CE 3.0?—exploring controversies in the conceptualization of the circular economy through a focus on history and resource value retention options. Resour Conserv Recycl 135:246–264. https://doi.org/10.1016/j.resconrec.2017.08.027
117. Reim W, Parida V, Örtqvist D (2015) Product-Service Systems (PSS) business models and tactics–a systematic literature review. J Clean Prod 97:61–75
118. Rennings K (2000) Redefining innovation—eco-innovation research and the contribution from ecological economics. Ecol Econ 32:319–332. https://doi.org/10.1016/s0921-8009(99)00112-3
119. Richards DJ, Allen B, Frosch RA (1994) The greening of industrial ecosystems: overview and perspective. In: Allenby BR, RDJ (eds) The greening of industrial ecosystems. National Academy Press, Washington
120. Robinson J (2004) Squaring the circle? Some thoughts on the idea of sustainable development. Ecol Econ 48(4):369–384
121. Schroeder P, Anggraeni K, Weber U (2019) The relevance of circular economy practices to the sustainable development goals. J Ind Ecol 23(1):77–95
122. Schuller T (2000) Social capital, human capital and sustainable development. Frameworks to measure sustainable development, vol 51
123. Serageldin I (1996) Sustainability and the wealth of nations. Paper presented at the international conference on environmentally sustainable development 1995, World Bank

124. Skene KR (2018) Circles, spirals, pyramids and cubes: why the circular economy cannot work. Sustain Sci 13(2):479–492
125. Smol M, Kulczycka J, Avdiushchenko A (2017) Circular economy indicators in relation to eco-innovation in European regions. Clean Technol Environ Policy 19:669–678. https://doi.org/10.1007/s10098-016-1323-8
126. Solow RM (1986) On the intergenerational allocation of natural resources. Scandinavian J Econ, 141–149
127. Stahel WR (1989) The limits to certainty: facing risks in the new service economy. Kluwer Academic Publishers, Dordrecht
128. The Natural Step (2000) The natural step framework guidebook. Retrieved from https://www.publicspaceinfo.nl/bibliotheek/natural-step-framework-guidebook/
129. The Natural Step (2020) The system conditions. Retrieved from https://thenaturalstep.org/approach/the-system-conditions/
130. Tibbs H (1992) Industrial ecology: an environmental agenda for industry. Whole Earth Rev 4(Winter):4–19
131. Toxopeus ME, De Koeijer BLA, Meij AGGH (2015) Cradle to cradle: effective vision vs. efficient practice? Procedia CIRP 29:384–389
132. Tukker A (2015) Product services for a resource-efficient and circular economy—a review. J Clean Prod 97:76–91. https://doi.org/10.1016/j.jclepro.2013.11.049
133. Tukker A, Butter M (2007) Governance of sustainable transitions: about the 4 (0) ways to change the world. J Clean Prod 15(1):94–103
134. Turner RK (1993) Sustainable environmental economics and management. Belhaven Press
135. United Nations (2020) The 17 goals. https://sdgs.un.org/goals
136. Unruh G (2008) The biosphere rules. Harvard Bus Rev 86(2):111–117, 138
137. Unruh G (2018) Circular economy, 3D printing, and the biosphere rules. Calif Manag Rev 60(3):95–111
138. VINNOVA (2001) Drivers of environmental innovation. VINNOVA Innovation in focus VF 2001:1. VINNOVA-Swedish governmental agency for Innovation Systems. Stockholm
139. van den Bergh JCJM, Truffer B, Kallis G (2011) Environmental innovation and societal transitions: introduction and overview. Environ Innov Societal Transitions 1(1):1–23. https://doi.org/10.1016/j.eist.2011.04.010
140. Vermunt D, Negro S, Verweij P, Kuppens D, Hekkert M (2019) Exploring barriers to implementing different circular business models. J Clean Prod 222:891–902
141. White R (1994) Preface. In: Allenby BR, Deanna RJ (eds) The greening of industrial ecosytems. National Academy Press, Washington
142. Williams A (2007) Product service systems in the automobile industry: contribution to system innovation? J Clean Prod 15:1093–1103. https://doi.org/10.1016/j.jclepro.2006.05.034
143. Witjes S, Lozano R (2016) Towards a more circular economy: proposing a framework linking sustainable public procurement and sustainable business models. Resour Conserv Recycl 112:37–44. https://doi.org/10.1016/j.resconrec.2016.04.015
144. Yang M, Smart P, Kumar M, Jolly M, Evans S (2018) Product-service systems business models for circular supply chains. Prod Plan Control 29(6):498–508
145. Yang M, Vladimirova D, Rana P, Evans S (2014) Sustainable value analysis tool for value creation. As J Manage Sci Appl 1(4):312–332
146. Zink T, Geyer R (2017) Circular economy rebound. J Ind Ecol 21(3):593–602. https://doi.org/10.1111/jiec.12545

Chapter 3
Defining the CE: A Review of Definitions, Taxonomies and Classifications

3.1 Introduction

This chapter provides a thorough literature review on existing definitions, classifications and taxonomies of the CE. This is a necessary exercise, as most researchers and practitioners recognize that the CE is an "umbrella concept". There are different approaches to circularity, and a commonly agreed definition of the CE currently does not exist.

The aim of this chapter is to perform a comprehensive literature review of the most important and widespread CE definitions, taxonomies and classifications, to analyse them individually, to identify commonalities and differences among them and to provide a critical appraisal of the CE definitions. This would allow readers to find major areas of agreement which may point towards a "core consensus" of the CE. Additionally, areas without agreements or even conflicting viewpoints may highlight different, non-mainstream or fringe understandings of the CE.

3.2 Methodology

An exhaustive literature review was undertaken to identify existing definitions and taxonomies of the CE. Given the high policy and practical relevance of the CE, the analysis of the literature was based on a literature review of both the academic and the so-called grey literature. For academic contributions, the search was undertaken with the help of the Web of Science (WoS), Scopus and Google Scholar tools. The search strategy comprised the following search parameters: "Circular Economy" and "definition" or "taxonomy" or "classification" applied to the title, abstract and keywords of articles. For grey literature contributions, which included semi-academic publications by think tanks, foundations, policy-makers or influential third-party

P. del Río et al., *The Circular Economy*, Green Energy and Technology,
https://doi.org/10.1007/978-3-030-74792-3_3

Table 3.1 Overview of the results (long list)

Search query[a]	Search engine				Total
	Web of Science (WoS)	Scopus	Google Scholar	Google	
CE and definition	188	197	40,000	1,560,000	**1,600,385**
CE and taxonomy	30	22	4,940	133,000	**137,992**
CE and classification	116	103	25,800	617,000	**643,019**
Total	**334**	**322**	**70,740**	**2,310,000**	**2,381,396**

Source: Own elaboration

[a]"CE (circular economy)" as shown in the table was introduced as "Circular Economy" into the search engines. The numbers shown in the table refer to the absolute number of results of each search query per search engine. Date of the search: 26 October 2020

Table 3.2 Overview of the results (final shortlist)

Number of unique contributions	Total
Group 1: original contribution	**27**
Group 2: amendments, adjustments or corrections to existing definitions	**20**
Total	**47**

Source: Own elaboration

stakeholders, the search was undertaken in the Google Search engine with the term "Circular Economy" in combination with the search terms mentioned above.

The literature search was performed in October 2020 and yielded the following results (long list) (Table 3.1).

The references obtained with the Web of Science (WoS) and Scopus were ordered according to the impact that they had, which was proxied by the number of received citations. All papers with 40 or more citations were included in the shortlist. It should be taken into account that this criterion favours high-quality papers as well as older ones, which is why specific attention was paid during the snowballing procedure (see below) in order to include highly relevant new papers with less than 40 citations. All other papers were manually screened (title, abstract, keywords) and included if they provided a relevant content, i.e. a definition, taxonomy or classification of the CE. This was the case for 66 papers. Both Google Scholar and Google rank search results by received references from other web sources through PageRank, which can be a proxy for received citations. The first 15 results of Google Scholar and Google Search were again thoroughly manually screened. Considerably more than 15 results were initially screened, yet they provided increasingly repeated results to the prior WoS and Scopus searches (in the case of Google Scholar) and less relevant contributions, i.e. more local or company-specific results, and also multiple sites of the Ellen MacArthur Foundation (EMF) (in the case of Google). Finally, it was decided to recur to the 15 highest ranked results only, and thus, they were added to the shortlist if they provided relevant content. Other contributions, such as corporate, policy-maker, press or opinion leader's websites that merely stated that the company, state or region had a CE strategy, or websites that mentioned the concept without providing further details, were not included in the shortlist. After screening, the shortlist contained 37 papers.

"Snowballing" was applied to this sample. This was especially relevant for a few review articles which pointed towards other highly relevant contributions with CE definitions or taxonomies that were not originally included in the shortlist. Therefore, the final list of relevant contributions was 47 (Table 3.2). All of these were thoroughly examined with a special focus on their contribution to the research objective.

The contributions were divided into groups. *Group 1* contained all contributions that provided an original (new) definition, taxonomy or classification of the CE, whereas *Group 2* contained all contributions that advanced an already existing definition, taxonomy or classification by providing amendments, adjustments or corrections to them.

The following table provides an overview of the results.

3.3 Circular Economy Definitions, Taxonomies or Classifications

Table 3.3 provides details on the content of the aforementioned 47 contributions to the literature, including the approach followed, the research scope, the focus of the paper, the CE levels considered and the CE definitions, taxonomies or classifications proposed. A brief comment on the findings of the particular contribution is also provided (see last column).

Work on CE definitions, taxonomies and classifications before 2014 is relatively scant in our sample (only 3 definitions have been included, one each from 2006, 2008 and 2011) but heavily increased thereafter, reaching a peak in 2018.[1] The reduction of publications in 2019 is a bit surprising. It may indicate a trend (i.e. the concept is gaining maturity, and the space for further definitions, classifications or taxonomies is narrowing), or it might simply be an outlier. Whatever the interpretation, it is clear that the concept has gained and is gaining momentum, attention and impact (Fig. 3.1).

The relevant contributions are concentrated in a few journals. Most of the academic articles are published in the Journal of Cleaner Production (16), followed by Resources, Conservation and Recycling (5) and the Journal of Industrial Ecology (4). Relevant articles were also published in Ecological Economics (3), Business Strategy and the Environment (2) and Sustainability (2) (Fig. 3.2).

Theoretical and review-oriented contributions clearly dominate, which is a logical result for an emerging concept. The academic research is mostly based on

[1]Note that the search did not cover the whole year 2020, but only until October 2020.

Table 3.3 List and features of the papers

Group	Citations	Authors	Title	Journal or source	Approach	Research scope	Focus	CE levels	CE definitions, taxonomies or classifications	Main insights from the paper on the CE
2	2069	Ghisellini et al. (2016)	A review on CE: The expected transition to a balanced interplay of environmental and economic systems.	Journal of Cleaner Production	Literature review	To provide a literature review on main CE features and perspectives.	Holistic	All	An academic and a policy definition of CE (from other authors) are given (Ghisellini et al. (2016).	The CE concept is rooted in prior academic concepts. It is highly policy relevant, and different countries approach the CE differently. CE implementation is in its early stages and not addressed in its totality. Firms have a key role to play in the CE.
1	1808	Geissdoerfer et al. (2017)	The CE – A new sustainability paradigm?	Journal of Cleaner Production	Literature review, bibliometric analysis	To identify the relationship between Sustainability and CE. To clarify the two concepts.	Holistic	None	CE definitions are provided from other authors (EMF 2013, Geng and Doberstein, 2008, Webster, 2015, Yuan et al., 2008, Bocken et al., 2016) However, an original CE definition is also elaborated by these authors: CE is "*a regenerative system in which resource input and waste, emission, and energy leakage are minimised by slowing, closing, and narrowing material and energy loops. This can be achieved through long-lasting design, maintenance, repair, reuse, remanufacturing, refurbishing, and recycling.*" (Geissdoerfer et al. 2017, p. 759).	The conceptual relationship between sustainability and CE remains unclear. Despite not being new, it has recently gained momentum amongst policy makers. CE itself is based on numerous previous concepts (Industrial Economics, Industrial Ecology, Cradle-to-cradle, Performance Economy, Biomimicry, etc.). The CE is seen as a precondition for sustainability.
2	1281	Kirchherr et al. (2017)	Conceptualizing the CE: An analysis of 114 definitions.	Resources, Conservation and Recycling	Literature review and theory building	To revise the theoretical contributions on the concept of CE and to classify them according to several	Concept of CE from different theoretical and practical viewpoints	All	No explicit definition of the CE is provided.	CE may mean different things to different people. The concept of CE is sometimes not well understood and essential parts of the concept are not taken into account.

(continued)

Table 3.3 (continued)

Group	Citations	Authors	Title	Journal or source	Approach	Research scope	Focus	CE levels	CE definitions, taxonomies or classifications	Main insights from the paper on the CE
						criteria				Most definitions refer to reduce, reuse and recycle activities, without addressing the need for a systemic shift.
2	1123	Tukker (2015)	Product services for a resource-efficient and CE - A review.	Journal of Cleaner Production	Literature review, bibliometric analysis, and theory building	An instrumental approach to the CE, that is, how the CE can be reached	Product service system (PSS) as an instrument towards the CE	Resource use oriented	No explicit definition of the CE is provided.	The paper addresses the "bigger picture" and places PSS in the context of sustainability and competitiveness.
1	1062	Murray et al. (2017)	The CE: An Interdisciplinary Exploration of the Concept and Application in a Global Context.	Journal of Business Ethics	Literature review	To summarize conceptualisations and origins of the CE, to contribute to the *"little formal academic debate"* (p. 370) and to evaluate CE potential in a sustainable business context	Business and policy	Holistic approach, rather focused on macro and partially meso levels. Connection to the 3R framework of reduction, reuse and recycling	*"The term CE has both a linguistic and a descriptive meaning. Linguistically it is an antonym of a linear economy […] By circular, an economy is envisaged as having no net effect on the environment; rather it restores any damage done in resource acquisition, while ensuring little waste is generated throughout the production process and in the life history of the product. The word circular has a second, inferred, descriptive meaning, which relates to the concept of the cycle. There are two cycles of particular importance here: the biogeochemical cycles and the idea of recycling of products."* (Murray et al. 2017, p.371).	The CE is not considered a new concept but a new word. The CE borrows from a wide range of earlier concepts. From a policy makers' perspective, the CE is instrumental to achieve some goals, i.e., recycling of valuable materials, job creation, reduction of greenhouse gas emissions etc. The CE is sometimes oversimplistic and misses the social dimension.
2	998	Lieder and Rashid (2016)	Towards CE implementation: A comprehensive	Journal of Cleaner Production	Literature review, framework	To provide an overview of existing research on CE, to	Resource scarcity, environmental	All. The R-framewor	These authors also consider several CE definitions from other authors (Geng and	Sustainability-related challenges are increasingly tackled from a CE-perspective.

(continued)

Table 3.3 (continued)

Group	Citations	Authors	Title	Journal or source	Approach	Research scope	Focus	CE levels	CE definitions, taxonomies or classifications	Main insights from the paper on the CE
			review in context of manufacturing industry.		development	elaborate a CE framework and to propose implementation strategies	impact and economic benefit in relation to the CE	k	Doberstein, 2008, Yuan et al., 2006, Stahel, 1982, EMF, 2013, Pearce and Turner, 1990)	The concept is not new and it is not clear. The antecedents of CE are diverse, both in areas and geographic scope.
1	827	Korhonen et al. (2018a)	CE: The Concept and its Limitations.	Ecological Economics	Theory building	To structure scientific research on CE. To define the concept of CE. To identify challenges that must be overcome so that CE can contribute to sustainability.	Holistic	All (implicitly)	"[CE] *is an economy constructed from societal production-consumption systems that maximizes the service produced from the linear nature-society-nature material and energy throughput flow. This is done by using cyclical materials flows, renewable energy sources and cascading1-type energy flows*" (Korhonen et al. (2018a, p.38).	Research on CE is *"superficial and unorganized"* (Korhonen et al. (2018a, p. 37). It has been led and applied mainly by practitioners and policy makers, not researchers. Ecological Economics is a concept from which CE may benefit at the macro level, whereas Eco-efficiency and Industrial Ecology are useful for the micro-level. Many other concepts provide input, too. Currently, several limits to the CE exist: thermodynamic, spatial-temporal system boundaries, physical economic growth, lock-in, intra- vs. inter-organizational strategies and physical flow limits.
1	816	Stahel (2016)	The CE. Nature.	Nature. International weekly journal of science.	Presentation and dissemination of a concept	(grey literature)	Holistic	None	*"A 'CE' would turn goods that are at the end of their service life into resources for others, closing loops in industrial ecosystems and minimizing waste (see 'Closing loops'). It would change economic logic because it replaces production with sufficiency: reuse what you can, recycle what cannot be reused, repair what is broken,*	The CE is an economic and societal trend. In order to achieve it, several concerted actions must be activated.

(continued)

Table 3.3 (continued)

Group	Citations	Authors	Title	Journal or source	Approach	Research scope	Focus	CE levels	CE definitions, taxonomies or classifications	Main insights from the paper on the CE
									remanufacture what cannot be repaired" Stahel (2016, p. 435)	
1	787	Yuan et al. (2006)	The CE: A new development strategy in China.	Journal of Industrial Ecology	Review	To provide a comment on CE	A geographic focus (China)	All	"*Although there is no commonly accepted definition of CE so far, the core of CE is the circular (closed) flow of materials and the use of raw materials and energy through multiple phases*" (Yuan et al. 2006, p. 5).	CE is an economic rather than an environmental strategy. No CE definition exists. The CE is based on many previous concepts. It is of high interest to policy makers.
1	554	Haas et al. (2015)	How Circular is the Global Economy? An Assessment of Material Flows, Waste Production, and Recycling in the European Union and the World in 2005.	Journal of Industrial Ecology	Framework development, quantitative study based on Eurostat data	To assess the circularity of global material flows	Global, resource-flow oriented	Macro	"*The CE is a simple, but convincing, strategy, which aims at reducing both input of virgin materials and output of wastes by closing economic and ecological loops of resource flows*" (Haas et al. (2015), p. 765).	There is a very low degree of circularity in global resource flows due to several reasons (accumulation of in-use stock and resource-use for energy generation). Eco-friendly design and the energy transition are thus currently main roads to a CE. Academically, the concept is not well defined. As a consequence, measurement is problematic.
1	525	Geng and Doberstein (2008)	Developing the CE in China: Challenges and opportunities for achieving 'leapfrog development'.	International Journal of Sustainable Development & World Ecology	Literature, grey literature, policy and business literature review	To describe the current state of CE and CE practices	Geographical perspective (China)	All	"*The [CE], is understood to mean the realisation of a closed loop of material flows in the Chinese economic system*" (Geng and Doberstein 2008, p. 231)	Natural and economic ecosystems can be much alike. The CE can solve environmental problems in China. The Chinese Government is interested and active in implementing the concept, yet there are barriers (related to policy, technology and public participation).
1	496	Sauvé et al. (2016)	Environmental sciences, sustainable	Environmental Development	Literature review, theory building	To outline and contrast three concepts:	Conceptual	None	"*The objective of the CE is to optimize the use of virgin resources, and reduce*	The success of the CE concept is due to the fact that it provides a basis for an action-

(continued)

Table 3.3 (continued)

Group	Citations	Authors	Title	Journal or source	Approach	Research scope	Focus	CE levels	CE definitions, taxonomies or classifications	Main insights from the paper on the CE
			development and CE: Alternative concepts for trans-disciplinary research.			Sustainable Development, environmental sciences and CE			*pollution and waste at each step, in as much as possible and desirable.*" (Sauvé et al. 2016, p. 52).	oriented basis and perspective to tackle sustainability problems. Nevertheless, there are still practical challenges related to the CE.
1	376	Gregson et al. (2015)	Interrogating the CE: the moral economy of resource recovery in the EU.	Economy and Society	Case study	To critically interrogate the concepet of CE	Geographical perspective (United Kingdom and also the EU)	None	"*The aim is to move away from the linear economic model, summarized as 'take make dispose' with raw materials in at one end and externalized wastes at the other*" (Gregson et al. 2015, p. 219).	The actual implementation of the CE is limited and fragile and mainly focused on recycling. CE reality is messy and several struggles for implementing the CE in practice exist.
1	332	Korhonen et al. (2018b)	CE as an essentially contested concept.	Journal of Cleaner Production	Theory building	To provide an overview of the concept and its antecedents. To suggest a CE research model.	Production and consumption systems, business and policy	All, with a focus on system functioning (macro) and individual artefacts and agents (micro). Physical flow of material and energy.	Several CE definitions and taxonomies are provided, and it is highlighted that no commonly accepted ones exist. A new definition is proposed: "*CE is a sustainable development initiative with the objective of reducing the societal production-consumption systems' linear material and energy throughput flows by applying materials cycles, renewable and cascade-type energy flows to the linear system*" (Korhonen et al. 2018b, p.547).	The CE is found to be a visionary concept, but research on it is only emerging. The CE is instrumental for policy and business to achieve sustainability goals.
2	283	Reike et al. (2018)	The CE: New or Refurbished as CE 3.0? — Exploring Controversies in the Conceptualization	Resources, Conservation and Recycling	Literature review, theory building	To identify the state of the art in CE research. To provide a "heuristic" of CE that is useful in practice.	Resource and product flows	The R-framework	Three perspectives on CE are given and summarized: waste, input-output/eco-efficiency and value retention. Also, CE is "*a regenerative*	The CE has gained much attention, which is related to its potential to achieve a sustainable society. Yet, the idea is not new and conceptual antecedents date back decades

(continued)

Table 3.3 (continued)

Group	Citations	Authors	Title	Journal or source	Approach	Research scope	Focus	CE levels	CE definitions, taxonomies or classifications	Main insights from the paper on the CE
			of the CE through a Focus on History and Resource Value Retention Options.						*system in which resource input and waste, emission, and energy leakage are minimized by slowing, closing, and narrowing material and energy loops. This can be achieved through long-lasting design, maintenance, repair, reuse, remanufacturing, refurbishing, and recycling (Geissdoerfer et al., 2017)"* (Reike et al. 2018, p. 249).	ago. Value retention of resources and products is key. Different "loops" (R's) exist for that aim.
1	276	Merli et al. (2018)	How do scholars approach the CE? A systematic literature review.	Journal of Cleaner Production	Literature review, bibliometric analysis	To provide an overview of academic contributions to the CE concept.	Theoretical contributions on CE	All (a discussion of previous classifications is provided)	Besides referring to the EMF's definition of CE, the authors provide their own definition as *"(CE) aims to overcome the take-make-dispose linear pattern of production and consumption, proposing a circular system in which the value of products, materials and resources is maintained in the economy as long as possible."* (Merli et al. 2018, p. 703)	The CE concept builds on many previous concepts and is thus not new. It is a concept to correct the current malfunctioning of the economic system. There is no agreement on it and much confusion exists. Most studies are practical in nature and research mainly focuses on macro-dynamics and firm circular process implementation in the context of cleaner production.
1	275	Zink and Geyer (2017)	CE Rebound.	Journal of Industrial Ecology	Review	To critically examine the CE concept.	Holistic	Rather macro	*"The core of the CE refers to three activities: reuse at the product level (such as "repair" or "refurbishment"); reuse at the component level (e.g., "remanufacturing"); and reuse at the material level ("recycling")"* (Zink and Geyer 2017, p. 2)	CE is neither a new nor an undisputed concept. The economic part and implications of the concept have often been overlooked. It may be the case that CE increases overall production which leads to a rebound effect.
1	252	Prieto-	Towards a	Journal of	Literature	To elaborate a	Holistic	Micro,	12 definitions of CE are given	Eco-innovations are an

(continued)

Table 3.3 (continued)

Group	Citations	Authors	Title	Journal or source	Approach	Research scope	Focus	CE levels	CE definitions, taxonomies or classifications	Main insights from the paper on the CE
		Sandoval et al. (2018)	consensus on the CE.	Cleaner Production	review	consensus on CE framework research. To identify the relationship between CE and eco-innovation		meso, macro, the R-framework	in a table. Also, an original definition is provided: The CE is *"an economic system that represents a change of paradigm in the way that human society is interrelated with nature and aims to prevent the depletion of resources, close energy and materials loops, and facilitate sustainable development through its implementation at the micro (enterprises and consumers), meso (economic agents integrated in symbiosis) and macro (city, regions and governments) levels"* (Prieto-Sandoval et al. 2018, p. 613).	instrument to reach the CE.
2	225	Loiseau et al. (2016)	Green economy and related concepts: An overview.	Journal of Cleaner Production	Literature review	To provide an overview of the many concepts that can be grouped under "green economy". To identify their contribution to weak and strong sustainability.	Analysis of the concepts of environmental economics ecological economics, cleaner production, waste hierarchy, bio-economy, industrial ecology, CE, nature-based solutions, dematerialization through product-	None	The authors use the EMF's definition, according to which the CE is *"an industrial economy that is restorative by design, and which mirrors nature in actively enhancing and optimizing the systems through which it operates (EMF, 2012)"* (Loiseau et al., 2016, p. 365).	CE is only one of the concepts amongst many which contribute to sustainability

(continued)

Table 3.3 (continued)

Group	Citations	Authors	Title	Journal or source	Approach	Research scope	Focus	CE levels	CE definitions, taxonomies or classifications	Main insights from the paper on the CE
							servicizing, life cycle assessment, and cost-benefit analysis			
1	225	Urbinati et al. (2017)	Towards a new taxonomy of CE business models.	Journal of Cleaner Production	Literature review, framework development and empirical analysis	To develop an understanding of the role of CE for business models	Business model and value-oriented perspective	System-based (macro) and artefact-based (micro). (Closed) loop oriented.	*"CE, indeed, bases on the establishment of closed production systems, where resources are reused and kept in a loop of production and usage, allowing generating more value and for a longer period."* (Urbinati et al. 2017, p. 487). Additionally, some existing principles for the CE are given.	Scholars, practitioners and policy makers struggle to create new business models or to adapt existing ones with respect to the CE. An explanatory business model (and value-oriented) framework is missing.
1	213	de Jesus and Mendonça (2018)	Lost in Transition? Drivers and Barriers in the Eco-innovation Road to the CE.	Ecological Economics	Literature review	To identify the role of eco-innovation for reaching the CE. To review drivers and barriers to CE.	Conceptual	None explicitly, some implicitly	The authors use the EMF (2012) definition of the CE (see above). An original definition of CE is also provided by the authors: the CE is a *"multidimensional, dynamic, integrative approach, promoting a reformed socio-technical template for carrying out economic development, in an environmentally sustainable way, by re-matching, re-balancing and re-wiring industrial processes and consumption habits into a new usage-production closed-loop system"* (de Jesus and Mendonça 2018, p. 76).	CE is a framework more than a disruptive approach to sustainability. The policy relevance is undeniable, but the concept is still poorly understood. It is unclear how the CE as a desired economic end-state can be reached. Eco-innovation is proposed as a transition mechanism which can transform the system towards a CE.

(continued)

Table 3.3 (continued)

Group	Citations	Authors	Title	Journal or source	Approach	Research scope	Focus	CE levels	CE definitions, taxonomies or classifications	Main insights from the paper on the CE
1	203	den Hollander et al. (2017)	Product Design in a CE: Development of a Typology of Key Concepts and Terms.	Journal of Industrial Ecology	Literature review, theory building	To identify guiding principles, strategies, and methods for circular product design and to identify how this differs from eco-design	Product design, material flow.	Micro (product) level	*"In a CE, the economic and environmental value of materials is preserved for as long as possible by keeping them in the economic system, either by lengthening the life of the products formed from them or by looping them back in the system to be reused"* (den Hollander et al. 2017, p. 517). This original definition is based on several Industrial Ecology definitions.	The aim of a zero-waste economy depends on product design for longevity. The economic value of products must be preserved or restored over time. Technological change but also business change (i.e., maintenance and repair, or recovery and reuse of products) are important.
1	201	Hu et al. (2011)	Ecological utilization of leather tannery waste with CE model.	Journal of Cleaner Production	Case study	To identify the CE applications in a specific sector/industry.	A specific sector (leather)	None, the R-framework	*"CE focuses on resource-productivity and eco-efficiency improvement in a comprehensive way, especially on the industrial structure optimization of new technology development and application, equipment renewal and management renovation"* (Hu et al. 2011, p. 221).	CE is a concept that was pushed by legislators early (i.e., Germany and China). Originally recycling-focused, CE now comprises many more aspects (i.e., the R-framework).
2	195	Homrich et al. (2018)	The CE umbrella: Trends and gaps on integrating pathways.	Journal of Cleaner Production	Literature review, bibliometric analysis, semantic analysis.	To identify research trends and gaps on CE. To identify if there is a convergence in the CE literature.	Analysis of definitions of CE.	None	Several definitions are presented in their Appendix A, the majority of which also came up during our search. The EMF's definition is center in the argument of the paper: The CE is *"an industrial system that is restorative or regenerative by intention and design (EMF, 2015)"* (Homrich et al. 2018, p. 526)	CE is a concept that originates from different fields and consensus or convergence of conceptualizations is missing. CE is often treated from a (resource) eco-efficiency perspective.
2	174	Govindan and	A systematic review on drivers,	International Journal of	Literature review	To provide an overview of drivers	Supply chain	Mainly meso	*"The central of CE is the circular (closed) flow of*	The CE is able to optimize production and consumption

(continued)

Table 3.3 (continued)

Group	Citations	Authors	Title	Journal or source	Approach	Research scope	Focus	CE levels	CE definitions, taxonomies or classifications	Main insights from the paper on the CE
		Hasanagic (2018)	barriers, and practices towards CE: a supply chain perspective.	Production Research		and barriers to the CE as well as practices within the CE.		level, but also micro and macro (implicitly)	*materials and the use of raw materials and energy through multiple phases (Franklin-Johnson, Figge, and Canning 2016) and an economy based on a "spiral-loop system" that minimises matter, energy-flow and environmental deterioration without restricting economic growth or social and technical progress (Geng et al. 2008)*" (Govindan and Hasanagic 2018, p. 281).	patterns. Several drivers and barriers exist to different CE practices. The role of policy makers is highlighted.
2	160	Pauliuk (2018)	Critical appraisal of the CE standard BS 8001:2017 and a dashboard of quantitative system indicators for its implementation in organizations.	Resources, Conservation and Recycling	Review of a Standard (BS 8001:2017), theory building	To elaborate a CE system definition that allows for the creation of CE indicators. To elaborate a dashboard of indicators.	BS 8001:2017 framework for implementing the principles of CE in organizations by the British Standards Institution	Micro (firm) level face to "systems thinking"	The CE is defined as an "*economy that is restorative and regenerative by design, and which aims to keep products, components and materials at their highest utility and value at all times, distinguishing between technical and biological cycles, where 'restorative' refers to spent resources being fed back into new products and services, and 'regenerative' refers to the enabling of living systems to heal and renew the resources that are consumed*" (Pauliuk 2018, p. 83).	The CE is instrumental in achieving sustainable business practices. CE is an umbrella concept, which takes a systems perspective. Very few specific guiding principles for the CE in firms exist. Firms have several possibilities to act and measure their efforts towards a CE.
2	149	Saidani et al. (2019)	A taxonomy of CE indicators.	Journal of Cleaner Production	Literature review, indicator and framework development	To develop measurement indicators of the CE. To develop a measurement framework to	Methodological / measurement-oriented	All	The reader is referred to the 114 definitions by Kirchherr et al. (2017). "*CE is defined as "an economic system that replaces the 'end-of-life' concept with reducing,*	CE is instrumental to achieve the goals of sustainable development. CE-related actions and measurement must be provided so that actors (businesses, policy makers)

(continued)

Table 3.3 (continued)

Group	Citations	Authors	Title	Journal or source	Approach	Research scope	Focus	CE levels	CE definitions, taxonomies or classifications	Main insights from the paper on the CE
						identify progress with regards to (economic system) sustainability.			*alternatively reusing, recycling and recovering materials in production/distribution and consumption processes. It operates at the micro level (products, companies, consumers), meso level (eco-industrial parks) and macro level (city, region, nation and beyond), with the aim to accomplish sustainable development, thus simultaneously creating environmental quality, economic prosperity and social equity, to the benefit of current and future generations*" (Saidani et al. 2019, p. 545).	may contribute to the CE and sustainability.
1	118	Moraga et al. (2019)	CE indicators: What do they measure?	Resources, Conservation and Recycling	Literature review, theory building	To elaborate a framework for categorizing CE strategies and indicators. To illustrate these at the micro and macro level.	Holistic (theory building) and applied ("CE monitoring Framework" in the European Union")	Micro and macro. The R-framework.	The authors propose two definitions of the CE: in a strict and more lenient sense: the "*sensu stricto focuses on the technological cycle of resources*" by "*slowing and closing resource loops*" (Moraga et al. 2019, p. 453). The "*sensu latu*" definition recognizes the CE as "*an economic model wherein planning, resourcing, procurement, production and reprocessing are designed and managed, as both process and output, to maximise ecosystem functioning and human well-being*" (Moraga	CE is an ill-defined and an umbrella concept incorporating different meanings. Despite this, it is widely embraced, especially by policy makers. Preserving materials (with strategies such as recycling) is the most widespread practice with regards to CE.

(continued)

Table 3.3 (continued)

Group	Citations	Authors	Title	Journal or source	Approach	Research scope	Focus	CE levels	CE definitions, taxonomies or classifications	Main insights from the paper on the CE
									et al. 2019, p. 453).	
2	116	Nußholz (2017)	Circular Business Models: Defining a Concept and Framing an Emerging Research Field.	Sustainability	Literature review	To frame circular business model research.	Resource efficiency and business model innovation	Unspecified economic resource and value flows. Firm business model perspective.	A definition based on 4 previous definitions is provided: *"The CE is a paradigm that suggests a redesign of the current linear economic system, largely based on linear resource flows, towards closed-loop resource flows that can preserve the embedded environmental and economic value in products over time. The CE has the potential to lead to increased resource efficiency and generate environmental gains through reduced raw material extraction and waste generation"* (Nußholz 2017, p. 1).	Circular business models (with regards to the R-framework) help firms to combine economic and environmental profit (business model innovation).
1	103	Geisendorf and Pietrulla (2018)	The CE and circular economic concepts-a literature analysis and redefinition.	Thunderbird International Business Review	Literature review	To revise existing CE definitions. To propose a revised definition.	Holistic	Micro, meso, macro. The R-framework	The authors refer to two CE definitions EMF (2016) and CE Action Plan (2015). An original definition is also provided: *"In a [CE], the value of products and materials is maintained, waste is avoided, and resources are kept within the economy when a product has reached the end of its life"* (Geisendorf and Pietrulla 2018, p. 779).	The academic field has currently different understandings of what the CE is. It has many conceptual antecedents and there is some confusion in the field.
2	99	Masi et al. (2017)	Supply Chain Configurations in the CE: A	Sustainability	Literature review	To identify commonalities in the CE	The supply chain	Meso level	The provided CE definition is based on previous definitions by the EMF and Murray et al.	The CE is a *"new label for an existing concept"* (Masi et al. (2017, p. 7). Most CE

(continued)

Table 3.3 (continued)

Group	Citations	Authors	Title	Journal or source	Approach	Research scope	Focus	CE levels	CE definitions, taxonomies or classifications	Main insights from the paper on the CE
			Systematic Literature Review.			implementation at the meso level in supply chains. To identify drivers and barriers.			(2017): *"The CE seeks to replace the "take-make-consume-dispose" patterns with closed-loops of material flows, made possible by combining a variety of different processes, such as maintenance, repair, reusing, refurbishing, remanufacturing, and recycling. A core assumption of the CE is therefore that the recovery of value from physical goods through the narrower cycles of re-use and refurbishment are superior both economically and environmentally to recycling and energy recovery"* (Masi et al. 2017, p. 2). In the review part, 8 more existing definitions are provided.	definitions are combinations of Cleaner Production and Industrial Symbiosis, but many other concepts are also roots for the CE. The CE is instrumental to achieve the goal of decoupling economic growth from environmental degradation, increasing system resilience, and preserving environmental, economic and social value. A series of drivers and barriers exists to implement the CE (financial, technological, societal, informational, institutional)
2	88	Niero and Olsen (2016)	CE: To be or not to be in a closed product loop? A Life Cycle Assessment of aluminium cans with inclusion of alloying elements.	Resources, Conservation and Recycling	Life-cycle assessment	To identify the role of production and recycling in the context of LCA	A specific sector: Aluminium products	Micro (product) level. A closed loop.	The authors refer to the EMF (2013) definition.	There are several technical suggestions to improve the recycling function for aluminium products for environmental performance and the CE.
2	86	Fisher et al. (2018)	Cloud manufacturing as a sustainable process manufacturing route.	Journal of Manufacturing Systems	Literature review and theory building	To investigate cloud manufacturing's role for sustainability and the CE (amongst others)	Cloud manufacturing and sustainable manufacturing	None explicitly. Resource-flow and product-level oriented	*"A CE is an alternative to a traditional linear economy (make, use, dispose) in which we keep resources in use for as long as possible, extract the maximum value from them whilst in use, then recover and regenerate products and*	Cloud manufacturing potentially contributes to the CE

(continued)

Table 3.3 (continued)

Group	Citations	Authors	Title	Journal or source	Approach	Research scope	Focus	CE levels	CE definitions, taxonomies or classifications	Main insights from the paper on the CE
									materials at the end of each service life [Waste and Resource Action Plan, 2017]. To create a sustainable manufacturing future, new manufacturing models need to be explored that support this circular approach." (Fisher et al. 2018, p.54)	
2	84	Millar et al. (2019)	The CE: Swings and Roundabouts?	Ecological Economics	Literature review	To review the CE literature in order to clarify the relationship between Sustainable Development and CE.	Holistic	All (implicitly)	"*No universal definition of the concept* [of CE] *exists in the literature both within and between schools of thought, the CE is generally understood by the business world as a model that is "restorative and regenerative by design, and aims to keep products, components, and materials at their highest utility and value at all times (EMF, 2017)*" (Millar et al. (2019, p. 13).	Sustainable development can serve to overcome current deficiencies of the (linear) economic system and provide economic prosperity, environmental improvements and social equity. CE, as an alternative yet related concept, is instrumental to that and may achieve sustainable development goals. On the other hand, both concepts are ambiguous and not well defined. As for the CE, numerous contradictions and knowledge gaps exist that may lead to wrong developments that are not different from the current linear economic functioning.
1	83	de Jesus et al. (2018)	Eco-innovation in the transition to a CE: An analytical literature review.	Journal of Cleaner Production	Literature review, theory building	To identify definitions of CE and eco-innovation (EI), the role of EI for CE at different levels and character traits of EI that contribute to the CE.	Holistic	All (micro, meso, macro)	Several transition-oriented "*CE-friendly concepts*" (de Jesus et al. 2018, p. 3002) are given, amongst them by Geng and Doberstein (2008), Standing Committee of the National People's Congress of China (2009), EMF (2014), EC (2014), EIO (2016),	The conventional economy creates severe systemic risks and irreversible environmental damage. The CE as a nature-inspired concept may be a solution as it minimizes negative and maximizes positive (restorative) aspects of the economy. EI is instrumental

(continued)

Table 3.3 (continued)

Group	Citations	Authors	Title	Journal or source	Approach	Research scope	Focus	CE levels	CE definitions, taxonomies or classifications	Main insights from the paper on the CE
									Lieder and Rashid (2016), Geissdoerfer et al. (2017), Kirchherr et al. (2017), de Jesus et al. (2018). Then, an original CE definition is provided: CE is *"an integrative concept for attaining "clean congruence" by guiding new institutional set-ups that match environmental considerations with socio-economic performance while promoting techno-economic development that is not depending on the consumption of finite resources"* (de Jesus et al. 2018, p. 3004) and *"an encompassing notion calling for specific actions towards the minimization of resource extraction, maximization of reuse, increased efficiency, enhanced waste recycling and the development of new business models."* (de Jesus et al. 2018, p. 3004).	in achieving the CE and, more generally, as a driver for sustainability transitions.
2	80	Hens et al. (2018)	On the evolution of "Cleaner Production" as a concept and a practice.	Journal of Cleaner Production	Literature review	To provide a review on Cleaner Production	Theoretical	None	The CE *"is inspired by ecological systems […]. By adopting of "closing-the-loop" production patterns, CE aims to increase the efficiency of resource use, with special focus on waste [i.e., EMF and Ghisellini et al. (2016)]"* (Hens et al. 2018, p. 3328)	Some aspects of cleaner production fit into the concept of CE. CE is a generic term rather than a specific concept.

(continued)

Table 3.3 (continued)

Group	Citations	Authors	Title	Journal or source	Approach	Research scope	Focus	CE levels	CE definitions, taxonomies or classifications	Main insights from the paper on the CE
1	69	Suárez-Eiroa et al. (2019)	Operational principles of CE for sustainable development: Linking theory and practice.	Journal of Cleaner Production	Literature review	To provide a review of CE and operational principles. To embed CE within the Sustainable Development framework.	Theoretical	None	7 existing definitions of CE are provided in a table (Suárez-Eiroa et al., 2019, p. 954) and an original definition is also given: The CE *"is a regenerative production consumption system that aims to maintain extraction rates of resources and generation rates of wastes and emissions under suitable values for planetary boundaries, through closing the system, reducing its size and maintaining the resource's value as long as possible within the system, mainly leaning on design and education, and with capacity to be implemented at any scale."* (Suárez-Eiroa et al. 2019, p. 958)	Both conceptual and practical discussions on the CE are ongoing. The CE is not a new concept. Still, there is no conceptual agreement of any kind. CE is especially prominent amongst policy makers.
2	51	Masi et al. (2018)	Towards a more CE: exploring the awareness, practices, and barriers from a focal firm perspective.	Production Planning & Control	Quantitative study (survey)	To study implementation of practices aligned with CE principles in firms. To study the firm within the supply chain. To identify barriers hindering implementation.	Worldwide (survey distributed via social media, n=77)	Micro (firm-level)	8 definitions of CE are given from other authors. All definitions and references are given in Table 3.2, (Masi et al., 2018, p. 542).	The transition towards the CE is already in motion. CE has different levels (micro, meso, macro). Existing micro-level studies have limitations (mainly with respect to scope). Barriers to implementing CE-related practices exist.
2	25	Ünal and Shao (2019)	A taxonomy of CE implementation strategies for manufacturing firms: Analysis of 391 cradle-to-	Journal of Cleaner Production	Empirical study with data from a database on 391 products in 187 firms	To provide a taxonomy of CE implementation strategies. To show how firms use their circular capabilities	Cradle-to-Cradle products	Micro level (firm and product)	The authors refer to the definition of Korhonen et al (2018)	The CE is a branch of sustainability science with the aim to reach the SDGs. CE has many conceptual antecedents. The CE is also a means to achieve firm competitiveness

(continued)

Table 3.3 (continued)

Group	Citations	Authors	Title	Journal or source	Approach	Research scope	Focus	CE levels	CE definitions, taxonomies or classifications	Main insights from the paper on the CE
			cradle products.			for competitive goals.				and can be directly linked to firm strategy.
1	18	Yuan et al. (2008)	Where will China go? A viewpoint based on an analysis of the challenges of resource supply and pollution.	Environmental Progress	Review	To provide a viewpoint on CE	A geographic focus (China)	All. The R-framework	*"In an ideal CE system, all the materials and energy are effectively utilized and therefore the environmental impacts of development on the ecosystem are reduced to the minimum. The reduction principle is aimed at reducing the inputs of materials and energy into the production and consumption processes"* (Yuan et al. 2008, p. 511)	In the case of China, the CE was embraced from a policy perspective in order to solve problems such as food scarcity, clean water and air, energy demand and raw material supply. CE was introduced top down via central economic planning instruments.
2	9	Ferasso et al. (2020)	CE business models: The state of research and avenues ahead.	Business Strategy and the Environment	Literature review, bibliometric analysis	To advance in the currently limited knowledge on circular business models.	Business models	Micro-level (firm, product, technology, strategy) but also meso-macro (networks, industry)	*"The CE is a cyclic system that aims to eliminate waste by turning goods that are at the end of their life cycle into resources for new ones"* and *"the aim of this kind of closed loop cyclic system is to eliminate waste by turning goods that are at the end of their life cycle into resources for new ones (Stahel, 2016)"* (Ferasso et al. (2020), p. 1 and 2).	CE is a key topic in the public debate on sustainability. For private actors, new business models allow for a transition of firms to the CE. CE principles comprise technical aspects (resource efficiency, waste generation or environmental impacts) as well as an economic transition perspective (i.e., through business models).
2	2	Bassi and Dias (2020)	Sustainable development of **small - and medium - sized** enterprises in the European Union: A taxonomy of CE practices.	Business Strategy and the Environment	Quantitative (data from the Flash Eurobarometer 441 survey)	To identify CE implementation practices in firms	EU-28 and small and medium-sized firms (SMEs)	Micro-level (firm)	The authors refer to the CE definitions of other authors (Geissdoerfer et al, 2017, Geng and Doberstein, 2008, Stahel, 1982 and EMF, 2015)	Academically, CE is criticised to be superficial and unsystematic.
1	Included from the general	Ellen MacArthur Foundation	Towards the CE.	https://www.ellenmacarthurfoundation.or	Presentation of a concept	(grey literature)	Holistic	None	*"The term 'CE' denotes an industrial economy that is restorative by intention and*	As opposed to the current (linear) economic system, the CE may offer environmental,

(continued)

Table 3.3 (continued)

Group	Citations	Authors	Title	Journal or source	Approach	Research scope	Focus	CE levels	CE definitions, taxonomies or classifications	Main insights from the paper on the CE
	Google search. The number of citations is not provided there	(2013b)		g/assets/downloads/publications/TCE_Report-2013.pdf					*design*" (Ellen MacArthur Foundation 2013b, p. 23).	social and economic benefits. Longevity and closing economic cycles are key. Different sectors face different opportunities and challenges.
1	Included from the general Google search. The number of citations is not provided there	Ellen MacArthur Foundation (2013c)	What is a CE?	https://www.ellenmacarthurfoundation.org/circular-economy/concept	Presentation of a concept	(grey literature)	Holistic	None	"*A CE aims to redefine growth, focusing on positive society-wide benefits. It entails gradually decoupling economic activity from the consumption of finite resources, and designing waste out of the system. Underpinned by a transition to renewable energy sources, the circular model builds economic, natural, and social capital. It is based on three principles:* - *Design out waste and pollution* - *Keep products and materials in use* - *Regenerate natural systems*" (Ellen MacArthur Foundation 2013c).	The CE has its origins in other historical and philosophical concepts. The two main spheres of the CE are the technical and the biological sphere. In both, loops must be closed.
1	Included from the general Google search. The number of citations is	Ellen MacArthur Foundation (2013a)	Infographic CE System diagram.	https://www.ellenmacarthurfoundation.org/circular-economy/concept/infographic	Presentation of a concept	(grey literature)	Holistic	None	"*A CE seeks to rebuild capital, whether this is financial, manufactured, human, social or natural. This ensures enhanced flows of goods and services. The system diagram illustrates the continuous flow of technical*	There are three principles of the CE (preserve natural capital, optimize resource use and foster system effectiveness). The technical and biological sphere allow for closing loops via different mechanisms.

(continued)

Table 3.3 (continued)

Group	Citations	Authors	Title	Journal or source	Approach	Research scope	Focus	CE levels	CE definitions, taxonomies or classifications	Main insights from the paper on the CE
	not provided there								*and biological materials through the 'value circle'"* (Ellen MacArthur Foundation 2013a)	
1	Included from the general Google search. The number of citations is not provided there	European Commission (2020)	EU CE Action Plan.	https://ec.europa.eu/environment/circular-economy/	Policy report	(policy literature)	Policy and legislation	All	Several parts of the CE are highlighted in different parts of the report tailored to the topic at hand. One definition related to resources that is given is: *"The CE can significantly reduce the negative impacts of resource extraction and use on the environment and contribute to restoring biodiversity and natural capital in Europe"* (European Commission 2020, p. 12)	The EU policy on CE fits in the EU Green Deal and offers immense strategic opportunities for the continent. Guidance for economic actors is key, mainly by policy makers, but also by finance. Many mechanisms that can be used are outlined in the report.
1	Included from the general Google search. The number of citations is not provided there	House of Commons (2014)	Growing a CE: Ending the Throwaway Society.	https://publications.parliament.uk/pa/cm201415/cmselect/cmenvaud/214/21402.htm	Policy report	(policy literature)	Policy and legislation	All	*"CE maximises the sustainable use and value of resources, eliminating waste and benefiting both the economy and the environment. It offers an alternative to the predominant current approach where resources are used for one purpose and then discarded. The idea is not new, and is associated with a range of concepts such as 'cradle to cradle' design and 'industrial ecology', which draw inspiration from biological cycles and emphasise the importance of optimising the use of resources in a system over*	Policy plays an important role in transiting the economy and society towards a CE. Taxation reform, funding of material recovery activities, the ban of certain economic waste-related action and cooperation with the industry on environmental standards or eco-design are recommended policy approaches.

(continued)

Table 3.3 (continued)

Group	Citations	Authors	Title	Journal or source	Approach	Research scope	Focus	CE levels	CE definitions, taxonomies or classifications	Main insights from the paper on the CE
									time. A CE includes a range of processes, or 'cycles', in which resources are repeatedly used and their value maintained wherever possible" (House of Commons 2014, p. 5).	

Source: Own elaboration

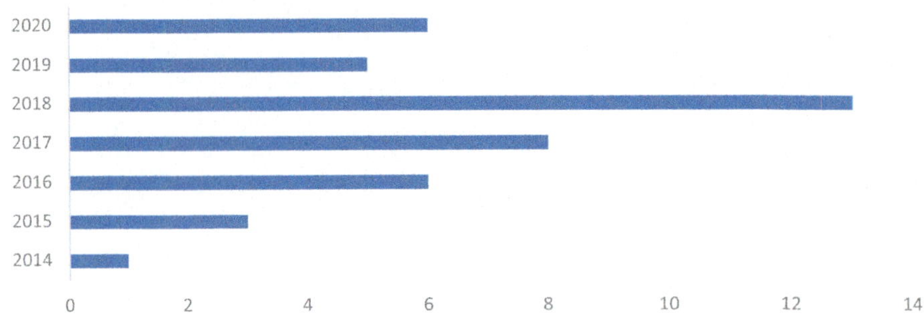

Fig. 3.1 Number of publications per year

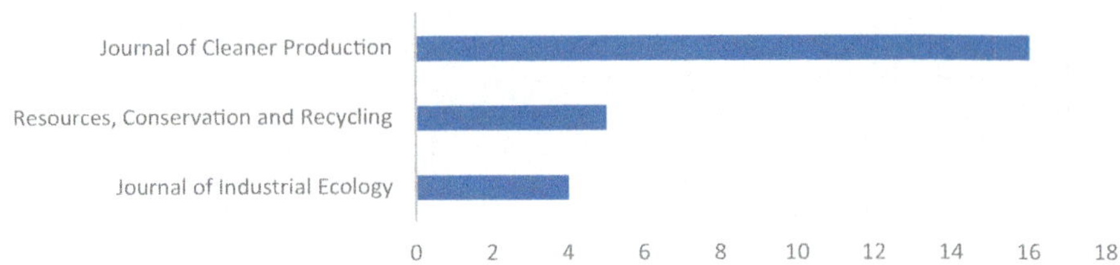

Fig. 3.2 Number of publications per journal

literature reviews (27) and theory building, concept or framework development (13). Only 10 studies were data-based contributions: bibliometric studies (5) and empirical data analysis (5). The grey literature contributes with concept presentations (6) and policy reports (5) (Fig. 3.3).

The provision of an overview of the CE concept is the aim or research scope of most contributions (29). This includes the revision, clarification or classification of existing CE contributions and also the work of contributions from the grey literature on CE concepts, most prominently by the EMF. Twelve contributions aim to provide guiding or implementation principles, 9 evaluate the potential and contribution of the CE to reach sustainability, and 7 assess drivers and barriers to the CE directly or through eco-innovation. Again, the provision of overviews, definitions, classifications or taxonomies is deemed a usual feature of an emerging field (Fig. 3.4).

Regarding the most relevant advantages of the CE contributions which are highlighted in the selected papers, policy relevance stands out as the single most important factor (18). Also, the goal orientation of the concept (i.e. it is instrumental for achieving sustainability) is frequently highlighted (10). To a lesser extent, it is appraised that CE provides a broader picture of the sustainability transition of the economy and society (7) and specifically that it is rooted in several earlier concepts (4), thus being multifaceted and providing conceptual flexibility (Fig. 3.5).

On the other hand, among the major criticisms, the following stand out: no clear academic definition of the CE exists (11), and as a consequence, the CE may mean

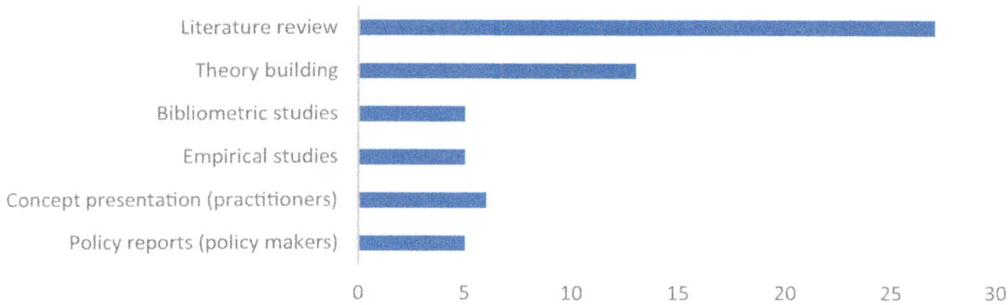

Fig. 3.3 Approaches followed in the selected contributions (number of publications per approach)

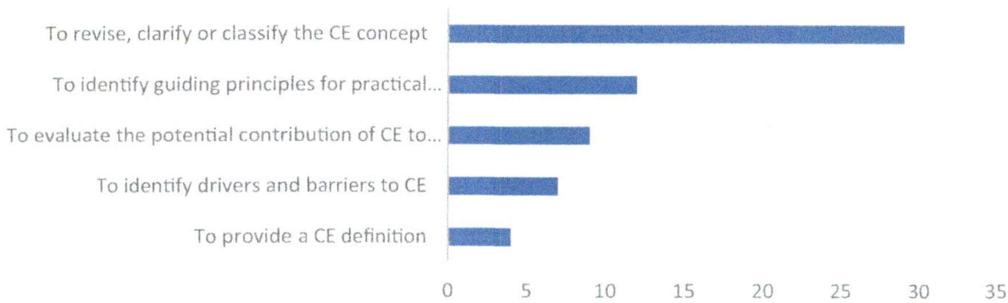

Fig. 3.4 Stated aims or research scopes (number of publications per stated aim or research scope)

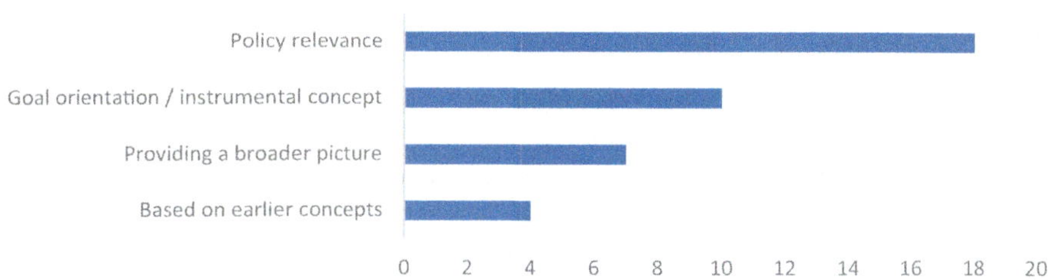

Fig. 3.5 Top highlighted advantages (number of publications that highlight certain advantages of the CE concept)

different things to different actors. Also, the concept is not new (10), the CE is only an umbrella concept incorporating already existing concepts without developing new content (9), and it is not well understood by economic actors, policy-makers and researchers (7) (see Sect. 2.7 for an in-depth discussion of these shortcomings) (Fig. 3.6).

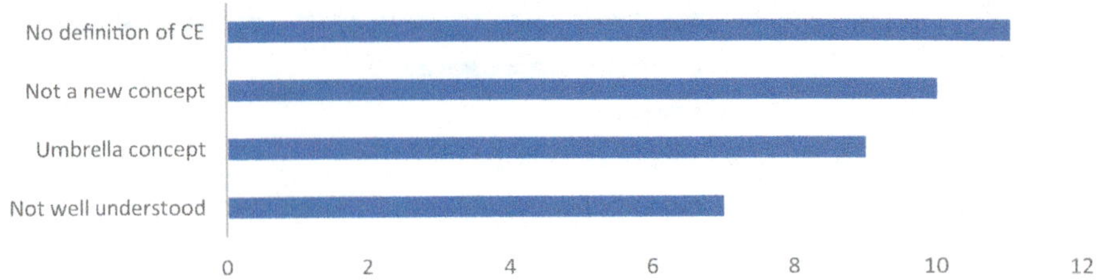

Fig. 3.6 Top highlighted shortcomings (number of publications that highlight certain shortcomings of the CE concept)

3.4 Synthesis of Definitions

Regarding how a CE could function, the vast majority of CE definitions adheres to the identification of a "system perspective of the CE" or the "closing cycles perspective" or even both (see also Sect. 4.1).

The system perspective states the CE may occur at different hierarchy levels: in companies or with respect to products at the micro-level, in eco-industrial parks or along value chains at the meso-level or in cities, regions or countries at the macro-level. According to this view, the CE is considered a multi-level framework, which means different things at different levels. The hierarchically closer a level is to a firm (i.e. the micro-level), the more leverage and room for manoeuvre the firm has, i.e. through developing innovations or changing business practices. It is thus generally easier to address CE at this level for individual actors. On the downside, the overall impact of CE initiatives at the micro-level may be very limited. They may not impact higher levels of the CE, and their contribution to systemic change and a transition of the economy to sustainability may also be modest.

The "closing cycles perspective", which represents the core principle of the CE, focuses on cycles that include both man-made products, components and materials and biological raw and processed materials. Different economic activities have been proposed to close cycles such as reduce, reuse and recycle ("3R"). More and more such R-activities have been added, and up to 10 Rs are proposed (see Chap. 4 for details).

Both the system perspective and the closing cycles perspective can be combined as they are mutually complementary. A few contributions do so explicitly, while some others do so implicitly. Broadly speaking, the system perspective identifies the levels of action in which CE initiatives can take place, while the closing cycles perspective identifies which specific CE-related action can be implemented at that level. And vice versa, as for a specific CE-related action, a certain economic level is addressed. For instance, in-house CE initiatives can be carried out by firms without external cooperation. In contrast, initiatives along the value chain require such cooperation. In short, the system perspective in combination with the "closing cycles perspective" frames the scope ("what") and mechanism ("how") with regard to the CE.

Regarding the aims and targets of the CE, many definitions build on the fact that CE is not an aim in itself. Instead, CE is instrumental for reaching sustainability in a broader sense. Sustainable development and the associated Sustainable Development Goals (SDGs) are commonly referred (see also Sects. 2.1 and 2.6). Other closely related aims are resource and energy efficiency, value retention, utility maximization, zero-waste or maximum use of wastes with regard to minimizing negative economic impacts on the environment. Some authors also state that the CE may positively contribute to the environment through creating restorative industrial systems and that positive development can regenerate nature and hence create environmental and social benefit. Most of these definitions are based on the understanding that economic development can be decoupled from environmental degradation and coupled to the rebuilding of natural and social capital.

Therewith, economic activity and economic artefacts are understood to form part of an economic system that, in turn, forms part of a broader global system. The economic perspective is thus widened to include the environmental and social perspectives.

While both the aims of the CE, its hierarchical levels and the associated general CE-related actions are relatively well defined, most CE definitions are silent on specific tools for involved actors (producers and consumers as economic actors and policy-makers as transition-encompassing and guiding actors). In a few cases, CE definitions identify concrete actions or tools but it is often not clear what involved actors can specifically do. Some CE definitions address this issue and "connect" CE to other concepts such as business models, firm strategy and eco-innovation. They make use of other concepts and their tools in order to operationalize the CE for economic actors.

We conclude that the CE is a two-sided concept: CE is a vision of how an economic system can be ideally sustainable, practically based on closed cycles of physical resource and energy flows at different hierarchical levels and by different actors in which, after each original use, subsequent use maintains or enhances the resource-based economic value and creates or enhances environmental and social value. The CE vision of closed cycles and retained value is connected to being an instrument which contributes to Sustainable Development and which involves a rupture with the current state of the linear economy. The instrumental part of CE is embedded in the eco-innovation concept and refers to the subset of targets which are related to closing cycles and retaining value, as mentioned in Chap. 2.

3.5 Strengths and Weaknesses: A Critical Appraisal of CE Definitions

The definitions, classifications and taxonomies of the CE highlight several strengths but also weaknesses that are inherent to the CE concept. Most commonly, the provision of a "broader picture" of sustainability transitions is appraised.

Especially, the policy-makers and businesses find it very attractive because it provides a clear perspective on things that should be done in order to operationalize sustainability transitions and make sustainability and competitiveness compatible. The different levels suggest the scope of activities that individual firms (micro-level), coordinated groups of firms (meso-level) or entire economies (macro-level) can undertake. They suggest the role of policies in guiding these actors towards desired action, and they are thus highly policy-relevant in this respect. Within each level, practical choices exist on how to reach a higher circularity. Thus, in essence, the CE guides policy-makers and businesses in a very general manner, yet it leaves enough room for flexible adaptation.

Being so flexible, it is a very attractive concept because it can easily be fitted to specific situations or goals. It provides simple criteria upon which decisions can be based, i.e. to replace linear (undesired) practices with circular (desired) ones. Even getting a little bit more circular is already a success. Furthermore, as the concept is well known and already present in a wider public debate, it is also of commercial interest for firms to engage in CE, and policy-makers can easily fit their goals (such as job creation) under their CE policy strategy. It is easy to “sell” a concept that does not call for curbing the economy but rather changing it towards a triple positive outcome (economic, environmental and social).

One of the main strengths of the concept is that it has already become very popular among policy-makers, who have adopted regulations in some countries in order to implement it (China, the EU and Germany, among others; see Chap. 7 for further details), in an effort to move towards sustainability. But the causation has probably also gone the other way around: the implementation of CE regulations in pioneering countries has undeniably spurred interest in the concept, both by policy-makers elsewhere, practitioners and academics. Indeed, its early policy achievements with regard to recycling in Germany and with regard to air and water quality as well as food security in China are at least partially responsible for the success of the CE concept.

On the downside, the CE concept is often criticized for being too broad and unspecific, and to provide little or even no extra value compared to earlier concepts. For some researchers, it is not clear what the CE really is and some even consider it too simplistic (not addressing issues with sufficient details) or raisin picking (not addressing all issues) (see Sect. 2.7 for details).

Lastly, it is recognized that the field moves slowly away from its initial fuzziness and towards (yet-to-be-reached) consensuses, because agreement begins to form along certain major avenues of the CE such as the system perspective and the closing cycles perspective.

References

1. Bassi F, Dias JG (2020) Sustainable development of small- and medium-sized enterprises in the European Union: a taxonomy of circular economy practices. Bus Strategy Environ. https://doi.org/10.1002/bse.2518
2. Bocken NMP, de Pauw I, Bakker C, van der Grinten B (2016) Product design and business model strategies for a circular economy. J Ind Prod Eng 33, 308–320
3. Ellen MacArthur Foundation (2013a) Infographic circular economy system diagram. Retrieved from https://www.ellenmacarthurfoundation.org/circular-economy/concept/infographic
4. Ellen Macarthur Foundation (2013) Towards the circular economy: economic and business rationale for an accelerated transition
5. Ellen MacArthur Foundation. (2013b) Towards the circular economy (1530-9290). Retrieved from https://www.ellenmacarthurfoundation.org/assets/downloads/publications/Ellen-MacArthur-Foundation-Towards-the-Circular-Economy-vol.1.pdf
6. Ellen MacArthur Foundation (2013c) What is a circular economy? A framework for an economy that is restorative and regenerative by design. Retrieved from https://www.ellenmacarthurfoundation.org/circular-economy/concept
7. European Commission (2020) EU circular economy action plan. A new circular economy action plan for a cleaner and more competitive Europe. Retrieved from https://ec.europa.eu/environment/circular-economy/
8. Ferasso M, Beliaeva T, Kraus S, Clauss T, Ribeiro-Soriano D (2020) Circular economy business models: the state of research and avenues ahead. Bus Strategy Environ. https://doi.org/10.1002/bse.2554
9. Fisher O, Watson N, Porcu L, Bacon D, Rigley M, Gomes RL (2018) Cloud manufacturing as a sustainable process manufacturing route. J Manuf Syst 47:53–68. https://doi.org/10.1016/j.jmsy.2018.03.005
10. Geisendorf S, Pietrulla F (2018) The circular economy and circular economic concepts-a literature analysis and redefinition. Thunderbird Int Bus Rev 60(5):771–782. https://doi.org/10.1002/tie.21924
11. Geissdoerfer M, Savaget P, Bocken NMP, Hultink EJ (2017) The circular economy—a new sustainability paradigm? J Clean Prod 143:757–768. https://doi.org/10.1016/j.jclepro.2016.12.048
12. Geng Y, Doberstein B (2008) Developing the circular economy in China: challenges and opportunities for achieving 'leapfrog development'. Int J Sustain Dev World Ecol 15(3):231–239. https://doi.org/10.3843/SusDev.15.3:6
13. Ghisellini P, Cialani C, Ulgiati S (2016) A review on circular economy: the expected transition to a balanced interplay of environmental and economic systems. J Clean Prod 114:11–32. https://doi.org/10.1016/j.jclepro.2015.09.007
14. Govindan K, Hasanagic M (2018) A systematic review on drivers, barriers, and practices towards circular economy: a supply chain perspective. Int J Prod Res 56(1–2):278–311. https://doi.org/10.1080/00207543.2017.1402141
15. Gregson N, Crang M, Fuller S, Holmes H (2015) Interrogating the circular economy: the moral economy of resource recovery in the EU. Economy and Society 44(2):218–243. https://doi.org/10.1080/03085147.2015.1013353
16. Haas W, Krausmann F, Wiedenhofer D, Heinz M (2015) How circular is the global economy?: An assessment of material flows, waste production, and recycling in the European Union and the world in 2005. J Ind Ecol 19(5):765–777. https://doi.org/10.1111/jiec.12244
17. Hens L, Block C, Cabello-Eras JJ, Sagastume-Gutierez A, Garcia-Lorenzo D, Chamorro C, Vandecasteele C (2018) On the evolution of "cleaner production" as a concept and a practice. J Clean Prod 172:3323–3333. https://doi.org/10.1016/j.jclepro.2017.11.082

18. den Hollander MC, Bakker CA, Hultink EJ (2017) Product design in a circular economy: development of a typology of key concepts and terms. J Ind Ecol 21(3):517–525. https://doi.org/10.1111/jiec.12610
19. Homrich AS, Galvão G, Abadia LG, Carvalho MM (2018) The circular economy umbrella: trends and gaps on integrating pathways. J Clean Prod 175:525–543. https://doi.org/10.1016/j.jclepro.2017.11.064
20. House of Commons (2014) Growing a circular economy: ending the throwaway society. Retrieved from https://publications.parliament.uk/pa/cm201415/cmselect/cmenvaud/214/214.pdf
21. Hu J, Xiao Z, Zhou R, Deng W, Wang M, Ma S (2011) Ecological utilization of leather tannery waste with circular economy model. J Clean Prod 19(2–3):221–228. https://doi.org/10.1016/j.jclepro.2010.09.018
22. de Jesus A, Antunes P, Santos R, Mendonça S (2018) Eco-innovation in the transition to a circular economy: an analytical literature review. J Clean Prod 172:2999–3018. https://doi.org/10.1016/j.jclepro.2017.11.111
23. de Jesus A, Mendonça S (2018) Lost in transition? Drivers and barriers in the eco-innovation road to the circular economy. Ecol Econ 145:75–89. https://doi.org/10.1016/j.ecolecon.2017.08.001
24. Kirchherr J, Reike D, Hekkert M (2017) Conceptualizing the circular economy: an analysis of 114 definitions. Resour Conserv Recycl 127:221–232. https://doi.org/10.1016/j.resconrec.2017.09.005
25. Korhonen J, Honkasalo A, Seppälä J (2018) Circular economy: the concept and its limitations. Ecol Econ 143:37–46. https://doi.org/10.1016/j.ecolecon.2017.06.041
26. Korhonen J, Nuur C, Feldmann A, Birkie SE (2018) Circular economy as an essentially contested concept. J Clean Prod 175:544–552. https://doi.org/10.1016/j.jclepro.2017.12.111
27. Lieder M, Rashid A (2016) Towards circular economy implementation: a comprehensive review in context of manufacturing industry. J Clean Prod 115:36–51. https://doi.org/10.1016/j.jclepro.2015.12.042
28. Loiseau E, Saikku L, Antikainen R, Droste N, Hansjürgens B, Pitkänen K, Thomsen M (2016) Green economy and related concepts: an overview. J Clean Prod 139:361–371. https://doi.org/10.1016/j.jclepro.2016.08.024
29. Masi D, Kumar V, Garza-Reyes JA, Godsell J (2018) Towards a more circular economy: exploring the awareness, practices, and barriers from a focal firm perspective. Prod Plan Control 29(6):539–550. https://doi.org/10.1080/09537287.2018.1449246
30. Masi D, Day S, Godsell J (2017) Supply chain configurations in the circular economy: a systematic literature review. Sustainability 9(9). https://doi.org/10.3390/su9091602
31. Merli R, Preziosi M, Acampora A (2018) How do scholars approach the circular economy? A systematic literature review. J Clean Prod 178:703–722. https://doi.org/10.1016/j.jclepro.2017.12.112
32. Millar N, McLaughlin E, Börger T (2019) The circular economy: swings and roundabouts? Ecol Econ 158:11–19. https://doi.org/10.1016/j.ecolecon.2018.12.012
33. Moraga G, Huysveld S, Mathieux F, Blengini GA, Alaerts L, Van Acker K, Dewulf J (2019) Circular economy indicators: what do they measure? Resour Conserv Recycl 146:452–461. https://doi.org/10.1016/j.resconrec.2019.03.045
34. Murray A, Skene K, Haynes K (2017) The circular economy: an interdisciplinary exploration of the concept and application in a global context. J Bus Ethics 140:369–380. https://doi.org/10.1007/s10551-015-2693-2
35. Niero M, Olsen SI (2016) Circular economy: To be or not to be in a closed product loop? A life cycle assessment of aluminium cans with inclusion of alloying elements. Resour Conserv Recycl 114:18–31. https://doi.org/10.1016/j.resconrec.2016.06.023
36. Nußholz J (2017) Circular business models: defining a concept and framing an emerging research field. Sustainability 9(10). https://doi.org/10.3390/su9101810

37. Pauliuk S (2018) Critical appraisal of the circular economy standard BS 8001:2017 and a dashboard of quantitative system indicators for its implementation in organizations. Resour Conserv Recycl 129:81–92. https://doi.org/10.1016/j.resconrec.2017.10.019
38. Pearce DW, Turner RK (1990) Economics of natural resources and the environment. Johns Hopkins Univ Press
39. Prieto-Sandoval V, Jaca C, Ormazabal M (2018) Towards a consensus on the circular economy. J Clean Prod 179:605–615. https://doi.org/10.1016/j.jclepro.2017.12.224
40. Reike D, Vermeulen WJV, Witjes S (2018) The circular economy: new or refurbished as CE 3.0?—Exploring controversies in the conceptualization of the circular economy through a focus on history and resource value retention options. Resour Conserv Recycl 135:246–264. https://doi.org/10.1016/j.resconrec.2017.08.027
41. Saidani M, Yannou B, Leroy Y, Cluzel F, Kendall A (2019) A taxonomy of circular economy indicators. J Clean Prod 207:542–559. https://doi.org/10.1016/j.jclepro.2018.10.014
42. Sauvé S, Bernard S, Sloan P (2016) Environmental sciences, sustainable development and circular economy: alternative concepts for trans-disciplinary research. Environ Develop 17:48–56. https://doi.org/10.1016/j.envdev.2015.09.002
43. Stahel WR (2016) The circular economy. Nature. Retrieved from https://www.nature.com/news/the-circular-economy-1.19594
44. Stahel WR, Reday-Mulvey G (1982) Jobs for tomorrow: the potential for substituting manpower for energy. Vantage Press
45. Suárez-Eiroa B, Fernández E, Méndez-Martínez G, Soto-Oñate D (2019) Operational principles of circular economy for sustainable development: linking theory and practice. J Clean Prod 214:952–961. https://doi.org/10.1016/j.jclepro.2018.12.271
46. Tukker A (2015) Product services for a resource-efficient and circular economy—a review. J Clean Prod 97:76–91. https://doi.org/10.1016/j.jclepro.2013.11.049
47. Ünal E, Shao J (2019) A taxonomy of circular economy implementation strategies for manufacturing firms: analysis of 391 cradle-to-cradle products. J Clean Prod 212:754–765. https://doi.org/10.1016/j.jclepro.2018.11.291
48. Urbinati A, Chiaroni D, Chiesa V (2017) Towards a new taxonomy of circular economy business models. J Clean Prod 168:487–498. https://doi.org/10.1016/j.jclepro.2017.09.047
49. Webster K (2015) The circular economy: a wealth of flows. Ellen MacArthur Foundation, Isle of Wight
50. Yuan Z, Bi J, Moriguichi Y (2006) The circular economy: a new development strategy in China. J Ind Ecol 10:4–8
51. Yuan Z, Jiang W, Liu B, Bi J (2008) Where will China go? A viewpoint based on an analysis of the challenges of resource supply and pollution. Environ Prog 27(4):503–514. https://doi.org/10.1002/ep.10300
52. Zink T, Geyer R (2017) Circular economy rebound. J Ind Ecol 21(3):593–602. https://doi.org/10.1111/jiec.12545

Chapter 4
The Micro-level Approach to the Circular Economy

4.1 The Levels of the Circular Economy

The CE is a multidimensional and multi-level concept. This multidimensionality is addressed by most authors in the CE literature. The analysis of the CE in a given setting has been approached from two different yet overlapping perspectives, the "systemic" and the "hierarchical" (or R-framework) approaches (see also Chap. 3). The former has emphasized the different levels of circularity, whereas the latter tries to identify best practices in each level. Both perspectives should be combined in any analysis of circularity practices.

Regarding the systemic perspective, the CE has often been characterized as a multi-level phenomenon. The previous literature has stressed that CE may occur and can be analysed at different levels, such as the micro-level (products, companies, consumers), meso-level (inter-firm networks, symbiosis association, (eco)-industrial parks, green supply chain management) and macro-level (city, province, region and nation) [28, 37]. The spatial differentiation of the CE is also present in many contributions. For example, Fang et al. [13] argue that "at the macro-level, the development of a CE emphasizes adjusting industrial composition and structure (…). At the meso-level, (the CE is about) applying industrial ecology concepts (…). At the micro-level, the CE will ensure that by-products are identified in individual enterprises and used effectively" [13, p. 318]. Likewise, Ghisellini et al. [19] claim that the implementation of the CE at the macro-level refers mostly to cities (e.g. ecocities), it focuses on the introduction of eco-industrial parks at the meso-level, and it is related to the adoption of cleaner production and eco-design at the micro-level.

Circular solutions are understood to replace existing linear solutions at each level, possibly involving different kinds of stakeholders at the corresponding level. The higher level is the *macro-level.* In an idealized situation, CE-type arrangements of the physical flows of materials and energy would reduce virgin inputs to the system and waste and emissions outputs from the system [29]. However, this ideal

P. del Río et al., *The Circular Economy*, Green Energy and Technology,
https://doi.org/10.1007/978-3-030-74792-3_4

of a single cyclic system is not realistic since, as Korhonen et al. [29, p. 42] argue, "CE-type projects that have been implemented and that will be implemented in the near future will always be local or regional at most since no global body for governance exists". At this level, industrial metabolism is emphasized, and minimization of materials and energy flows are stressed from a policy-making point of view. From an academic perspective, the focus is on the analysis of the biological analogy applied to the whole industrial system.

On the *meso-level*, inter-firm level collaboration and synergies are emphasized. These are enabled through geographic proximity [31], with economic agents being integrated in symbiosis [18].

On the *micro-level*, the attention is on the circular models, practices and technologies implemented by individual actors (in this case, firms) [5]. Firms are important actors for the realization of a CE [23]. "Firms' activities largely determine the optimization of the 'inner circles' of the CE which relate to reducing material and energy consumption, increasing recycling and reuse, and expanding product lifetime" [23, p. 2]. On the other hand, "the CE approach has also attracted the attention of many firms" [23, p. 1] since it can increase the efficiency of production processes or allow firms to show their sustainability efforts [23]. As stressed by Kiefer et al. [26] and mentioned throughout this book, since the contributions on the micro-level are scarce, there is a call for more CE studies at this level [15, 19, 31, 43, 45].

Regarding the "hierarchical perspective", as mentioned in the previous section, a main distinguishing feature of the CE concept is "value retention", i.e. keeping resources within the economy by retaining the added value in products for as long as possible, extracting their maximum value and eliminating waste [44]. By closing loops and making resource use circular, resources are not lost, but are instead used repeatedly [14].

The identification of a hierarchy of activities has led researchers to focus on those which maximize the extent of circularity, i.e. what Dijksma and Kamp [11, p. 23] call "full circularity". The "butterfly figure" from the Ellen MacArthur Foundation, for instance, proposes a hierarchical arrangement of reuse, repair, refurbishment, remanufacturing, repurpose and, finally, recycling [4]. The smaller the loop (activity wise and geographically) the more profitable and resource efficient it is [24]. For example, the inner circles (product reuse, remanufacturing and refurbishment) demand less resources and energy and are also more economic than conventional recycling of materials as low-grade raw materials [30]. Most high-level policy-making (e.g. European Commission) favours reuse over recycling in their "waste hierarchies" although firms, in practice, tend to favour recycling over refurbishment [14].

Several contributions have proposed different types of circular practices without an explicit hierarchization. However, most carry out a systematization of the different practices using the traditional "R-framework". Despite the differences between schools of thought, the core of the CE refers to the "R" activities in practical terms, whether 3 (as in [49]), 9 (as in [38]) or 10 (as in [40]). This R-framework involves multiple pathways for the uptake of CE principles, which are made possible through eco-innovations.

The most simple, popular and easy to remember description of the practical approach of the CE concept is the 3Rs: reduction, reusing and recycling (see, for example, [33]). It is the most commonly employed (35–40% of definitions in the sample of [28]).

The 9Rs framework was developed by Potting et al. [38, p. 5). The authors considered the following circularity strategies within the production chain, with the following order of priority:

- R0 (*refuse*, which consists of making the product redundant by abandoning its function or by offering the same function with a radically different product).
- R1 (*rethink*, which refers to making product use more intensive through, for example, sharing products or by putting multifunctional products on the market).
- R2 (*reduce*, which is about increasing efficiency in product manufacturing or use by consuming fewer natural resources and materials).
- R3 (*reuse* by another consumer of discarded products which are still in good condition and fulfil their original function).
- R4 (*repair* and maintenance of a defective product, so it can be used with its original function).
- R5 (*refurbish*, which refers to restoring an old product and bring it up to date).
- R6 (*remanufacture* or use parts of a discarded product in a new product with the same function).
- R7 (*repurpose* or use parts of a discarded product in a new product with a different function).
- R8 (*recycle*, process materials to obtain the same (high grade) or lower (low grade) quality).
- R9 (*recover*, incineration of materials with energy recovery).

Similarly, Reike et al. [40] distinguish between 10 Rs: R0 (Refuse), R1 (Reduce), R2 (Resell, reuse), R3 (Repair), R4 (Refurbish), R5 (Remanufacture), R6 (Repurpose), R7 (Recycle materials), R8 (Recover energy) and R9 (Remine). Rs closer to R0 are deemed better options from a CE point of view.

Obviously, as mentioned above, both approaches to the CE (the systemic and the hierarchical one) are not isolated from each other and should not be used separately. On the contrary, they are related, and, indeed, they are often used in combination.

4.2 A Focus on the Micro-level. What Circular Economy Practices?

This book focuses on the micro-level of the CE, which refers to individual actors, particularly companies [46, 48]. At this level, companies are focused on their own improvement processes and eco-innovation development or uptake in order to "close the loop" [19, 23, 39]. Several types of CE practices (or circular eco-innovations) can be implemented in firms, including eco-design and cleaner production strategies, resource efficiency initiatives and sustainable production and consumption methods [7]. There are indeed many examples of specific firms undertaking this type of efforts, as shown by the Ellen MacArthur Foundation (2013), among others.

The importance of the micro-level and its relative neglect in the literature (compared to other topics and levels) justifies dedicating an exclusive focus on this level. As argued by Franco [15, p. 835], the CE practices developed and adopted by firms are "pre-requisites for a successful deployment of the circular economy".

Although part of the CE literature has tried to support firms in the implementation of circular processes [35], there is a common agreement among many authors that the focus on the CE at the micro-level has been scarce and, particularly, that the analysis of the antecedents of CE implementation at this level remains a largely unexplored topic [1, 7, 15, 25, 42, 45, 19, 31, 43]. For example, de Jesus et al. [7] observe that the micro-level still represents the smallest corpus in the CE literature. Similarly, according to Lieder and Rashid [31], the literature on micro-level eco-innovation (EI) contributions to sustainability and the CE is "extremely thin". Aranda-Usón et al. [1, p. 2] argue that, although, some studies in the CE literature at the micro-level have been conducted, "conceptual discussions of the CE are still in their infancy among scholars, and the literature in the micro field is only emerging". Similarly, Scarpellini et al. [42, p. 2] observe that "research focused on the micro level, particularly on firms' specific capabilities and their CE involvement, remains scant". Franco [15] also noted the lack of research on the micro-level.

However, several authors have devoted a specific attention to the micro-level circular innovations developed or adopted by firms. Arguably, the focus has been on the following three aspects: (i) what circular practices have been adopted, (ii) what the drivers and barriers to such adoption have been and (iii) what the impacts of such adoption on firm variables (productivity, performance, employment...) have been. These three aspects are connected, particularly the first and the second ones (what are the determinants and barriers to the uptake of given circular practices?) and the first one and the third one (what are the corporate impacts of the adoption of a given circular practice?). This subsection focuses on the first aspect, whereas the next chapter addresses the second. The third issue is also taken into account, but not measured in this book (see [23] for an analysis of this topic).

The selection of the papers below is based on the general literature review performed in Chap. 3 and is useful both for this chapter (focusing on the uptake of CE practices at the micro-level) and Chap. 5 (which is devoted to the analysis of the drivers and barriers to the uptake of those CE practices). Those contributions on the CE with a micro-level perspective were chosen. To do this, we read the title, abstract and key words of all those papers and made an initial selection based on their apparent focus on the micro-level and the use of an empirical approach. In addition, we expanded the number of possible papers with a micro-level focus using snowballing techniques, i.e. looking at the titles of papers in the references of the initially selected contributions. For the final selection, all those papers should include either (i) an empirical investigation of the CE practices developed or adopted by firms at the micro-level (this chapter) or (ii) the drivers and barriers to such development or adoption (Chap. 5). We then read the papers and kept those which met at least one of the above two conditions.

We finally ended up with 24 papers [1, 2, 3, 5, 6, 8, 9, 10, 15, 16, 18, 20, 21, 22, 23, 25, 26, 27, 32, 36, 41, 42, 45, 47]. The aim was to identify which CE practices were considered at the firm level and which ones have been implemented the most. Thus, the main insights from each of the selected papers on the types of CE practices which were adopted by firms are provided below, whereas the drivers and barriers to such adoption are considered in the next chapter.

Cainelli et al. [5] used data from the European Community Innovation Survey (CIS) on 60,000 service and manufacturing firms in nine European countries in the 2006–2008 period. The adoption of three types of environmental innovations which were closely related to the CE and resource efficiency was considered: (i) reduced material use per unit of output; (ii) recycled waste, water or materials and (iii) improved recycling of product after use [5, p. 2]. Their results showed that the most adopted environmental innovations was (ii) (19% of firms), followed by (i) (13.6%) and (iii) (13%).

The aim of Horbach and Rammer [23, p. 4] was to "analyze whether firms that engage in CE innovations experience positive or negative results in terms of sales growth and employment" [23, p. 2]. To do so, they used data from the German part of the CIS in 2014, which allowed the identification of CE innovations at the firm level. The authors found that 27% of all firms in Germany reported CE innovations during 2012–2014. Process-related innovations were more frequent than product-related ones. Regarding process-related CE innovations, 10.6% of firms had reduced energy use per unit of output. This was the single most important activity, followed by recycled waste, water or materials for own use or sale (6.4%) and reduced material use/use of water per unit of output (4.8%). Regarding product-related CE innovations, the most frequent innovation was reduced energy use (7.3% of firms), followed by extended product life through longer-lasting/more durable products (3.7%) and improved recycling of product after use (3.2%).

Kiefer et al. [26], who analysed the relationship between EI and CE, carried out an extensive literature review to search for variables and indicators that allowed them to quantify the concepts of EI and CE and to quantitatively model their relationships. Existing suitable variables and indicators were used. This was the case for EI characteristics. A quantitative 5-point Likert scale was created to differentiate between the existing levels of the CE. Within firms, the survey targeted innovation-related decision makers who were asked on the variables related to EIs. On the other hand, it was difficult for managers in firms to estimate the impacts a given EI had on CE, as this went far beyond firm boundaries. With the aim of reducing motivational and unmotivated biases and to ensure maximum robustness of the analyses, the variable "level of circularity" asked for an open, textual description ("Please describe the impact that the EI has had"). These descriptions allowed the authors to allocate them to one of the defined ordinal scale levels. Their findings suggested that only systemic EIs contributed to a global CE, while other EI types could even act as barriers. At lower levels, such as sector/region and firm, some EI types contributed to circularity. Eco-efficiency stood out in this context.

Surprisingly, upscaling an EI from a lower level to a global circularity level was not possible, and technological novelty and radicality as well as cooperation were not drivers of the CE.

Gusmerotti et al. [22] used a questionnaire-based survey and a cluster analysis to classify the implementation of the CE in 841 Italian companies. They identified five clusters: "information-oriented companies", "linear companies", "green marketers", "optimizers" and "circular companies", and considered 15 CE practices (or "items") drawn from the literature. They asked firms how they had performed with respect to them (on an 11-point Likert scale, ranging from 0% up to 100%). Their results showed that the respondents in the different clusters performed differently with respect to the aforementioned items. For example, respondents in the cluster of "linear companies" performed poorly in all aspects investigated in the questionnaire, whereas respondents in the cluster of "circular companies" had a good performance in all those aspects.

Ormazabal et al. [36] focused on the degree of implementation of the CE by SMEs, including their willingness to work in a symbiotic relationship with other companies. The article was based on an online survey of 95 SMEs in the regions of Navarre and the Basque Country in Spain. The first part of the survey was organized in three groups of questions according to the phases of the CE cycle: take-transform (suppliers compliance with environmental legislation, environmental criteria for suppliers, environmental criteria for consumption and production improvements, use of biodegradable materials and circularity of materials), use (after sales services, rental services and maintenance) and recovery (use of waste heat, reuse of industrial wastes, reclaim of the used products from customers, by-products selling). The authors then asked firms whether they never or always took the practices in those phases into account (with five possibilities in the middle). The results show that, for the take-transform phase, 42% of the participants never or rarely used any environmental criteria for supplier selection, while just 17% of participants continuously used environmental criteria to select their suppliers. "42% of the companies reported that they usually try to reduce the consumption of raw materials while designing and to improve their processes" [36, p. 161]. Regarding the use phase, the SMEs surveyed "are not yet prepared to implement circular business models, such as leasing instead of just selling a product and ending the relationship with clients or offering services that prolong their products' life cycle" [36, p. 161]. Concerning the recovery phase, the responses indicated that "more than 41% of SMEs never or rarely reach the recovery phase by using waste heat, recirculating their own industrial sources, using or selling by-products, or reclaiming used products from their customers" [36, p. 161].

Aranda-Usón et al. [1] contributed to the measurement of the CE at the micro-level from a territorial perspective and analysed how companies adopt the CE principles internally. The authors performed a literature review and classified the 12 CE-related practices performed by businesses that had been analysed in the literature into four groups: (I) Waste treatment and recycling (which included environmental impact, energy efficiency and industrial waste recycling); (II) Dematerialization, secondary raw materials and waste recovery (including renewable energy, dematerialization, recyclability and secondary raw materials); (III) Eco-design (which included eco-design-durability, eco-design-multifunction and eco-innovation) and (IV) Industrial ecology and/or symbiosis (internal recycling, energy waste valorisation and symbiosis). They then asked 52 industrial and non-industrial firms located in the region of Aragon (Spain) to identify the CE-related activities that they performed. The results showed that most firms carried out activities in the first group (between 61% and 82%), whereas only a minority of firms (between 5% and 23%) adopted practices included in group 4. Groups 2 and 3 had intermediate levels of success in this regard. The authors concluded that "a certain incremental tendency can be appreciated through analysis of the specific activities that have been introduced at the micro-level in terms of the CE" [1, p. 9].

Garcés-Ayerbe et al. [16] used the European Commission Flash Eurobarometer 441 [12] to analyse CE practices and behaviour in a sample of 10,618 European companies between 2013 and 2015. Firms were asked whether they had performed any of the following activities: (1) replanning of the way water is used to minimize usage and maximize re-usage; (2) use of renewable energy; (3) replanning energy usage to minimize consumption; (4) minimizing waste by recycling and reusing waste or selling it to another company and; (5) redesigning products and services to minimize the use of materials or use recycled materials. Around ¾ of the firms stated that they had implemented or were implementing at least one of those CE activities ("in-going firms"), whereas ¼ stated that they had not implemented any of them ("no-going firms") [16, p. 7]. The CE activity most often performed by firms was recycle and reuse (77% of firms), followed by minimization of energy consumption (55%), redesign (46%), minimization of water use (or maximization of water re-usage) (25%) and use of renewable energy (23%). The authors indicated that there was a progressive process in the implementation of CE activities, from reactive to proactive behaviour and from control to prevention activities.[1]

The aim of Rizos et al. [41] was to increase knowledge and understanding of the barriers and enablers experienced by SMEs when implementing CE business models. They used a sample of 30 case studies on SMEs from the 52 case studies included in the GreenEcoNet Web platform.[2] Each of those 30 SMEs had strategies that included one or more green solutions. The most common type of green solution in their sample was a green technology/product (70% of SMEs), followed by organizational methods and (green) business plans (50%). Other types of green solutions were training (20%), information technology (7%), networking and communication (7%) and financing (3%). Each of the case studies also belonged to

[1]"CE behavior is a gradual process that starts by implementing material recycling and reuse measures. The next step is to put into practice measures to minimize power consumption and to redesign products. As a last step, the most proactive firms in implementing CE measures also rethink their water use and turn to renewable energy" [16, p. 12].

[2]The GreenEcoNet web platform is "a web platform financed by the European Commission and developed by six European research organisations with the objective of showcasing examples of SMEs that have successfully made a change towards a green business model" [41, p. 6].

one or more technology areas. Resource efficiency (41% of case studies) was the most represented technology area, followed by waste treatment and recycling (16%), materials (10%) and energy production (10%) [41].

Zamfir et al. [47] assessed the adoption of CE practices in European SMEs. As other studies, they used the micro-data from the Flash Eurobarometer 441 with 10,618 European companies (for a discussion of the CE practices considered in this Eurobarometer, see [16] above). They found that almost ¾ of SMEs had undertaken some CE activities in the three-year period covered by the study. The most widespread CE practices were recycling, reusing or selling waste to other companies (55% of SMEs) and the reduction of energy consumption by replanning its usage (38%). This was followed by the redesign of the products and services of the firm in order to reduce the use of materials or to use recycled materials (34%), the minimization of the usage of water by replanning how water was used (19%) and the use of renewable energy (16%) [47].

The starting point in García-Quevedo et al. [17] was the observation that, despite the potential benefits of CE activities, their implementation remains relatively rare. They also used the European Commission's Eurobarometer Survey 441 and confirmed that the most commonly adopted practices by the SMEs were "those aimed at minimizing waste by recycling or reusing waste or selling it to another company (59%) and improving energy efficiency (43%). In contrast, SMEs are less likely to implement actions to replan water usage (20%) and to make a predominant use of renewable energy (18%)" [17, p. 2456].

Bassi and Dias [3] also used the Flash Eurobarometer 441 and confirmed the findings of previous studies which used the same database. They found that "73.2% of the firms undertook or were in the process of undertaking at least one CE activity in the past three years; however, the situation varies greatly across countries" [3, p. 531]. As in other studies, SMEs adopted CE practices to a different degree. Minimizing waste by recycling or reusing waste or selling it to another company was the most adopted CE practice (55.4% of firms have adopted or are about to adopt this policy), followed by replanning energy usage to minimize consumption (37.7% of SMEs), redesigning products and services to minimize the use of materials or using recycled material (34.4%), replanning the way water is used to minimize usage and maximize re-usage (18.8%) and the use of renewable energy (15% of firms) [3, p. 531]. These results were further confirmed by Demirel and Danisman [8], who also used the Flash Eurobarometer 441 to show that the most common CE activity introduced by SMEs was minimizing waste (39% of firms), followed by replanning energy (26%), redesigning products and services (22%), using renewable energy (13%) and replanning water (12%).

Although Katz-Gerro and López Sintas [25] also used the Flash Eurobarometer 441 survey to confirm previous findings, their analysis showed that firms in some countries (e.g. Finland and Ireland) adopted the five specific CE activities more frequently. They also found that there were "systematic differences between countries in both the type of activities adopted and the frequency with which their firms engage in specific activities" [25, p. 488]. A very interesting finding of this paper is that "there is a ranking of CE activity adoption observed in all patterns (activity path dependency), with companies differing in the degree to which they are involved in those activities (level of path dependency). These findings contrast with the alternative configurational possibility, which suggests that companies adopt particular and differing patterns of CE activities that are independent of each other" [25, p. 489].

Diaz Lopez et al. [10] analysed how changes in business models can support resource efficiency measures (REMs) implemented by companies. REMs referred to "technical and organisational measures such as the use of more resource-efficient technologies, the design of products that use less materials and energy over their life cycles, or taking back product components for re-use in new products" [10, p. 21]. An analytical framework was developed which consisted of a classification of REMs, business model changes (BMCs), radicalness of change and implementation barriers (IBs). This framework was applied to 143 analysed cases (and dominant types of REMs) in the literature. The 143 REMs were classified into three categories: supply side measures (cleaner production, eco-efficiency, green supply chain management, pollution control and waste management), demand side measures (functional sales, green products, green services, service instead of products, service substitutes and take back management) and life cycle measures (cradle-to-cradle, CE and industrial symbiosis). The authors showed that the variety of REMs implemented was high and that specific categories such as cleaner production or green products did not dominate.

Scarpellini et al. [42] analysed the previous business routines and activities that could facilitate the introduction of a CE. In a survey of 89 Spanish firms with a size above 50 employees, firms were asked about several variables in order to explore the intersection between eco-innovation and the CE-related activities introduced by businesses. Five groups of eco-innovation inputs and outcomes in the context of the CE were selected: (1) Eco-innovation investments; (2) eco-design; (3) circular energy; (4) circular R&D and (5) circular material loops.[3] The authors provided evidence that these "CE-related activities behave similarly to eco-innovation" [42, p. 11], highlighting the importance of the latter for the former. Specifically, at the micro-level in firms, environmental capabilities that are needed for eco-innovations were also positively related to CE activities [42].

Sousa-Zomer et al. [45] used a case study approach of a single firm in an emerging economy (Brazil) to analyse how the adoption of cleaner production (CP) practices influenced the implementation of the CE by the firm. The authors concluded that CP practices fostered the implementation of CE principles in the firm. In particular, the company implemented a range of CP practices and principles (material input, design, production, delivery, consumption and end-of-life resource management) that contributed to the implementation of the new circular business model. It implemented a new business strategy focused on the leasing of water purifiers which represents a use-oriented product–service system.

[3]These five broad categories include many items (see [42] for details).

Franco [15] focused on three practices (sustainable product design, sustainable supply chain and reverse logistics) in the European textile industry using eight case studies from cradle-to-cradle (C2C) certified companies in Germany, Switzerland, Austria and Italy. The authors reached interesting conclusions regarding the impacts between different stages of the value chain, i.e. upstream and downstream. According to Franco [15, p. 841], "innovations in basic materials upstream of the value chain, in particular, facilitated the development of innovations in component parts and finished products downstream, while demand for circular products pulled by manufacturers and retailers downstream stimulated manufacturing as well as the provision of textile services from 'sandwich spectators' upstream".

Liu and Bai [32] explored firm awareness and behaviour in developing the CE. They carried out a survey and interviewed 157 manufacturing firms from Bohai Rim, Tianjinin (China). The firms' engagement (awareness and actual behaviour) with regards to reducing, reusing and recycling both materials and energy was measured. CE awareness was proxied by several variables: knowledge about the CE generally and the 3Rs specifically, agreement on whether the CE should be considered (a part of) business ethics and willingness to engage in waste regeneration and reduction, as well as minimization of natural resource consumption and waste production. Actual CE behaviour was proxied by purchase of environmentally sensitive raw materials, minimization of resource consumption, waste disposal techniques, eco-industrial inter-firm cooperation, use of cleaner production auditing and existence of a CE management department. The results showed that, although firms had generally a good understanding of the CE, a positive view about it, and a strong willingness to operate under the principles of the CE [32], actual firm behaviour was quite different and much more linear. Most firms did not have a CE management department, cooperate with other firms or perform cleaner production audits.

Guldmann and Huulgaard [21] focused on circular business model innovations at the micro (firm) level. Accordingly, they carried out 12 case studies in Denmark, covering different firm sizes, ages, customer segments and sectors of activity. The authors stated that circular business models extended linear ones in several respects: value recreation and redelivery, and value recapture within the extended value proposition, through preservation of embedded value at the highest level of utility, slowing or closing of resource loops and extended and intensified product use, among others [21].

Dey et al. [9] investigated how the CE enhances firm sustainability using a sample of 130 SMEs from the West Midlands region in the UK. Data were collected from a survey, focus groups and case studies and were used for performing structural equitation modelling. Several CE fields of action were investigated: materials and source selection, inbound storage and transportation (take), eco-design, lean practices, total energy and renewable energy consumption, well-being and equality (make), outbound storage and transportation (distribute), after sales service, repair, reuse, carbon offsetting (use), recycle and reverse logistics (recover). The three dimensions of sustainability were proxied by productivity, turnover, cost and growth (economic), energy and resource efficiency and waste reduction (environmental) and employee turnover, accident reduction and carbon offsetting (social performance). The results showed that CE fields of action were mostly related to better economic performance (take, make, distribute, use, recover) but much less to better environmental or social performance (make, use), highlighting a strong economic focus of the CE in SMEs.

Barreiro-Gen and Lozano [2] focused on the implementation of the CE in organizations in order to answer the question of "how circular" the CE is. They investigated the 4Rs of reduction, repairing, remanufacturing and recycling with the help of a survey to 5,922 organizations worldwide taken from the Global Reporting Initiative (GRI) list and 256 answers sets (with a clear dominance of EU organizations). Data were quantified on 5-point Likert scales. Their results showed that organizations engaged more in some Rs (reducing and recycling) than others (repairing and remanufacturing) and that organizations that engaged in one R tended to also engage in other Rs, e.g., there were positive correlations between the 4Rs. Also, an internal focus was mostly preferred over an external one. Generally, private firms engaged more in the 4Rs than public sector or civil society organizations. Furthermore, not all CE activities were claimed by organizations, whereas other non-CE activities were put under the label of the Circular Economy.

Colucci and Vecchi [6] provided evidence on CE implementation in the fashion industry. The paper was based on a product life cycle analysis through case studies of 4 Italian fashion firms. The data were collected through semi-structured interviews and other company information, such as financial statements or corporate websites. In that context, the following loops for the CE were identified: product-life extension (design for durability), reuse (preservation of product-based value), remanufacturing (return to new or better products) and recycling (of materials) [6]. Furthermore, sustainability practices in these companies were identified, in particular, the selection of local suppliers that are sustainable and implementation of retail models that minimize environmental footprints and preserve the environment.

Finally, Ghisetti and Montresor [20] focused on finance and the adoption of CE practices in SMEs, using data from the 441 Flash Eurobarometer survey for 2,318 SMEs within the EU in 2016. The results showed that SMEs had different financing mechanisms at hand and that they used them differently for their CE initiatives. These initiatives includedcircular innovation modes (new products or processes), circular use modes (circular use of existing products, i.e. through PSS, maintenance or add-on services) and circular output modes (recycling, waste reduction and elimination). These CE initiatives had different risk profiles and, thus, financial requirements. The authors found that traditional funding was overall more important and beneficial to SMEs for all initiatives in that context than new ways of funding, as often promoted recently by policy-makers. They concluded that facilitating equity, debt and publicly supported funding (as traditional ways of funding) for SMEs should be the priority if the aim was to activate SME engagement in the CE.

To sum up, the above-mentioned literature provides several insights on the adoption of CEIs by firms:

(1) It is possible to identify different CE practices which can be implemented at the micro-level (firms). As stressed by Aranda-Usón et al. [1, p. 9], "the level of adoption of the CE by businesses can be measured using a set of indicators able to define the volume of the CE-related activities performed by businesses".
(2) However, the types of activities adopted are diverse, and a common classification has not been adopted. A first, main distinction is between CE practices (specific activities such as reusing, remanufacturing, recycling…) and CE business models. Although they are obviously related, some authors focus on the former, whereas others pay attention to the latter. Regarding the CE practices, there is not an agreement on how to classify them, and surprisingly, little connection with the "R" hierarchies (3 Rs, 6 Rs, 9 Rs or 10 Rs) is made in many of those papers. The fact that some contributions use the same database (the Flash Eurobarometer 441 from the European Commission) leads to some homogeneity regarding those practices, but a uniform classification does not exist.
(3) Some papers use their own-built surveys, but many draw on the aforementioned European Commission database. Own-built surveys have the advantage that they adapt better to the specific context under study (sector, country). On the other hand, it is difficult to compare the results from different studies using different databases.
(4) There is a clear focus on a certain type of firms (SMEs) as well as a geographical focus (EU Member States).
(5) Regarding the types of practices, the evidence shows that waste treatment, resource efficiency and reduction of energy consumption are the most common CE practices adopted by the firms. In contrast, measures such as replanning water usage and use of renewable energy are relatively scarce. There is a trend to adopt incremental practices (at least at this incipient stage of the CE), whereas the implementation of the more radical ones is less common. The only notable exception is Diaz Lopez et al. [10], who conclude that "we did not find that specific categories such as cleaner production or green products dominate, despite the fact that the literature often suggests such REMs are easier to implement than more complex REMs like industrial symbiosis or cradle-to-cradle" [10, p. 32].

References

1. Aranda-Usón A, Portillo-Tarragona P, Scarpellini S, Llena-Macarulla F (2020) The progressive adoption of a circular economy by businesses for cleaner production: an approach from a regional study in Spain. J Clean Prod 247:1–12. https://doi.org/10.1016/j.jclepro.2019.119648
2. Barreiro-Gen, M., & Lozano, R. (2020). How circular is the circular economy? Analysing the implementation of circular economy in organisations. Business Strategy and the Environment. https://doi.org/10.1002/bse.2590

3. Bassi F, Dias JG (2019) The use of circular economy practices in SMEs across the EU. Resour Conserv Recycl 146:523–533. https://doi.org/10.1016/j.resconrec.2019.03.019
4. Bocken N, Olivetti EA, Cullen JM, Potting J, Lifset R (2017) Taking the circularity to the next level: a special issue on the circular economy. J Ind Ecol 21(3):476–482. https://doi.org/10.1111/jiec.12606
5. Cainelli G, D'Amato A, Mazzanti M (2020) Resource efficient eco-innovations for a circular economy: evidence from EU firms. Res Policy 49(1):1–11. https://doi.org/10.1016/j.respol.2019.103827
6. Colucci M, Vecchi A (2020) Close the loop: evidence on the implementation of the circular economy from the Italian fashion industry. Bus Strategy Environ. https://doi.org/10.1002/bse.2658
7. de Jesus A, Antunes P, Santos R, Mendonça S (2018) Eco-innovation in the transition to a circular economy: an analytical literature review. J Clean Prod 172:2999–3018. https://doi.org/10.1016/j.jclepro.2017.11.111
8. Demirel P, Danisman GO (2019) Eco-innovation and firm growth in the circular economy: evidence from European small- and medium-sized enterprises. Bus Strategy Environ. https://doi.org/10.1002/bse.2336
9. Dey PK, Malesios C, De D, Budhwar P, Chowdhury S, Cheffi W (2020) Circular economy to enhance sustainability of small and medium-sized enterprises. Bus Strategy Environ 29(6):2145–2169. https://doi.org/10.1002/bse.2492
10. Diaz Lopez FJ, Bastein T, Tukker A (2019) Business model innovation for resource-efficiency, circularity and cleaner production: what 143 cases tell us. Ecol Econ 155:20–35. https://doi.org/10.1016/j.ecolecon.2018.03.009
11. Dijksma S, Kamp H (2016) A circular economy in the Netherlands by 2050. Ministry for the Environment and Ministry of Economic Affairs
12. European Commission (2016) Flash Eurobarometer 441. https://data.europa.eu/data/datasets/s2110_441_eng?locale=en
13. Fang Y, Côté RP, Qin R (2007) Industrial sustainability in China: practice and prospects for eco-industrial development. J Environ Manage 83(3):315–328
14. Figge F, Thorpe AS, Givry P, Canning L, Franklin-Johnson E (2018) Longevity and circularity as indicators of eco-efficient resource use in the circular economy. Ecol Econ 150:297–306. https://doi.org/10.1016/j.ecolecon.2018.04.030
15. Franco MA (2017) Circular economy at the micro level: a dynamic view of incumbents' struggles and challenges in the textile industry. J Clean Prod 168:833–845. https://doi.org/10.1016/j.jclepro.2017.09.056
16. Garcés-Ayerbe C, Rivera-Torres P, Suárez-Perales I, Leyva-de la Hiz D (2019) Is it possible to change from a linear to a circular economy? An overview of opportunities and barriers for European small and medium-sized enterprise companies. Int J Environ Res Public Health 16(5):1–15. https://doi.org/10.3390/ijerph16050851
17. García-Quevedo J, Jové-Llopis E, Martínez-Ros E (2020) Barriers to the circular economy in European small and medium-sized firms. Bus Strategy Environ. https://doi.org/10.1002/bse.2513
18. Geng Y, Fu J, Sarkis J, Xue B (2012) Towards a national circular economy indicator system in China: an evaluation and critical analysis. J Clean Prod 23(1):216–224
19. Ghisellini P, Cialani C, Ulgiati S (2016) A review on circular economy: the expected transition to a balanced interplay of environmental and economic systems. J Clean Prod 114:11–32. https://doi.org/10.1016/j.jclepro.2015.09.007
20. Ghisetti C, Montresor S (2020) On the adoption of circular economy practices by small and medium-size enterprises (SMEs): does "financing-as-usual" still matter? J Evolut Econ 30(2):559–586. https://doi.org/10.1007/s00191-019-00651-w
21. Guldmann E, Huulgaard RD (2020) Barriers to circular business model innovation: a multiple-case study. J Clean Prod 243:1–13. https://doi.org/10.1016/j.jclepro.2019.118160

22. Gusmerotti NM, Testa F, Corsini F, Pretner G, Iraldo F (2019) Drivers and approaches to the circular economy in manufacturing firms. J Clean Prod 230:314–327. https://doi.org/10.1016/j.jclepro.2019.05.044
23. Horbach J, Rammer C (2019) Circular economy innovations, growth and employment at the firm level: empirical evidence from Germany. J Ind Ecol. https://doi.org/10.1111/jiec.12977
24. Kalmykova Y, Sadagopan M, Rosado L (2018) Circular economy—from review of theories and practices to development of implementation tools. Resour Conserv Recycl 135:190–201. https://doi.org/10.1016/j.resconrec.2017.10.034
25. Katz-Gerro T, López Sintas J (2018) Mapping circular economy activities in the European Union: patterns of implementation and their correlates in small and medium-sized enterprises. Bus Strategy Environ https://doi.org/10.1002/bse.2259
26. Kiefer CP, Río P, Carrillo-Hermosilla J (2021) On the contribution of eco-innovation features to a circular economy: a microlevel quantitative approach. Bus Strategy Environ 1-17. https://doi.org/10.1002/bse.2688
27. Kirchherr J, Piscicelli L, Bour R, Kostense-Smit E, Muller J, Huibrechtse-Truijens A, Hekkert M (2018) Barriers to the circular economy: evidence from the European Union (EU). Ecol Econ 150:264–272. https://doi.org/10.1016/j.ecolecon.2018.04.028
28. Kirchherr J, Reike D, Hekkert M (2017) Conceptualizing the circular economy: an analysis of 114 definitions. Resour Conserv Recycl 127:221–232. https://doi.org/10.1016/j.resconrec.2017.09.005
29. Korhonen J, Honkasalo A, Seppälä J (2018) Circular economy: the concept and its limitations. Ecol Econ 143:37–46. https://doi.org/10.1016/j.ecolecon.2017.06.041
30. Korhonen J, Nuur C, Feldmann A, Birkie SE (2018) Circular economy as an essentially contested concept. J Clean Prod 175:544–552. https://doi.org/10.1016/j.jclepro.2017.12.111
31. Lieder M, Rashid A (2016) Towards circular economy implementation: a comprehensive review in context of manufacturing industry. J Clean Prod 115:36–51. https://doi.org/10.1016/j.jclepro.2015.12.042
32. Liu Y, Bai Y (2014) An exploration of firms' awareness and behavior of developing circular economy: an empirical research in China. Resour Conserv Recycl 87:145–152. https://doi.org/10.1016/j.resconrec.2014.04.002
33. Liu L, Liang Y, Song Q, Li J (2017) A review of waste prevention through 3R under the concept of circular economy in China. J Mater Cycles Waste Manage 19(4):1314–1323
34. Martínez-Cerna Economía circular y políticas públicas. Retrieved from https://www.kas.de/documents/273477/273526/Econom%C3%ADa+Circular+y+Pol%C3%ADticas+Públicas.pdf/e7d98c0f-423c-947c-fe3e-6a83ae5fb7c3?version=1.1&t=1580245377248
35. Merli R, Preziosi M, Acampora A (2018) How do scholars approach the circular economy? A systematic literature review. J Clean Prod 178:703–722. https://doi.org/10.1016/j.jclepro.2017.12.112
36. Ormazabal M, Prieto-Sandoval V, Puga-Leal R, Jaca C (2018) Circular economy in Spanish SMEs: challenges and opportunities. J Clean Prod 185:157–167. https://doi.org/10.1016/j.jclepro.2018.03.031
37. Pauliuk S (2018) Critical appraisal of the circular economy standard BS 8001:2017 and a dashboard of quantitative system indicators for its implementation in organizations. Resour Conserv Recycl 129:81–92. https://doi.org/10.1016/j.resconrec.2017.10.019
38. Potting J, Hekkert M, Worrell E, Hanemaaijer A (2017) Circular economy: measuring innovation in the product chain. PBL Publishers
39. Prieto-Sandoval V, Jaca C, Ormazabal M (2018) Towards a consensus on the circular economy. J Clean Prod 179:605-615. https://doi.org/10.1016/j.jclepro.2017.12.224
40. Reike D, Vermeulen WJV, Witjes S (2018) The circular economy: new or refurbished as CE 3.0?—exploring controversies in the conceptualization of the circular economy through a focus on history and resource value retention options. Resour Conserv Recycl 135:246–264. https://doi.org/10.1016/j.resconrec.2017.08.027

41. Rizos V, Behrens A, van der Gaast W, Hofman E, Ioannou A, Kafyeke T, … Topi C (2016) Implementation of circular economy business models by small and medium-sized enterprises (SMEs): barriers and enablers. Sustainability 8(11):1–18. https://doi.org/10.3390/su8111212
42. Scarpellini S, Valero-Gil J, Moneva JM, Andreaus M (2020) Environmental management capabilities for a "circular eco-innovation." Bus Strategy Environ. https://doi.org/10.1002/bse.2472
43. Scarpellini S, Portillo-Tarragona P, Aranda-Usón A, Llena-Macarulla F (2019) Definition and measurement of the circular economy's regional impact. J Environ Plan Manag 62(13):2211–2237. https://doi.org/10.1080/09640568.2018.1537974
44. Smol M, Kulczycka J, Avdiushchenko A (2017) Circular economy indicators in relation to eco-innovation in European regions. Clean Technol Environ Policy 19:669–678. https://doi.org/10.1007/s10098-016-1323-8
45. Sousa-Zomer TT, Magalhães L, Zancul E, Campos LMS, Cauchick-Miguel PA (2018) Cleaner production as an antecedent for circular economy paradigm shift at the micro-level: evidence from a home appliance manufacturer. J Clean Prod 185:740–748. https://doi.org/10.1016/j.jclepro.2018.03.006
46. Yuan Z, Bi J, Moriguichi U (2008) The circular economy. A new development strategy in China. J Ind Ecol 10:4–8
47. Zamfir A-M, Mocanu C, Grigorescu A (2017) Circular economy and decision models among European SMEs. Sustainability 9(9). https://doi.org/10.3390/su9091507
48. Zhu Q, Geng Y, Lai KH (2010) Circular economy practices among Chinese manufacturers varying in environmental-oriented supply chain cooperation and the performance implications. J Environ Manage 91(6):1324–1331. https://doi.org/10.1016/j.jenvman.2010.02.013
49. Zink T, Geyer R (2017) Circular economy rebound. J Ind Ecol 21(3):593–602. https://doi.org/10.1111/jiec.12545

Chapter 5
Drivers and Barriers to the CE: A Micro-/Meso-Level Analysis

An appropriate analysis of the adoption of CE innovations (CEIs) should be based on the application of an analytical framework which takes into account the wide array of determinants which influence their uptake. As mentioned in a previous chapter, CE innovations are a subset of all eco-innovations which, in turn, are a subset of all innovations. Therefore, such analytical framework should consider the barriers and drivers of innovation in the general innovation literature, but also take into account the particularities of eco-innovations and CE innovations.

The literature on the determinants to CEIs at the micro-level (firms) is relatively tiny but rapidly emerging. Some contributions are more comprehensive and address all the possible determinants, whether external or internal to the firm, and also take into account the characteristics of the specific practices or "Rs" in the CE framework mentioned in previous chapters. Others focus on a specific driver or barrier. Most of these contributions have been mentioned in the previous chapter when referring to the CE practices that firms develop or adopt.

In this chapter, we first review the literature on the determinants of CEIs at the micro-level. A synthesis on the methods as well as the results of relevant papers with respect to the drivers and barriers initially considered and those which are shown to be more relevant is provided. The selection of those papers with a focus on the CE at the micro-level has already been described in Chap. 4. All the papers mentioned in that chapter are included, but a couple of them which did not mention the CE practices adopted but which analysed the drivers and barriers have been added. Then, we put those determinants in a broader context, i.e. the drivers and barriers to the development and uptake of eco-innovations, which offer useful insights on the different types of determinants which should be considered. Recall that, according to our view, CEIs are a subset of EIs. This allows us to build an analytical framework which considers the different determinants of CEIs, based on the existence of drivers and barriers which are internal and external to the firm, as well as the characteristics of the CEIs.

P. del Río et al., *The Circular Economy*, Green Energy and Technology,
https://doi.org/10.1007/978-3-030-74792-3_5

Cainelli et al. [11] provided evidence on the role of (i) environmental policy and (ii) green demand drivers to sustain the adoption of RE-oriented eco-innovations. The authors included several variables as determinants of the adoption of those innovations by firms in 9 EU countries, such as existing environmental regulations or taxes on pollution, market demand from customers for CEIs, internal R&D, whether the firm belonged to a business group, whether the reference market was national, EU or global, whether the headquarters of the business group were located in the same country, whether the firm was subject to the EU emissions trading scheme (ETS) and its sales in 2006. They showed the relevance of environmental policies and demand in driving the adoption of CEIs. However, some heterogeneity could be observed regarding the role of policy as a determinant of adoption: "product-related innovation in recycling and innovations related to the after-use are suggested to be strongly affected by policy, while innovations related to the reduction of material inputs show a weaker policy-related influence". Interestingly, "R&D drives general innovation adoption, but the absorptive capacity it generates seems irrelevant to sustain specific typologies of eco innovations, for which policy and demand appear to be key drivers" [11, p. 10].

Ormazabal et al. [49] started from the assumption that the implementation of the CE is encouraged by environmental management, which incentivizes firms to innovate in their business models towards CE practices [49]. The authors identified 9 potential barriers to the CE by firms (lack of financial support, inadequate information management systems, lack of proper technology, lack of technical resources, lack of financial resources, lack of consumer interest in the environment, lack of support from public institutions, lack of qualified professionals in environmental management and lack of commitment on the part of the organizations' leaders) and 4 drivers (the increase of prestige, cost reduction and financial benefits, recovery of the local environment and the sustainability of the company in the market). In a survey, firms were asked about the importance of the aforementioned nine barriers. Lack of support from public organizations, insufficient financial resources and lack of customer interest in the environment were the most important barriers, whereas lack of leaders' commitment and the lack of qualified people were not regarded as a problem for CE implementation [49]. Regarding the drivers, increasing prestige and environmental recovery were considered as great benefits of CE implementation. In contrast, companies were neither fully convinced of the contribution of the CE to the sustainability of the company over the long term nor that the CE could bring them tangible benefits in terms of cost reductions or financial profits [49]. Finally, market sustainability was the worst rated opportunity.

Scarpellini et al. [52] stressed the role of internal environmental management capabilities as drivers of circular eco-innovations. The authors made an important distinction between formal and informal environmental management systems (EMS), with the latter referring to specific environmentally effective capabilities. They analysed the previous business routines and activities that could facilitate the introduction of a CE in a survey of 89 Spanish firms with a size above 50 employees. The statistical analysis was based on econometric modelling (partial least squares (PLS) structural equation modelling). Their most significant result was that, in contrast to formal EMSs, the effect of informal environmental management tools had an indirect impact on CE performance and helped to intensify circular material loops [52].

In the study of Gusmerotti et al. [34], 821 Italian firms were asked to indicate, on a 5-point Likert scale, their level of agreement with ten statements regarding the motivations (drivers) which had influenced the firm's decision to adopt environmental initiatives: (1) increasing efficiency by reducing costs; (2) improving the corporate image; (3) acquiring a competitive advantage; (4) increasing customer satisfaction; (5) reducing the dependence of the company on raw materials; (6) reducing the risks related to the phases involved in supplying raw materials; (7) complying with legal requirements; (8) anticipating future legal obligations; (9) reducing the company's environmental impact; and (10) reducing the environmental footprint of the company's products. The authors, who focused on drivers but not on barriers, grouped those drivers into four categories (economic, regulatory, environmental and resource risks). They found that economic drivers influenced such adoption. However, drivers related to regulatory pressure, resource exploitation risks and the pursuit of environmental values did not have a significant influence.

Garcés-Ayerbe et al. [30] distinguished among the barriers to CE practices and behaviour for "in-going" firms (e.g., those which had implemented or were implementing at least one CE measure) and "no-going" firms (e.g., those that had not implemented any CE activities). They first asked "in-going firms" about the barriers that they had faced when undertaking CE activities. Five barriers were listed: (1) lack of human resources; (2) lack of expertise to implement these activities; (3) complex administrative or legal procedures; (4) cost of meeting regulations or standards; and (5) difficulties in accessing finance. "No-going firms" were asked about the reasons why they had not performed any CE-related activity. The possible reasons were: (1) lack of human resources; (2) lack of expertise to implement these activities; (3) no clear idea about cost benefits or improved work processes; (4) no clear idea about investment required; (5) complex administrative or legal procedures; (6) cost of meeting regulations or standards; and (7) difficulties in accessing finance. According to their results, "in-going firms find more barriers related to regulations, standards and procedures, while no-going firms find barriers related to investment and searching for financing" [30, p. 9].

García-Quevedo et al. [31] used a cross-sectional survey of European SMEs and a multivariate probit model to identify the perception of firms about the main barriers they faced in the development or adoption of CE activities. They focused on two sets of barriers: those related to a lack of resources (human and financial) and capabilities (expertise) and those related to the regulatory framework (administrative procedures and the costs of meeting the regulations).[1] Their results

[1]The authors used the lack of human resources, lack of expertise and difficulties in accessing finance to capture the lack of resources or capabilities. They used complex administrative procedures and the cost of meeting regulations or standards to capture regulatory barriers.

indicated that the most important obstacle for firms to be engaged in CE activities was the complexity of administrative/legal procedures and the costs of meeting regulations/legal standards, followed by the lack of human resources. They distinguished between barriers that reflected the degree of difficulty of implementing CE activities and the learning experience associated with such processes (so-called revealed barriers) and those that were considered insurmountable (so-called deterring barriers). In this respect, regulatory obstacles and the lack of human resources were considered revealed barriers, whereas the lack of expertise in new technologies and the capability to change the mindset to face the long term were deterring barriers. The authors also found that being engaged in more than one CE activity had effects on a firm's perception of financial obstacles and that learning effects made the barrier "lack of expertise" lose importance when a firm was engaged in more than one CE activity. Interestingly, the authors stressed the need to distinguish between different CE activities, since "the perception of barriers differed substantially across these activities. Firms undertaking a disruptive innovation redesigning products and services to minimize the use of materials are more likely to perceive all barriers as important. However, firms implementing such activities as minimizing waste, replanning energy usage, and using renewable energy only perceive those obstacles related to administrative procedures and regulations" [31, p. 2450].

Moktadir et al. [47] proposed a decision support tool (best-worst method) for evaluating the challenges to CE practices. It was used to assess the challenges to CE practices in the leather industry in Bangladesh. Six case companies and six experts from major leather companies in this country were invited to evaluate the challenges to CE practices. "Initially, several potential challenges to CE practices were determined according to literature review, and were subjected to several rounds of reviews by leather industrial managers to develop the framework" [47, p. 11].[2] The authors ended up with a final list of 8 challenges to CE practices in this industry: "lack of technological advancement, lack of financial support from authorities, absence of strong legislation toward CE, lack of reverse logistics facility, lack of communication framework, lack of awareness of CE, lack of pressure from social community, and lack of long-term strategic goals" [47, p. 11]. The study findings revealed that, in the final ranking results, "lack of financial support from authorities" was assigned the highest weight. This was followed by "lack of technological advancement", "absence of strong legislation towards the CE", "lack of awareness of CE", "lack of long-term strategic goals", "lack of communication platforms",

[2]The authors performed a literature review and initially considered the following potential challenges to the implementation of CE practices: lack of technological advancement, lack of financial supports from authorities, absence of strong legislation towards CE, complexity in reconfiguring of liner system to circular system, lack of reverse logistics facility, lack of communication framework, lacking standardization of recycled products, lack of awareness of CE, lack of pressure from social community, lack of accessibility on real data, limited willingness to collaborate in the value chain, lack of environment management commitment, lack of waste management facility, lack of guidelines for quality of refurbishment products, lack of facility of circular procurement, uncertainty of return and profit, deficient firm framework to adopt CE practices and lack of market mechanisms for recovery.

"lack of reverse logistics facilities" and, finally, "lack of pressure from the social community".

Rizos et al. [51] analysed whether SMEs that had successfully introduced circularity into their business models had faced different types of barriers. In order to identify potential barriers to the adoption of CE business models, a literature review was initially conducted. Based on this review, barriers were categorized as follows: company environmental culture, lack of capital, lack of government support/ effective legislation, lack of information, administrative burden, lack of technical and technological know-how and lack of support from the supply and demand network. The results showed that "lack of support supply and demand network" and "lack of capital" were the two most relevant barriers, with at least 50% of the SMEs mentioning those barriers. They were followed at a considerable distance by "lack of government support", "administrative burden", "lack of technical know-how", "lack of information", "other barriers" and "company environmental culture", with percentages ranging from 25% to 8%. Regarding the drivers, company environmental culture was by far the most relevant enabler, with 2/3 of all SMEs mentioning it. This was followed at a long distance by networking, support from the demand network, financially attractive, recognition, personal knowledge and government support, with percentages ranging from 33 to 3%.

Zamfir et al. [56] applied the decision tree method in order to uncover relationships between characteristics of European SMEs and their behaviour in relation to the CE. They showed that the most important factors influencing the decision of companies to adopt CE practices were the country in which they operate, the sector of activity and the level of investment in R&D. "On the other hand, even within countries that offer more favorable conditions for stimulating SMEs to adopt CE practices, their behavior varies significantly across sectors and in relation to the company's turnover" [56, p. 12]. Additionally, this paper identified the CE activities that SMEs undertook in order to improve their economic performance. "Out of five potential types of circular economy activities to be implemented by European SMEs, only re-planning the energy usage to minimize consumption does not influence the economic performances of the companies" [56, p. 13].

Kirchherr et al. [43] presented the results of a study on CE barriers in the EU with 208 survey respondents and 47 expert interviews. The authors considered four categories of barriers to the CE which, in turn, included several specific barriers: (1) *cultural* (lacking awareness and/or willingness to engage with CE), which encompassed a hesitant company culture, limited willingness to collaborate in the value chain, lacking consumer awareness and interest and operating in a linear system; (2) *regulatory* (lacking policies in support of a CE transition) encompassed limited circular procurement, obstructing laws and regulations and lacking global consensus; (3) *market* (lacking economic viability of circular business models), which included low virgin material prices, lacking standardization, high upfront investment costs and limited funding for circular business models; and (4) *technological* (lacking proven technologies to implement CE), which included lacking ability to deliver high-quality remanufactured products, limited circular designs, too few large-scale demonstration projects and lack of data (e.g. on impacts).

The results showed that cultural barriers (particularly "lacking consumer interest and awareness" and "hesitant company culture") were perceived by businesses and policy-makers as the most relevant barriers to the CE. These were followed by "market barriers which, in turn, are induced by a lack of synergistic governmental interventions to accelerate the transition towards a CE" [43, p. 264], suggesting that there were important interactions between barriers. In contrast, the authors found that technological barriers were not among the most pressing CE barriers.

Bassi and Dias [7] explored the adoption of five CE practices by SMEs in the EU with the help of multilevel ordinal probit models that control for within- and between-variability across EU countries. They found that size, total turnover, percentage of turnover devoted to R&D and type of activity were the main determinants of such adoption. Interestingly, the authors found differences across the type of activity, firm characteristics and countries. The type of activity included the distinction between products and services and the type of market (business to business vs. business to consumers). Differences across categories were observed with, for example, firms selling services directly to consumers being the most likely to adopt CE practices. Regarding the company features, the authors found that "enterprises with few resources may be able to afford practices such as reduction of waste but not more demanding redesigning practices" [7, p. 531]. Finally, their results showed that CE measures across EU countries were very heterogeneous, with differences in the level of adoption both "within countries due to firms' characteristics—dimension, age, turnover, type of activity—and between countries: environmental and energy-saving practices are not given the same attention everywhere in Europe" [7, p. 524].

Diaz Lopez et al. [26] analysed 143 cases on the implementation of several resource efficiency measures (REMs). The authors identified the types of measures that companies implemented when they aimed to realize resource efficiency. They characterized business model changes that could support the implementation of REMs and considered several barriers to their implementation that were reported in the cases, i.e. institutional, market, organizational, behavioural and technological. The authors found that all those barriers could play a role. However, they could not "single out a factor that is dominant for specific REMs. Indeed, [they] could not identify a pattern in which REMs related to a large scope and high degree of change encountered more implementation barriers than others" [26, p. 32], despite the *a priori* common perception that they were more complex to implement. In their words, "simple statements such as 'radical REMs are more difficult to implement than simple REMs' could not be confirmed" [26, p. 33].

Katz-Gerro and López Sintas [38] analysed whether the patterns of CE activities adopted by SMEs were independent from past choices or activity-dependent. They showed that, in contrast to previous studies arguing that CE activities were independent from each other, seven patterns of engagement in the CE could be identified in which activities were systematically interdependent. Further, they showed that these patterns were associated with the organizational properties of SMEs: "The interdependence among CE activities suggests that minimizing waste may be the easiest activity to implement; hence, this activity may provide entrepreneurs and managers with not only the experience necessary to convince themselves of the benefits of implementing CE activities but also the knowledge needed to develop dynamic capabilities for the implementation of additional CE activities" (Katz-Gerro and López Sintas [38, p. 494].

Sousa-Zomer et al. [54] assessed the implementation of the CE at the micro-level by focusing on cleaner production principles and practices in a Brazilian home appliance manufacturing firm. The case study specifically considered the implementation of a circular business model that was based on a product–service system and aggregated data from 8 semi-structured interviews, direct observations in the firm and public company information. The results showed that the novel business model required a wide range of changes related to "material input, design, production, delivery, consumption, and end-of-life resource management" [54, p. 744]. Cooperation along the value chain was introduced and intensified, intra-firm organizational and production processes were changed, and material and natural resource (water) use for minimal life cycle environmental impact were addressed. Drivers included the implementation of new technologies, employee training, sharing of information with stakeholders and internal efficiency gains (production and organization). Public policy (mainly waste-related) was also supportive. The authors identified two additional drivers: that all involved stakeholders were able to generate additional or new "value" and that all CP practices and principles were connected and produced synergies among them.

Guldmann and Huulgaard [33] assessed the barriers to circular business model innovations with an analysis of 12 case studies in Denmark across different company sizes (2 start-ups, 3 micro, 3 small and 4 large firms), industries [wholesale or manufacturing of apparel (3), textiles (2), furniture (3), machinery and mechatronics (4)] and customer segments (8 B2B and 4 B2C). Personal meetings and digital correspondence or phone calls with individuals within the companies following an unstructured interview approach allowed the authors to collect data, which were triangulated with follow-up semi-structured interviews and company reports. The following types of barriers were encountered: (1) barriers at the organizational level included a narrow focus of existing sustainability strategies (i.e. on efficiency), low management commitment, fear for (low) economic profitability and cannibalization with existing offerings of the firms, lack of existing knowledge and skills in-house, lack of knowledge about regulation, difficulties to establish cross-organizational collaborations and requirements for (new) product design. (2) Barriers at the value chain level were related to investments of resources (financial, physical but also human), complex management issues of closed-loop resource cycles and the quality of resource input and productive output. Reluctance for building value networks and missing trust, hindering cooperation, were also identified as barriers. (3) Barriers at the employee level were mostly experience and knowledge-related as well as related to missing management support, existing structures that were not adequate for circular business model innovations or hesitancy to pursue new activities in general. (4) Barriers at the market and institutional level mainly referred to regulations that de-incentivize labour-intensive R-processes or classify recaptured goods as waste, making their processing difficult. Also, taxation and (lack of) funding were identified as barriers in this category. Generally, the most important barriers to circular business model innovation were encountered at the organizational level, followed by the value chain level, the employee level and, finally, the market and institutional level. The single most important barrier was the "lack of resources, knowledge or competencies in-house". Additionally, "prevailing linear business model structures and thinking" and "time requirements to build up new partnerships and trust" were also important individual barriers [33]. Nevertheless, significant differences were observable in these barriers across firms due to company-related factors (firm size, sector, customer segment) and other context factors.

Dey et al. [25] focused on the CE in 130 manufacturing SMEs in the West Midlands (UK). Specifically, they addressed the following three research questions: "How are CE fields of action related to sustainability performance? What are the issues, challenges, and opportunities of adopting CE in SMEs? And what key strategies, resources, and competences facilitate effective implementation of CE in SMEs?" [25, p. 2145]. Both quantitative and qualitative data were collected using a mixed-methods approach based on a survey, a focus group and case studies. A wide array of barriers was identified from the previous literature and grouped in two main categories, i.e. external (lack of financial support, lack of customers' support, lack of technology, lack of public institutional support, lack of professionals in environmental management) and internal (lack of information system, lack of technical and financial resources and lack of management commitment). The identified drivers included "increased image, cost reductions, business growth, emission reduction, productivity, sustainability and social well-being" [25, p. 2152]. The results of the study showed that the main specific barriers for the SMEs under study were the limited scope regarding material selection and eco-design, high financial requirements for "lean practices", carbon footprint reductions and switching to renewable energy supply, as well as difficulties in switching away from linear business operations [25]. Also, the lack of support from public institutions was a barrier to better employee well-being regarding the social dimension of the CE. On the other hand, specific drivers included the "availability of regenerative materials, competent suppliers, state-of-the-art technology and facilities, trained manpower, Third Party Logistics service providers, renewable energy sources, communication infrastructure, and facilities and technologies for reverse logistic" [25, p. 2162].

Barreiro-Gen and Lozano [6] investigated the CE on the micro-level, focusing on the 4 Rs in 256 organizations of various types (firms, public sector and civil society organizations), size and location. They found that around three quarters of these organizations were somehow actively involved in the CE. Specific drivers for their CE-related actions were age of the organization (the longer an organization has been involved in sustainability, the more effective its implementations are) and internal focus (i.e. not depending on external cooperation or networks). Additionally, awareness for and understanding of CE principles were drivers. However, the results showed that the organizations did not always perceive their actions to be related to the CE, or claimed that their actions were related to the CE when in fact that was not the case. As a general barrier, the authors highlighted the currently low level of inter-organizational cooperation [6].

Based on 4 case studies, Colucci and Vecchi [15] identified barriers to the implementation of CE practices in firms in the Italian fashion industry. These barriers were related to innovation (challenging processes, unavailability of technologies, difficulty to scale innovations and long R&D times), consumers (unreliable certifications, consumers' attitude and low understanding of rental models), techno-economic aspects (product quality, environmental impact and price) and business processes and models (take-back systems, difficulties in cooperation, difficulties in prototyping and customization). The authors underlined the importance of the attitude of customers as a key barrier to the CE. Furthermore, the supply chain was central in implementing CE practices, which is why the authors believed that addressing cooperation with relevant stakeholders could mitigate several barriers [15].

Ghisetti and Montresor [32] investigated the role of finance in the adoption of CE practices by SMEs. They used data from the Flash Eurobarometer 441 from 2015, upon which econometric analyses were performed. The results showed that financial variables were significant to explain the uptake of CE practices and acted either as drivers or barriers. Traditional finance was not a decisive barrier to the CE. Both internal (equity) and external (debt) financing were significant drivers. Public funding was also relevant. Alternative (new) forms of financing were even a barrier to the CE [32].

Franco [29] aimed to answer two research questions: (a) which factors hinder established firms' ability to go fully circular? and (b) how do these factors interact with each other in order to move firms and industries towards a circular production system? The authors carried out an analysis of the textile industry in Europe with the help of multiple case studies. They identified several factors along the product value chain which acted as either drivers or barriers to firm's willingness to develop a circular product. Interestingly, the authors also analysed the influence of power relationships between buyers and their suppliers on their willingness to co-innovate. The authors do not find evidence of a consumer demand-pull but that "the dynamics of different actors throughout the product's lifetime, from raw material production to recovery activities, matter. The CE system, as portrayed by this research, could be characterized as a positive feedback loop that could either make the system grow exponentially (especially on the manufacturing side) or shrink it to prevent take off" [29, p. 843]. The authors warned that, given the time delays "it will not be possible to establish a CE quickly. Contrary to popular belief, this industrial change will not emerge suddenly and will be the result of well-coordinated actions initiated at different parts of the system" [29, p. 842].

The findings of Demirel and Danisman [24] revealed "that a significant threshold investment (i.e., higher than 10% of revenues) into circular eco-innovations is required for SMEs to benefit from investing into the CE" [24, p. 1]. Therefore, these high initial investments represented an important barrier to the participation of SMEs in the CE. The authors were nevertheless sceptical of the positive contribution of the CEIs to SMEs since their results showed that "the majority of circular eco-innovations fail to boost the growth rates of SMEs, with the exception of investments into eco-design innovations" [24, p. 1]. Finally, equity finance for CE activities (i.e. angel and venture capital investments) was found to contribute positively to the growth of SMEs. This was in contrast to traditional forms of debt and grant finance.

Liu and Bai [45] investigated the role of firm awareness and behaviour in the development of CE-oriented solutions in 157 firms in China. Their findings indicated that, although firms have a good understanding of the CE, view it positively and show a high willingness to act, inter-firm cooperation was very low and systematic CE management in firms was largely lacking. Specific actions were not implemented in a significant manner, and dedicated CE departments or teams had not been created. The results highlighted large gaps between awareness and actual behaviour in firms. This was due to several obstacles: structural barriers (inefficient management, organizational structures, short-term orientation and bureaucracy hindering change generally, hierarchies and inflexibility generating path dependencies and hindering innovation and low/no resource dedication to CE-related initiatives), contextual barriers (low market pressure to engage in the CE, market uncertainty and low willingness to pay for greener products) and cultural barriers (strong risk aversion, lack of clear leadership commitment, dominance of imitation strategies and existing silos between firm planning and operation).

Finally, the Ellen MacArthur Foundation [28] stressed the role of non-financial barriers, which limit the uptake of CE opportunities. These barriers include "unintended consequences of existing regulations (e.g. definitions of waste that hinder trade and transport of products for remanufacturing), social factors such as a lack of experience among companies and policymakers to detect and capture CE opportunities, and market failures such as imperfect information (e.g. for businesses to repair, disassemble and remanufacture products) and unaccounted externalities (e.g. carbon emissions)" [28, p. 1].

Overall, some observations can be inferred from a cross-cutting analysis of the aforementioned papers:

1. Most studies have a clear geographical and sectoral focus. Analyses have mostly been carried out in European countries, although there are some contributions in a developing or emerging country setting. The assessment of the drivers and barriers to the development or adoption of CE practices has mostly been undertaken in manufacturing, with some attention being devoted to specific sectors (e.g. the textile sector). Finally, SMEs have received much attention in this context.
2. A certain unbalanced focus on the analysis of drivers and barriers can be observed. Whereas all papers assess the barriers to the development or uptake of CE practices, the analysis of drivers has received slightly less attention.
3. There is a wide array of barriers (and drivers), and different typologies have been proposed in the literature. There is a lack of consensus on the classification of the barriers to the CE and a lack of systematization of those barriers. Furthermore, the terminology clearly differs across studies, which makes it

difficult to compare across them and identify a common pattern regarding the most relevant ones.

4. Despite the previous remark, barriers tend to focus on policy, administrative procedures, market take-up (including customer awareness), access to finance and lack of awareness by the firm, more than on technology and coordination-of-actors issues. Drivers focus on economic benefit (including firm growth) and green image rather than on environmental drivers.
5. Drivers and barriers are most often considered isolated from each other, despite some research showing that they may interact in complex ways, leading to synergies and/or conflicts [41].

Regarding point 3 above, the eco-innovation (EI) literature provides relevant lessons in this regard and its insights should be further considered in this book, allowing those determinants to be grouped in several broader categories. The reason is that, as several authors observe [11, 32, 42], CE practices represent a particular case of EI, with similar enablers and barriers. Indeed, the studies reviewed in the first part of this chapter show that barriers to the CE are internal and external to the firm, but also that their relevance depends on the type of CE being considered. This suggests that a classification into three broad groups (factors internal to the firm, factors external to the firm and the characteristics of the CE practice being implemented) could be useful for those purposes. This links to previous contributions in the EI literature, some of which follow such classification.

The literature on the drivers and barriers to the uptake of EIs which, as mentioned above, includes CE innovations, is relatively abundant (see [5, 8, 19, 36] for overviews of this literature). Several classifications of barriers to eco-innovation have been proposed in this literature. For example, Horbach [35] groups the drivers into three broad categories: regulation and policy determinants, supply-side determinants (technological capabilities, cost savings, appropriability conditions) and demand-side determinants (consumers' preferences for environmentally friendly products). However, we use the classification in our previous work, which distinguishes between factors internal and external to the firm and characteristics of the technologies (CE practices) (see [13, 20, 21] for details).[3]

A systemic framework, integrating different approaches which highlight different determinants to eco-innovation, was initially developed and applied to some eco-innovation cases in [22]. The approaches being combined include the resource-based view (RBV) of the firm, the dynamic capabilities, evolutionary economics, the systems of innovation perspective, environmental economics and the corporate environmental strategy literature. We use this framework, which has been further improved by including institutional theory [41] and adding a "features of the technologies" dimension [20, 21].

This systemic framework is adapted and used in this book to analyse the barriers and drivers to CE practices in different firms in different sectors and countries (see

[3]The rest of this section heavily draws on previous research by the authors, including del Río [20, 21], Carrillo-Hermosilla et al. [13], del Río et al. [22, 19] and Keshminder and Río [41].

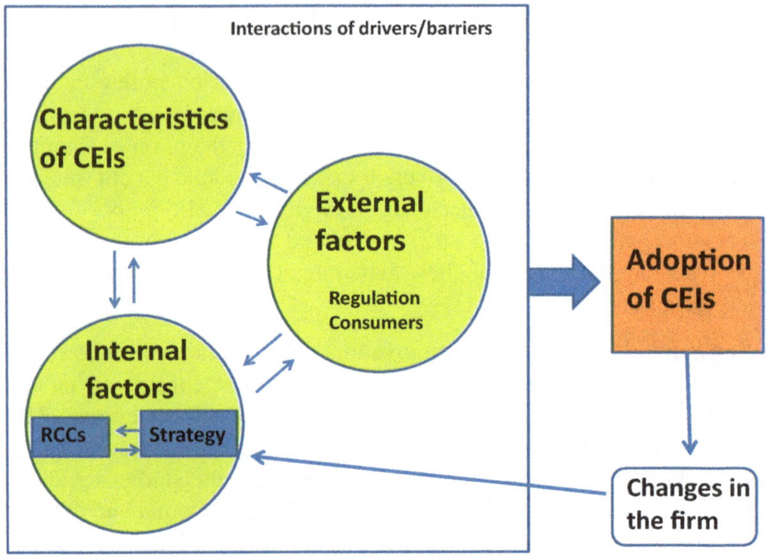

Fig. 5.1 Determinants of the development and adoption of CE innovations (CEIs) *Source* Adapted from del Río et al. [22]

Chap. 6). The framework has been adapted in two respects. On the one hand, rather than relating to "environmental innovation" or "eco-innovation" broadly, we take a narrower focus on CE-related innovations. On the other hand, in addition to the internal and external drivers, an explicit consideration of the third category of determinants of adoption has been included in order to take into account the specificities of those CE innovations (CE innovations features). The rest of this chapter discusses some of the specific determinants that would be included in the aforementioned three broad categories of determinants. Figure 5.1 summarizes the analytical framework used in this book. It should be taken into account that those determinants are likely to be interrelated and interact between each other in complex ways, as illustrated by some case studies in the next chapter. The drivers and barriers below are not isolated from each other, but interact sometimes in complex ways, leading to synergies, complementarities and conflicts (what Kemp and Dijk [40] call "a web of constraints"). Indeed, Keshminder and del Río [41] show that there are direct and indirect effects between the different drivers and barriers. Although the focus here is on the adoption of CEIs, the general framework which distinguishes between the three types of factors (internal and external to the firm, as well as the features of EIs), also apply to the development of CEIs.

External factors

The oldest literature on eco-innovation traditionally focused on the external drivers and, most importantly, on the role of regulation (see, e.g., [3, 10, 37, 44, 48, 50]). Firms take decisions influenced by the information received and the pressures exerted by outside forces, i.e. as a response of their interactions with external actors, including public policy-makers, competitors, equipment and input suppliers, industrial associations and chambers of commerce, insurance firms, final consumers/industrial clients, environmental NGOs, green parties, civil society, the mass media, public and private research centres and financial institutions [20]. Compared to EIs in general, such external factors, including the influence of supply chains and relationships with suppliers, play a particularly relevant role in the development or adoption of circular EIs (e.g. CEIs).

- *Regulation*

  Public policies, and environmental regulation in particular, are usually regarded as the most powerful pressure on firms to develop or adopt EIs [41], and this could also be the case with CEIs. The relevance of public policies is related to the triple externality problem, which is specifically faced by eco-innovation (see Chap. 2, [18, 21, 50]). This suggests that both environmental and innovation policies are relevant in this regard. The different types of environmental policies are usually classified into command-and-control (environmental or technological standards) or incentive or market-based (taxes, subsidies or emission permits). Relevant innovation-based policies could include grants or tax incentives for firms developing a given CEI. Not only specific instruments are important for the success of those policies, but also the existence of attractive framework conditions (long-term targets and policy stability), as well as the specific design elements of the instruments (see Chap. 7 for further details).
- *Demand-side pressures (consumers)*

  Environmentally aware consumers may encourage the development and uptake of CEIs if they demand products or services from firms which either manufacture or provide them using any of the circular practices mentioned in Chap. 4 (and, particularly, the Rs). However, there is still an open debate on the strength of this market-pull effect of those consumers on eco-innovation in general (and, thus, on CEIs) (see [19] for a detailed discussion).
- *Pressures of other stakeholders: financial institutions (banks), insurance companies,* etc.

  Financial institutions are increasingly requiring a good environmental track record for the firms they lend money to. This encourages the uptake of environmentally friendly practices in those firms, including CEIs.

Internal factors

Although the initial contributions on the literature on eco-innovation paid strong attention to the role of public policies, and the influence of internal factors was under-researched, these internal factors have gained ground in the last years and there is already a relatively abundant empirical literature on the drivers and barriers of EIs which include these internal factors in their analysis.

To be fair, the literature on corporate environmental management had long ago stressed the importance of the proactive environmental strategies of companies which positively influence the adoption of measures which reduce the environmental impact of products and processes (see, e.g., [1, 4, 53]). According to several authors [9, 53], a proactive environmental strategy represents a critical driver for eco-innovations. However, strategy is constrained by and is dependent upon the profile of the company's resources [9].[4]

Therefore, the literature on EI has taken these insights into account and has recently moved one step further to include the effects of organizational capabilities on the development and/or adoption of EIs. In particular, del Río et al. [22] combined a resource-based view (RBV) of the firm with other approaches (e.g. dynamic capabilities) to provide a theoretical framework which took the internal factors to the firm into account in a comprehensive manner. They considered the influence of a broad array of resources, capabilities and competences (RCCs), which were important drivers of business strategies and innovation performance. These RCCs include in-house knowledge, customer relationships, financial reserves, physical resources, reputation, motivation, attitude (top management commitment), human resources, personal contacts and networking [41]. RCCs influence the development and uptake of EIs in general and CEIs in particular. And this influence is both direct and indirect through their impact on environmental strategies.

The rest of this subsection further discusses some of these key drivers.

- *In-house knowledge and human resources*
  Firms with a strong knowledge base, i.e. with highly knowledgeable human resources, would more likely develop or adopt CE innovations, given their greater exposure to external knowledge flows and higher absorptive capability, which allows them to more easily adopt a new innovation [19]. Firms with higher investments on R&D are more likely to have such absorptive capacity. Horbach et al. [36] argue that, as a relatively new technology field, eco-innovations are characterized by higher innovation intensities. On the other hand, a strong knowledge base on existing technologies related to a linear economy may discourage CEIs.
- *Financial resources*
  The existence of a financially healthy situation in the firm makes the adoption of CEIs more likely, since the firm can devote sufficient financial resources for the adoption of new equipment or to finance changes in internal production processes. As noted in Demirel and Danisman [24], the participation of firms in the CE may be constrained by high initial investments. Some prior studies show that firms generally prefer internal over external finance for eco-innovation processes [24].

[4] "Resources give the company leeway in choosing the best strategy in response to the external environments and at the same time are critical determinants of knowledge creation and organizational capabilities" [9, p. 8].

- *Physical resources*
  The existence of an installed base which is difficult to change may act as an important barrier to the adoption of CE innovations, as suggested in Kiefer et al. [42], but this also depends on the degree of change required by those innovations, i.e. on the degree of compatibility of those innovations with respect to the existing products, processes and organization of the firm. This driver/barrier is closely related to the degree of change required by the new CE innovations (i.e. to the features of the innovations being adopted; see below).
- *Reputation*
  A good reputation of the firm with respect to environmental behaviour, treatment of staff and relationships with society at large may make links with other stakeholders easier and allow them to be more open to the changes caused by the adoption of CE innovations.
- *Motivation, attitude (top management commitment)*
  The environmentally proactive attitude of managers in the firm is likely to facilitate the adoption of CE-related innovations, which are supposed to reduce the environmental impacts of production or consumption activities (in addition to leading to cost savings). Top management commitment can thus be critical for the involvement of companies in the CE.
- *Networking (cooperation)*
  There is abundant evidence in the eco-innovation literature suggesting that cooperation with other stakeholders encourages innovation and adoption of environmental innovations (see, e.g., [17, 23]) and this can also be expected to be the case for CE-related innovations. It is widely acknowledged that cooperation intensity is greater in EI than in other innovations [8, 12, 17]. Indeed, this is probably a much more relevant driver of CEIs than EIs in general, given that the Rs require the involvement of different types of stakeholders.

Characteristics of the technologies

The degree of disruption in the firms that the new CE innovations entail with respect to existing production processes (including the degree of complexity and change and compatibility with existing production processes/business models) can be expected to influence the speed of their diffusion. Some innovations are easier to adopt (drop-in innovations), while, for others, this is much more difficult if they entail substantial changes in the company [39]. Following [20, 21], certain characteristics of CEIs may influence their development and adoption and the inertia to use existing technologies ("lock-in"), including their complexity (which may require additional training for the existing workforce), their compatibility with the existing production system (if the new technology involves changes in key system components), the life cycle of the firm's capital (new innovations are more likely to be developed/adopted if they do not involve the scrapping of already made investments) and high upfront costs resulting from development/adoption (innovations that do not require major initial investments are more attractive) [21, p. 863].

In this discussion on the contribution of different EI types to the CE, the classical distinction in the EI literature between incremental and radical EIs is relevant. The former refer to the gradual modification or redesign of organizations, processes and products. Radical EIs entail the introduction of alternatives or completely new organizational methods, products, processes or marketing [16] (see also Chap. 2).

A main topic in the CE literature at the micro-level is the extent to which incremental EIs contribute to the CE.[5] Some authors argue that the transition towards the CE in general and, in particular, the adoption of CEIs by firms take place in a gradual manner, starting initially from incremental EIs [2, 30], which can easily be dropped in existing systems [14]. In addition, several authors argue that the implementation of the CE is indirectly encouraged by the adoption of incremental EIs, since these positively impact the dynamic (organizational) capabilities of firms which, in turn, allow them to implement higher-level CE practices (see, e.g., [38, 52]). In contrast, the literature on innovation and EI shows that incremental changes may lock out more radical ones [21, 55]. Indeed, [42] suggest that incremental EIs may lead to a risk of lock-in in lower circularity levels.

The cost of the technologies is another important variable in this context. The cost savings which will be generated by the adoption of the new CEIs (real or perceived) are one of the most relevant features of the CEIs which are likely to influence their adoption. Obviously, they are a main driver for all innovations, whether eco-innovation or general innovation.

Finally, as suggested by the EI literature, sectoral specificities are likely to affect the adoption of new CE innovations because technological opportunities, market structures influencing innovation rates, the features of innovation processes and the degree of environmental impacts and stakeholder pressure, among others, are sector-specific [12, 13, 17, 23, 27, 46].

To sum up, the following Box 5.1 includes the list of the drivers and barriers to the adoption (and development) of CE innovations considered in this book. The case studies in the following chapter show the influence of those determinants on such adoption.

Box 5.1. Drivers and barriers to the adoption of CEIs considered in this book

Internal Factors to the Firm

- In-house knowledge and human resources.
- Financial resources.
- Physical resources.
- Reputation.
- Motivation, attitude (top management commitment).
- Networking (cooperation).

[5] See Kiefer et al. [42] for a full discussion.

External Factors to the Firm

- Public policies.
- Consumers.
- Financial institutions.

Features of the CEI

- Costs and expected benefits.
- Compatibility with existing installed bases.
- Degree of radicality of the technology.

References

1. Aragón-Correa JA, Rubio-López EA (2007) Proactive corporate environmental strategies: myths and misunderstandings. Long Range Plan 40:357–381. https://doi.org/10.1016/j.lrp.2007.02.008
2. Aranda-Usón A, Portillo-Tarragona P, Scarpellini S, Llena-Macarulla F (2020) The progressive adoption of a circular economy by businesses for cleaner production: an approach from a regional study in Spain. J Clean Prod 247:1–12. https://doi.org/10.1016/j.jclepro.2019.119648
3. Ashford NA, Ayers C, Stone RF (1985) Using regulation to change the market for innovation. Harvard Environ Law Rev 9:419
4. Bansal P, Roth K (2000) Why companies go green: a model of ecological responsiveness. Acad Manag J 43(4):717–736
5. Barbieri N, Ghisetti C, Gilli M, Marin G, Nicolli F (2016) A Survey of the literature on environmental innovation based on main path analysis. J Econ Surv 30:596–623. https://doi.org/10.1111/joes.12149
6. Barreiro-Gen M, Lozano R (2020) How circular is the circular economy? Analysing the implementation of circular economy in organisations. Bus Strategy Environ. https://doi.org/10.1002/bse.2590
7. Bassi F, Dias JG (2019) The use of circular economy practices in SMEs across the EU. Resour Conserv Recycl 146:523–533. https://doi.org/10.1016/j.resconrec.2019.03.019
8. Belin J, Horbach J, Oltra V (2011) Determinants and specificities of eco-innovations—an econometric analysis for the French and German industry based on the Community Innovation Survey
9. Berrone P, Gelabert L, Fosfuri A, Gomez-Mejia L (2007) Can institutional forces create competitve advantage? An empirical examination of environmental innovation. Working paper, Madrid, Spain
10. Bhatnagar S, Cohen M (1997) The impact of environmental regulation on innovation: a panel data study. Retrieved from http://www.vanderbilt.edu/vcems/papers/innovate.pdf
11. Cainelli G, D'Amato A, Mazzanti M (2020) Resource efficient eco-innovations for a circular economy: Evidence from EU firms. Res Policy 49(1):1–11. https://doi.org/10.1016/j.respol.2019.103827

12. Cainelli G, Mazzanti M, Montresor S (2012) Environmental innovations, local networks and internationalization. Ind Innovation 19(8):697–734. https://doi.org/10.1080/13662716.2012.739782
13. Carrillo-Hermosilla J, del Río P, Könnölä T (2009) Eco-innovation: when sustainability and competitiveness shake hands. Palgrave Macmillan, Hampshire
14. Carrillo-Hermosilla J, Del Río P, Könnölä T (2010) Diversity of eco-innovations: reflections from selected case studies. J Clean Prod 18:1073–1083. https://doi.org/10.1016/j.jclepro.2010.02.014
15. Colucci M, Vecchi A (2020) Close the loop: evidence on the implementation of the circular economy from the Italian fashion industry. Bus Strategy Environ. https://doi.org/10.1002/bse.2658
16. de Jesus A, Antunes P, Santos R, Mendonça S (2018) Eco-innovation in the transition to a circular economy: An analytical literature review. J Clean Prod 172:2999–3018. https://doi.org/10.1016/j.jclepro.2017.11.111
17. de Marchi V (2012) Environmental innovation and R&D cooperation: empirical evidence from Spanish manufacturing firms. Res Policy 41:614–623. https://doi.org/10.1016/j.respol.2011.10.002
18. del Río P (2004) Public policy and clean technology promotion. The synergy between environmental economics and evolutionary economics of technological change. Int J Sustain Dev 7(2):200–216
19. del Río P, Peñasco C, Romero-Jordán D (2016b) What drives eco-innovators? A critical review of the empirical literature based on econometric methods. J Cleaner Prod 2158–2170
20. del Río P (2005) Analysing the factors influencing clean technology adoption: a study of the Spanish pulp and paper industry. Bus Strategy Environ 14:20–37
21. del Río P (2009) The empirical analysis of the determinants for environmental technological change: a research agenda. Ecol Econ 68:861–878. https://doi.org/10.1016/j.ecolecon.2008.07.004
22. del Río P, Carrillo-Hermosilla J, Könnölä T, Bleda M (2016) Resources, capabilities and competences for eco-innovation. Technol Econ Dev Econ 22:274–292. https://doi.org/10.3846/20294913.2015.1070301
23. del Río P, Peñasco C, Romero-Jordán D (2015) Distinctive features of environmental innovators: an econometric analysis. Bus Strategy Environ 24:361–385
24. Demirel P, Danisman GO (2019) Eco-innovation and firm growth in the circular economy: evidence from European small- and medium-sized enterprises. Bus Strategy Environ. https://doi.org/10.1002/bse.2336
25. Dey PK, Malesios C, De D, Budhwar P, Chowdhury S, Cheffi W (2020) Circular economy to enhance sustainability of small and medium-sized enterprises. Bus Strategy Environ 29(6):2145–2169. https://doi.org/10.1002/bse.2492
26. Diaz Lopez FJ, Bastein T, Tukker A (2019) Business model innovation for resource-efficiency, circularity and cleaner production: what 143 cases tell Us. Ecol Econ 155:20–35. https://doi.org/10.1016/j.ecolecon.2018.03.009
27. Díaz-López FJ (2008) A tailored method for eco-innovation strategies and drivers (in the South). In: DIME international conference of innovation, sustainability and policy, pp 1–49
28. Ellen MacArthur Foundation (2015) Delivering the circular economy: a toolkit for policymakers. Delivering the circular economy: a toolkit for policymakers, vol 177. https://doi.org/10.1038/531435a
29. Franco MA (2017) Circular economy at the micro level: a dynamic view of incumbents' struggles and challenges in the textile industry. J Clean Prod 168:833–845. https://doi.org/10.1016/j.jclepro.2017.09.056
30. Garcés-Ayerbe C, Rivera-Torres P, Suárez-Perales I, Leyva-de la Hiz D (2019) Is it possible to change from a linear to a circular economy? An overview of opportunities and barriers for European small and medium-sized enterprise companies. Int J Environ Res Public Health 16(5):1–15. https://doi.org/10.3390/ijerph16050851

31. García-Quevedo J, Jové-Llopis E, Martínez-Ros E (2020) Barriers to the circular economy in European small and medium-sized firms. Bus Strategy Environ. https://doi.org/10.1002/bse.2513
32. Ghisetti C, Montresor S (2020) On the adoption of circular economy practices by small and medium-size enterprises (SMEs): does "financing-as-usual" still matter? J Evol Econ 30 (2):559–586. https://doi.org/10.1007/s00191-019-00651-w
33. Guldmann E, Huulgaard RD (2020) Barriers to circular business model innovation: a multiple-case study. J Clean Prod 243:1–13. https://doi.org/10.1016/j.jclepro.2019.118160
34. Gusmerotti NM, Testa F, Corsini F, Pretner G, Iraldo F (2019) Drivers and approaches to the circular economy in manufacturing firms. J Clean Prod 230:314–327. https://doi.org/10.1016/j.jclepro.2019.05.044
35. Horbach J (2008) Determinants of environmental innovation—new evidence from German panel data sources. Res Policy 37:163–173. https://doi.org/10.1016/j.respol.2007.08.006
36. Horbach J, Rammer C, Rennings K (2012) Determinants of eco-innovations by type of environmental impact—the role of regulatory push/pull, technology push and market pull. Ecol Econ 78:112–122. https://doi.org/10.1016/j.ecolecon.2012.04.005
37. Jaffe AB, Palmer K (1997) Environmental Regulation and Innovation: a panel data study. Rev Econ Stat 79:610–619. https://doi.org/10.1162/003465397557196
38. Katz-Gerro T, López Sintas J (2018) Mapping circular economy activities in the European Union: patterns of implementation and their correlates in small and medium-sized enterprises. Bus Strategy Environ. https://doi.org/10.1002/bse.2259
39. Kemp R (1994) Technology and the transition to environmental sustainability. Futures 26:1023–1046. https://doi.org/10.1016/0016-3287(94)90071-X
40. Kemp R, Dijk M (2013) Analytical framework of drivers and barriers to resource efficiency (Maastricht University, Deliverable 1.1., Issue. https://www.ucl.ac.uk/polfree/publications
41. Keshminder JS, Río P (2019) The missing links? The indirect impacts of drivers on eco-innovation. Corp Soc Responsib Environ Manag. https://doi.org/10.1002/csr.1789
42. Kiefer CP, Río P, Carrillo-Hermosilla J (2021) On the contribution of eco-innovation features to a circular economy: a microlevel quantitative approach. Bus Strategy Environ 1–17. https://doi.org/10.1002/bse.2688
43. Kirchherr J, Piscicelli L, Bour R, Kostense-Smit E, Muller J, Huibrechtse-Truijens A, Hekkert M (2018) Barriers to the circular economy: evidence from the European Union (EU). Ecol Econ 150:264–272. https://doi.org/10.1016/j.ecolecon.2018.04.028
44. Lanjouw JO, Mody A (1996) Innovation and the international diffusion of environmentally responsive technology. Res Policy 25:549–571. https://doi.org/10.1016/0048-7333(95)00853-5
45. Liu Y, Bai Y (2014) An exploration of firms' awareness and behavior of developing circular economy: an empirical research in China. Resour Conserv Recycl 87:145–152. https://doi.org/10.1016/j.resconrec.2014.04.002
46. Mazzanti M, Zoboli R (2006) Examining the factors influencing environmental innovations
47. Moktadir MA, Ahmadi HB, Sultana R, Zohra F-T, Liou JJH, Rezaei J (2020) Circular economy practices in the leather industry: a practical step towards sustainable development. J Clean Prod 251:1–13. https://doi.org/10.1016/j.jclepro.2019.119737
48. Norberg-Bohm V (1999) Stimulating 'green' technological innovation: an analysis of alternative policy mechanisms. Policy Sci 32(1):13–38
49. Ormazabal M, Prieto-Sandoval V, Puga-Leal R, Jaca C (2018) Circular economy in Spanish SMEs: challenges and opportunities. J Clean Prod 185:157–167. https://doi.org/10.1016/j.jclepro.2018.03.031
50. Rennings K (2000) Redefining innovation—eco-innovation research and the contribution from ecological economics. Ecol Econ 32:319–332. https://doi.org/10.1016/S0921-8009(99)00112-3
51. Rizos V, Behrens A, van der Gaast W, Hofman E, Ioannou A, Kafyeke T, Topi C (2016) Implementation of circular economy business models by small and medium-sized enterprises (SMEs): barriers and enablers. Sustainability 8(11):1–18. https://doi.org/10.3390/su8111212

52. Scarpellini S, Valero-Gil J, Moneva JM, Andreaus M (2020) Environmental management capabilities for a "circular eco-innovation". Bus Strategy Environ. https://doi.org/10.1002/bse.2472
53. Sharma P, Sharma S (2011) Drivers of proactive environmental strategy in family firms. Bus Ethics Q 21
54. Sousa-Zomer TT, Magalhães L, Zancul E, Campos LMS, Cauchick-Miguel PA (2018) Cleaner production as an antecedent for circular economy paradigm shift at the micro-level: evidence from a home appliance manufacturer. J Clean Prod 185:740–748. https://doi.org/10.1016/j.jclepro.2018.03.006
55. Unruh GC (2002) Escaping carbon lock-in. Energy Policy 30:317–325. https://doi.org/10.1016/S0301-4215(01)00098-2
56. Zamfir A-M, Mocanu C, Grigorescu A (2017) Circular economy and decision models among European SMEs. Sustainability 9(9). https://doi.org/10.3390/su9091507

Chapter 6
Drivers and Barriers to Circular Practices at the Micro-Level: Case Studies

In order to illustrate the drivers and barriers to the adoption of CE innovations at the micro-(firm) level, in this chapter, we present case studies of firms in different sectors. All case studies follow the same structure (Box 6.1). The selection of case studies aimed to represent a diverse, wide array of CE innovations; i.e., it is intended to cover most of the CE activities in the R-framework proposed by Reike et al. [37](see Chap. 2), such as refuse (R0), reduce (R1), resell and reuse (R2), repair (R3), refurbish (R4), remanufacture (R5), repurpose (R6), recycle materials (R7), recover energy (R8) and remine (R9), in different sectors and for different geographical areas (countries). Furthermore, we made sure that both successful cases and failures were considered. With this set up, the following case analyses are described subsequently:

1. Too Good To Go.
2. Rubicon Global.
3. IKEA.
4. Herrenknecht.
5. German construction sector/Kaspar Kraemer.
6. Camper.
7. Rebattery.
8. Upcycling the Oceans (ECOALF).
9. Madaster platform.
10. REVOV.

Box 6.1 Structure of the case studies

1. **Introduction**
   Background on the company and sector, and other relevant aspects of the institutional environment influencing the development or adoption of CE practices.

P. del Río et al., *The Circular Economy*, Green Energy and Technology,
https://doi.org/10.1007/978-3-030-74792-3_6

2. **Circular practices**
   Description of the circular economy practices developed or adopted by the firms.
3. **Drivers/barriers**
   Identification of drivers and barriers to the development or adoption of a given practice, based on secondary sources, company reports, company websites or interviews. The assumption is that such development and adoption are generally related to multiple factors. Some are internal to the firm (resources, dynamic capabilities and competences), whereas others are rather external (regulation, pressure of consumers…) or linked to the particular features of the CE practice (see Chap. 5). The interaction/interrelation between those factors (drivers and barriers) is shown to the extent possible.
4. **Lessons learnt**
   Here, a final discussion of the case study and the implications for both private and public policy-makers are provided.

6.1 Case Studies

6.1.1 Case Study 1. Too Good To Go

Introduction

Founded in 2015, Too Good To Go served its first meal in Copenhagen in March 2016. The initial idea of the founders was to focus on food that became waste at the end of buffets. While developing this concept, founders quickly realized that it could be extended to all kinds of food service providers such as restaurants and cafes, bakeries and hotels [47]. The vision behind Too Good To Go has remained the same since the beginning: inspiring and empowering everyone to fight food waste together.

The company, headquartered in Copenhagen, has local offices in 14 countries (Netherlands, France, Denmark, Portugal, Belgium, Poland, Switzerland, Austria, Spain, Sweden, Norway, Germany, Italy and the UK). It remains one entity, with everything gathered under one global holding. The company generates revenue from two main streams, the business partners active on the platform, who pay a yearly subscription to Too Good To Go, and a small commission fee for each meal sold.

Circular practices

The rationale behind Too Good to Go is simple: to connect consumers with businesses whose products would otherwise have gone unsold and been disposed of. Too Good To Go has saved 29 million meals and avoided the equivalent of more than 72,000 tonnes of greenhouse gas emissions (around 15,000 vehicles driven in one year). Through a community of 18 million users and 38,000 restaurants, supermarkets and cafes in 14 countries, the company was managing to save one meal per second just before the Covid-19 pandemic [47].

After four years, Too Good To Go is the world's largest Business-To-Consumer Platform aiming to fight food waste. This is done via a mobile app in which businesses can add the food surplus they have and consumers can see the offer available. The application is mostly intended for its use by restaurants, bakeries, supermarkets, hotels and canteens. For Too Good To Go, this is a "win-win-win solution" with a positive impact on the environment, allowing businesses to make money out of food which would otherwise be wasted while new customers and consumers can access food at affordable prices and reduce food waste [47].

After downloading the app, users have access to a range of meals available nearby. They can either view what's close by or search for specific meals with different options, such as collection time, location or type of food (for instance, vegan or vegetarian). Once they select their option, users receive a receipt which needs to be presented at the shop in order to receive the food bag. Typically, consumers will have access to a 3–5 euro "magic bag" with an original value of 10–15 euro; i.e., they are able to buy food that's worth three times the amount they pay [47].

When businesses pre-estimate the amount of surplus food that will be available, they do it according to their general planning and the demand the day before. In cases the store sells every meal and is left without surplus, the customer's order is cancelled and he/she is reimbursed.

Regarding other types of waste, such as the packaging used to contain the food, the company encourages its partners to allow consumers to bring their containers as much as possible. On the mobile application, consumers can easily access information, store by store, as to whether they can do this. For some stores, it is not possible to do so either because the food has to be packaged well beforehand—the case for most supermarkets—or because national or local regulations do not allow it. In these cases, Too Good To Go offers to provide the store with packaging made out of FSC3 and/or kraft paper [47].

All businesses joining the platform are in direct communication with Too Good To Go staff and benefit from an onboarding session with the company's team. To maintain the quality of food and experience on the app, Too Good To Go also works with partners who have received below-expectation user reviews to improve the experience for both parties. Additionally, the app keeps evolving and adding more functionalities, such as the vegetarian option or the possibility to bookmark your favourite stores [47].

Drivers/barriers

The key driver for founders was finding a solution to a problem: one-third of all food produced today ends up in a bin which, at best, feeds animals or is recycled and, at worst, is sent to landfill or incineration. This problem is recognized widely in society. Not only does this issue pose serious ethical and social questions, but it also deeply threatens the environment [23]. Food waste is responsible for 10% of all global greenhouse gas emissions, and 28% of agricultural lands worldwide are used to produce food whose destiny is to be ultimately wasted. At the European level, the average citizen wastes around 92 kg of food every year, contributing to one-third of the yearly waste generation per capita. Furthermore, the financial cost of food waste is estimated to be 143 billion euros per year in Europe [48].

Therefore, if food waste has an economic cost, preventing it brings economic benefits. That is the bet the Too Good To Go founders took. By creating a system where food surplus from restaurants, hotels, supermarkets and bakeries is sold at a lower price, the goal was to generate revenue from food that would have otherwise been wasted. By doing so, the company effectively acts on around 17% of the total food waste generated in Europe by providing beneficial solutions at the food service, wholesale and retail levels.

Also, business can benefit from the solution. Too Good To Go provides a solution for food service providers to sell their food surplus which otherwise would have been thrown away at the end of the business day. For businesses, the motivations behind joining the platform range from the environmental impacts of food waste to optimizing the general functioning costs or corporate social responsibility guidelines.

The app is just one way the company fights food waste, as it also directly encourages households, schools and policymakers to change their behaviour and aims to influence legislation that will reduce food waste further. The company's overall vision is "a planet with no food waste". To achieve this, it is actively empowering and inspiring everyone to fight food waste together by building a movement comprised of four pillars. In addition to its direct impact, achieved through the app, it also has an indirect impact through the four pillars, each with different targets to be met at the end of 2020 [47]:

- 1st pillar: It specifically targets households, as almost half of the food wasted in Europe takes place at this stage. The pillar provides educational messages with tips and tricks that can reduce food waste daily by adopting better buying, storing and cooking practices. The overall goal is also for citizens to gain an understanding of the value of food and to make the issue more visible.
- 2nd pillar: It targets businesses, asking them to go beyond just retail and food services to address food waste and losses taking place further upstream in the food value chain. It includes plans to improve the sustainability agendas of the 38,000 businesses partners the company already works with.

- 3rd pillar: It focuses on schools, targeting younger generations with the creation of educational toolkits that contain exercises and guides for teachers.
- 4th pillar: It focuses on public affairs. The company is willing to engage with policy-makers to make sure that the appropriate regulatory framework is adopted to reduce food waste and enable change to make food systems more sustainable (e.g. to allow consumers to bring their containers to reduce packaging).

Lessons learnt

While this solution is around software technology, its innovation is more related to interpreting the markets and connecting their different parts. Hence, this case provides an example of the importance of understanding the societal needs and demand in innovating for the circular economy. By identifying a concrete problem in food chains which cause severe environmental impacts and understanding the importance of the scalability of the solution, the founders developed an online app for connecting businesses and consumers to help them reduce waste. This intermediary role offers a model suitable for scaling up. The app and the platform approach, in general, offer an opportunity to extend the impact beyond the mere matching of supply and demand and contributing to wider awareness raising in society.

6.1.2 Case Study 2. Rubicon Global

Introduction

In 2008, Nate Morris and Marc Spiegel started Rubicon Global in Kentucky as they saw an opportunity to build a cloud-based, full-service waste and recycling platform to help companies reduce costs and increase sustainability by improving their waste and recycling practices. Rubicon states that its mission is to end waste, in all of its forms, by helping its partners find economic value in their waste streams and execute their sustainability goals [42].

In 2016, the company, headquartered in Atlanta, nearly doubled in size to more than 300 employees and was named a Next Billion-Dollar Startup by Forbes and one of the World's Most Innovative Companies by Fast Company. In 2017, Rubicon Global was honoured with the Ecolab Award for Circular Economy Digital Disruptor at the Annual Meeting of the World Economic Forum. Under Morris's leadership, in 2020, Rubicon has become a driver for change across the waste and recycling industry, managing 3,300,000+ Unique Service Locations across all 50 U.S. states, and in 20 countries [42]. The company has become the largest third-party vendor in the U.S. waste and recycling business.

Circular practices

Rubicon Global is a technology company that provides a suite of software-as-a-service (SaaS) products for waste, recycling and smart city solutions and collects and analyses data for businesses and governments worldwide for industries like restaurants, grocery, convenience and drug stores, retail, property management, manufacturing, construction and demolition and distribution and logistics.

Rubicon operates as a multi-sided platform bringing together customers who want to get rid of waste, recyclers, haulers and landfills. While these players bring in the hard assets, Rubicon has chosen to focus on connecting and streamlining such activities via their online platform, improving transparency and efficiency for all the players in the system. On the one hand, whereas customers and recyclers may see opportunities for circular practices, haulers may be more focused on eco-efficiency via improved logistics and pooling efforts for economies of scale. On the other hand, the same system may serve landfill operators, who need more tonnages. Still, Rubicon benefits from diverting waste from landfills rather than having a business model dependent on landfill tonnage [43].

As of 2020, the Rubicon platform serves and connects over 3,300,000 service locations worldwide and the network of over 7000 independent haulers [42]. Programmes managed with the platform include cardboard, plastic, paper, metal, glass, electronics recycling, construction and demolition, organics recycling (food waste, wood waste, etc.) and single-stream recycling solutions. Also, Rubicon experts manage commodity markets, zero-waste programs and other sustainability offerings across the portfolio.

Most recently, Rubicon has developed a smart city solution—RUBICONSmartCity™—that helps municipal governments improve their waste and recycling operations while transforming their fleets into roaming data centres that can help improve quality of life and deliver better government services through data analytics. The solution has been extended to more than 50 cities across the USA [42].

Rubicon bills customers on an annual subscription basis with three primary sources of revenue, including a fee based on the composition and amount of waste, a management fee for specialized software services (invoicing, data reporting, etc.) and a diversion bonus based on the amount of tonnage hauled that did not go to a landfill [43].

As Rubicon has grown, management has introduced a set of advanced software features, including automation of hauler scheduling, invoicing and metrics reporting. Using technologies such as visual recognition and machine learning, the company conducts an initial screening of a client's waste streams to identify types of waste and quantities, develops a waste separation system and then tailors a waste collection schedule. This helps customers improve their recycling rates, lower the costs by reducing the frequency of waste collection and sometimes earn extra income from selling the recyclable products (e.g. cardboard, paper).

As part of its mission, Rubicon educates its customers' employees on waste separation and recycling. It connects clients with its independent hauler network, which offers competitive prices, on-demand pickups, billing transparency and even a report on the customers' recycling efforts. It also collaborates with other companies along the circular economy value cycle to create sustainable offerings for its small business customers, such as Michelin, which offers discount pricing on new commercial tires and retreads, and TerraCycle, an expert in hard-to-recycle waste.

Drivers/barriers

The very beginning of the company was driven by the interest to solve environmental problems and to modernize the waste management sector. While working in China for the Kentucky state government earlier in his career, Morris was shocked by the incredible amount of waste and lack of solutions. Upon his return to the USA, he reconnected with Spiegel, whose family had been in the waste and recycling business for more than a century and questioned if there was a better, more sustainable way to deal with the global waste problem.

Their political connections and the established position and reputation in the sector provided an excellent basis to develop the business and convince investors and other partners to join the venture. Their commitment and capacity to win others to the project led to a successful growth path. Most recently, Rubicon has announced a strategic partnership with French-based Suez Environment to collaborate on technology and sustainability. Suez led Rubicon's round of funding, which has raised more than $50 million and brought Rubicon's post-money valuation to $800 million [42]. Rubicon continues to develop technology and data to change the global waste industry and the traditional model of waste collection based on the landfill.

Partnerships have played a relevant role in the development of the company. For instance, a technology pilot program with Odakyu Group in Japan and Helvetia Environment, Switzerland's waste management market leader, has allowed piloting circular economy solutions. Furthermore, a partnership agreement with EarthCam, the leading technology company in the construction industry, has allowed the use of video to facilitate corporate responsibility through AI-based automated waste, recycling and sustainability programs. Recently, Rubicon partnered also with the global safety science company UL to extend third-party validation services such as UL's standards for circularity, recycled content and waste diversion to Rubicon's customers and collaborators, while helping UL customers identify and access Rubicon recycling and waste reduction services across the sustainable material management value chain [45].

The global commercial waste management industry stood at 120 Bn euros in 2018 and is projected to show substantial growth with a compound annual growth rate of 6.7% [42]. Growth in restaurant chains, hotels and commercial buildings across several parts of the globe is increasing waste generation, which is fuelling the demand for efficient waste management systems. Growth in consumer awareness for waste management, coupled with increased efforts at the government level, is projected to boost industry demand. However, high costs associated with waste management and lack of existing infrastructure is likely to hamper market growth in some countries. The strong drivers in the sector also create a positive business environment for cloud-based waste management solutions [11].

The company is also well positioned with respect to the drivers related to sustainability and corporate responsibility. Many citizens, politicians and business leaders are concerned about low recycling rates and other indicators of poor environmental stewardship. Even in the early steps, Morris believed that the shift towards sustainability would have a profound impact on the waste management industry. He knew Rubicon's mission of promoting sustainability through diverting waste from landfills would be key in attracting the right investors, employees and customers to the company [43].

Lessons learnt

This case provides interesting insights about how a conventional waste management sector can benefit from a new player focused on serving existing players to manage their operations more efficiently and connecting with others, with benefits to the economy and the environment. Especially the company′s choice to focus on the platform business model that relies on the hard assets of other players offers a scalable pathway with the potential to have a wider impact on the economy. The new solutions for the cities that create opportunities to benefit from big data and artificial intelligence may lead to new more systemic solutions that were not possible before. Despite the incentives for the reuse of waste, the platform itself may still offer opportunities for circular practices, improving the efficiency and competitiveness of linear practices and leading to increased use of landfills rather than closing the loops. Hence, such advances in the sharing economy might well benefit from proactive policymaking and regulations that would orient the current practices towards circular practices.

6.1.3 Case Study 3. IKEA

Introduction

Over six decades, IKEA went from the woods of southern Sweden to being a major retail experience in more than 50 markets around the world. In 2019, IKEA attracted 2.5 billion website visits and 957 million visits to 433 IKEA stores. The number of IKEA co-workers worldwide amounted to 211,000 [27]. Total retail sales, which included sales of IKEA products, food and services to IKEA customers, amounted to €41.3 billion [28].

The IKEA sustainability strategy *People & Planet Positive* [25], launched in 2012, included a commitment to create a positive impact for people, society and the planet. In the words of its CEO, Torbjörn Lööf, "we want to enable more people to live sustainable lives within the limits of the planet. We want to reduce greenhouse gas emissions in the atmosphere. And we want to create opportunities for people to take better care of themselves, their families and communities" [25, p. 7]. In 2017, IKEA created its first "design for circularity" guide [26], which defined how circular design could enable their products to be reused, refurbished, remanufactured and recycled, and what demands it placed on their product design process. Further to their product design, IKEA embarked on a transformation journey in 2018 to become a circular business by 2030. In order to do so, it established four commitments to guide its approach [24, p. 22]:

1. By 2030, every IKEA product would be designed from the very beginning according to their circular design principles, to be reused, refurbished, remanufactured and recycled.
2. It would only use renewable or recycled materials, aiming to eliminate virgin fossil materials and to send nothing to landfills.
3. IKEA would develop new ways to acquire, care for and pass on their products, enabling customers to be part of the solution.
4. It committed to take the lead to achieve this transformation and work together with other businesses, NGOs, governments and customers to change the global agenda.

In 2018, more than 60% of the IKEA product range was based on renewable materials, like wood and cotton, and nearly 10% contained recycled materials [24, p. 8]. It had a long way to go to reach the goal of 100% renewable or recycled material by 2030. Finding enough clean recycled materials was a challenge.

Circular practices

To tackle this challenge, in parallel with its circular design strategy, IKEA started exploring (along with its franchisees) how its business could support the transition to a circular economy and provide new services that would enable its customers to prolong the life of its products and pass them on in a convenient way when they are no longer used [24, p. 17].

Such practices corresponded to the third of the abovementioned commitments in its strategy to become a circular business in 2030, with regard to passing on and reselling products [24, p. 17]. In its initial approach in this direction, IKEA Spain was inspired by the textile business, the retail sector which was at that time the most advanced concerning circularity. Following the example of recovery and recycling initiatives in firms such as Inditex or H&M, it began to experiment on a small scale with household textiles in the catalogue of IKEA products: pillows, duvets, duvet covers, curtains, towels, etc. In accordance with those responsible for sustainability in IKEA, its consumers already expected a similar initiative on its part.

Nevertheless, it seems clear that the commitment of IKEA and its actions in this third way of passing on and reselling should have gone beyond the textile segment of its product range, extending it to furniture, which constituted the fundamental core of its business and represented 4% of the solid waste in rubbish dumps. In a pioneering move in the company,[1] the IKEA sustainability team in Spain, led at that

[1] In the Belgian headquarters of IKEA a similar initiative arose, in which clients were presented with the proposal to extend the life of their products, reselling them, repairing them, presenting them to an acquaintance or donating them to the community.

time by Mercedes Gutiérrez, promoted in 2016 a project baptized as “Save the furniture”.[2] A multidisciplinary group of employees from different areas of the firm participated in its launch: services, legal, sales, administration, communication, store workers, etc. The project also benefited from the external support of Soulsight, a consultancy firm specialized in design thinking. This supported the IKEA team in the phases of exploration, market research, analysis and coordination of the focus groups, in which clients (IKEA Family Members), experts, members of NGOs and representatives from the Madrid City Council participated.

As the result of these analyses, the team concluded that consumers in the Spanish furniture market were strongly sensitive to price, which was consistent with the fact that 46% of households had a relatively low monthly income, around €1500, according to their own estimations. Spanish society also displayed a clear tendency to reuse its furniture, giving it to friends or family or storing it when it was no longer in use. It was estimated that the average family accumulated furniture and belongings in its junk room with an approximate worth of €2000.

The team promoting the “Save the furniture” project also concluded that an increasing market in the buying and selling of second-hand products via digital channels was being consolidated. Prominent in this market were platforms such as Wallapop, a Spanish company founded in 2013, or Vibbo. The latter company was launched in 2015 by Schibsted Spain, which was part of the Norwegian communications company Schibsted Media Group, to rename the generalist marketplace of classified announcements “Segundamano.es”, which had a 37 years’ experience in the market of buying and selling second-hand products in Spain. A non-structured search by the team promoting the “Save the furniture” project for IKEA furniture offered by private individuals in Vibbo returned figures of around 14,000 products.

In short, it was clear that there existed a parallel market for second-hand furniture with a sufficiently interesting volume, in which the “Save the furniture” team decided that IKEA should be a participant, rather than struggling against trends in favour of the sale of new furniture. The initiative therefore arose from an “outside in” approach, on the basis of a detected reality and social necessity. To address it, it was decided that a solution for clients should be used, which would be both agile and adapted for IKEA. This initiative permitted reconciliation of the intentions to circularize the company with a concrete and real business opportunity.

The pilot implementation of the project started in 2016 in the three IKEA stores which at that time operated in the Madrid region. This market was selected for its importance in terms of size and for the greater relative penetration of digital tools among its consumers in comparison with the rest of the country.

The “Save the furniture” initiative was proposed to IKEA clients as a new service intended to give a “better future to used furniture, a second opportunity”. It comprized the following four “solutions to prolong the life of IKEA products”[3]:

[2]https://www.ikea.com/es/es/campaigns/salvemos-los-muebles-pubc88453a1.

[3]https://www.ikea.com/es/es/campaigns/salvemos-los-muebles-pubc88453a1.

– "Sell your furniture": the client could sell the furniture that it no longer used to IKEA via its online platform (whether in stock or not) in the following categories: chests of drawers, tables, chairs, showcases, desks, shelves and wardrobes. The required conditions were that it had to be IKEA furniture, should not have been modified and had to be already assembled when supplied by the client to one of the participating stores. The sales receipt was not necessary.
– "Repair your furniture": It offered the client the possibility to obtain screws or loose parts for some of its products, in screw dispensing machines or in the "Bargains Section" of stores. Alternatively, clients could request these replacement parts via an online questionnaire, in order to receive them at home.
– "Care for your furniture": It offered clients advice on the care and cleaning of their IKEA products, to prolong their useful life, minimizing the consumption of water and energy.
– "Customize your furniture": It encouraged clients to personalize their furniture, sharing the versions of "post-designers" via their website and the social networks.

A proof of the success of this initiative was its international replication from the Spanish market to the rest of the IKEA group. The following early adopters were the Chinese and Japanese markets. Finally, the standardisation and global diffusion of these practices in the group were led by IKEA UK, under the new denomination "Circular Hub".

Drivers/barriers

Among the difficulties or barriers faced by this initiative, the role of regulation stands out. As stated by a representative of IKEA management[4]: "The regulations are not clear. Companies pay because they generate future waste. What happens if we assume the inverse logistics and revalue this future waste? On another point, the second-hand market is not regulated; today buying and selling between private individuals is performed without any regulation. When companies offer this service, we are obliged to pay VAT and to formalize a contract with the legal person. There aren't any subsidies or premiums to accelerate the uptake of the circular economy. Returns on investment are inexistent today, a great volume is required to make it profitable".

The expectations from the consumers of IKEA were a driver which favoured this initiative. They took for granted the environmental commitment of the company and expected its implication in circular practices. In the particular context of the Spanish market for second-hand furniture, a business opportunity and a trend towards multi-channelling could be observed, for which IKEA was required to offer a response. However, in the online channel, it was necessary to gain the attention of a clientele accustomed to using strongly consolidated platforms and mobile applications for their purchase of second-hand goods, including furniture. As a recent newcomer to the second-hand market, it was necessary to invest in in-store communication and in the social networks.

[4]Telephone interview on April 30, 2020 with Arturo García, Country Sustainability Manager IKEA Ibérica.

In more general terms, the IKEA business model did not initially envisage the circular economy: the company was dimensioned with a base on flows of exit merchandise, and establishing a system of inverse logistics did not prove easy. "In the end, behind reselling there is a digital market: it was necessary to develop channels, services, training, communication, it was necessary to redefine how, where, what, etc. A great effort in digitalization and multi-channelling, costly in time and money, was required", the company declared.[5]

Faced with these difficulties, IKEA signed an alliance with the platform Vibbo in 2016, which initially gave the company support with regard to a more rapid and simple categorization in the portal search engine for second-hand IKEA furniture, although from the beginning Vibbo wished to be autonomous. In fact, the launch of its own application was foreseen in 2020, but this was temporarily postponed due to the health crisis derived from Covid-19.

An additional difficulty for such inverse logistics was found in the effort required from clients, who had to transport themselves the assembled furniture to one of the stores. IKEA did not have its own services to offer this option to clients. It was also not economically viable to have available external services for this occasional transport of bulky objects from households to stores. With regard to textiles, stores did not have the necessary infrastructure for the treatment of waste. The objective was to ensure a sufficient volume and send it for sorting to the IKEA textile plant in Valls (Catalonia), which also received raw materials from all over the world, especially synthetic, viscose or polyester fibres.

The initiative "Save the furniture" enjoyed the support of another company's department (the sales team), although initially this team found it somewhat difficult to understand how sales of second-hand furniture could favour long-term sales of new products via client loyalty. It also counted upon the support of financial staff due to its clearly positive impact on the operating account of the company, as it increased the efficiency in the cost lines, reducing the costs of waste management, at the same as it resulted in highly productive second-hand sales. But, above all, the initiative counted on the enthusiasm and commitment of top IKEA management.

Lessons learnt

According to the company management, "in circular economics, design is key, but the retail sector is the meeting point between company ambition and the requirements of society in each of its markets".[6] This reflection shows the importance of approximating business circularity beyond design, bearing in mind the adaptation to the local context of the company objectives and resources. On this point, this IKEA initiative followed a demand-pull approach, with necessity and social reality being the origin of the opportunity for certain circular practices (e.g. passing on and reselling products).

It is also interesting to see how such practices of second-hand products do not necessarily "cannibalize" the conventional business of new product sales. This case

---

[5]Interview with Arturo García.

[6]See Footnote 5.

study demonstrates clearly that these are markets with distinct consumers and volumes, and thus, the circular economy is shown to be a way of opening business opportunities which would otherwise be neglected. What is more, extending the relationship with the client beyond the initial transaction of the new product, accompanying him or her and even compensating him or her at the end of its useful life, offers opportunities for companies to improve engagement and customer retention.

In addition, this case study shows the importance of having an absorptive capacity which permits the company to take inspiration from beyond the circular practices of its competitors in the same sector. Thus, IKEA paid attention to the initiatives in the retail sector which were most advanced at that time regarding circularization, namely textiles. This adaptation of external innovations was also executed progressively, starting on a small scale with a specific segment of its product portfolio, the recycling of household textiles. The company extended the circular practices to the core of its catalogue (furniture) only once it had developed greater knowledge on them.

The case study also shows the operational difficulties of reselling and establishing an inverse logistics system, which required a great effort in digitalization and multi-channelling, which is both time-consuming and expensive. Nevertheless, from a more strategic perspective and a wider horizon, this circular economy project demonstrated the compatibility between the economic and environmental objectives of the company. It strengthened its brand positioning not only by demonstrating its commitment to sustainability, but also by generating a greater confidence for consumers on product quality and durability and, similarly, in access.

6.1.4 Case Study 4. Herrenknecht[7]

Introduction

Herrenknecht AG is an industrial manufacturer of mechanized tunnel boring machines (TBMs) based in Lahr, Germany. With its approximately 5.000 employees, it regularly reaches yearly turnovers of over 1 billion euros. TBMs are used to mechanically excavate long-range large-diameter tunnels. There are different types of TBM technology and their use is fundamentally conditioned by the type of soil or rock and groundwater. Herrenknecht usually acts as a provider to construction companies that operate the TBM and excavate the tunnel themselves. As such, the TBM manufacturing business is almost exclusively project-based. The adequacy of a TBM and its underlying technology is conditioned by the

[7]Based on personal interview on January 10th, 2020, with Mr. Achim Kühn, Head of group marketing, member of the supervisory board and member of the executive board. Place: Herrenknecht HQ in Lahr, Germany. Duration: 1.5 h.

aforementioned geological conditions, which is why "standardization" of TBMs and their 1:1 reuse is almost impossible.

Examples of Herrenknecht tunnels include the Gotthard Base Tunnel, Yangtze River Crossing or the Madrid M-30 circumvention tunnel system, which had the biggest diameter of a specific TBM technology at the time.

Herrenknecht is considered a technology leader in the market, offering high-quality, safe and efficient TBMs. In recent years, other "Western" TBM manufactures have progressively dropped out of the market and currently main competitors are Chinese State-owned enterprises and Japanese technology conglomerates.

After several expansionist decades in global underground construction with high growth rates in the TBM manufacturing business, especially driven by the South of Europe (new railway lines, highways and metro systems) and China and other Asian countries (infrastructure development boom), the past and present decades are characterized by very high and increasing competition levels. This is combined with strategic/political lock-out of foreign TBM manufacturing companies from home markets (especially in the case of China), fierce price-based competition and "political competition".[8]

Regulation is an important factor in the tunnelling business. It comprises rules for designing underground infrastructure, TBM operation, management of mined soil/rock, etc. The regulation affecting tunnelling is more safety- than environmentally-motivated.

Environmental activism exists in some European countries but is generally focused on a few very large-scale construction projects and is not a major issue. The sustainability characteristics of products and services are not decisive issues in TBM-related value chains, especially downstream towards TBM customers.

Circular practices

Due to the project specificity of TBMs, the recirculation of parts, subsystems or the entire system was not an issue until recently. Even today, construction companies in some countries and some customers generally are generally reluctant to purchase anything but new TBMs.

On the other hand, it is a common practice for TBM manufactures to buy the TBMs back after finishing their initial use as clients usually have not any secondary use for them. This is usually a contractual obligation agreed upon when selling the TBM. As a consequence, at buy-back, Herrenknecht registers a TBM inflow to its stocks and a financial outbound payment. The TBM is physically transported to the company's facilities in Kehl, Germany. The difficulty was that Herrenknecht increasingly accumulated TBM stock, occupying space and financial resources, with almost no business value.

[8]In the Chinese Belt and Road initiative, infrastructure in many Asian and European countries is financed by Chinese institutions and the pressure to realize any procurement with Chinese companies is very high.

Against this increasingly pressing difficulty, Herrenknecht decided to engage in recirculating activities with the aim of reconditioning the TBMs for secondary uses. At present, the company has two main yet related circular activities: Remanufacturing and refurbishment. Following the definition and guidelines by the International Tunnelling and Underground Space Association (ITA), remanufacturing refers to reconditioning parts, subsystems or entire TBM systems to an "as new" quality, so that they can perform a complete, new, secondary life cycle. In contrast, refurbishment refers to extensive maintenance and repair to prolong the first life cycle substantially. This case study focuses on Herrenknecht's remanufacturing activities.[9]

The company remanufactures mainly large subsystems (assembly lines), smaller subsystems or individual parts. These can subsequently be used, if permitted by the new customer, in the manufacturing of "new" TBMs. In order to overcome the existing reluctance of customers to accept anything but new parts, a very large effort is put into the remanufacturing process. All parts and subsystems are given an entire "new life" (setting the counter to 0; i.e., if a new component works for 10.000 h, the remanufactured component will again work for at least 10.000 h). A "performance promise" is given by the company: the remanufactured component works at least equally well (or better) than a new one. This promise is kept by a strict quality control of each individual remanufactured component used in the new TBM (manufacturers of new parts often perform only statistical quality controls on a certain percentage of their output). Additionally, the company issues the same legal guarantees as the manufacturer of the new components. Within given ranges, the new TBM with remanufactured components may considerably differ in technical specifications from the original TBM.

The remanufacturing process is entirely realized in-house at a specialized facility close to the company's headquarters in Kehl (Germany). There, more than 10.000 components are remanufactured each year by 100 persons specifically dedicated to this area.[10] The remanufacturing process is precisely defined and embedded in a process consisting of six consecutive steps. First, the incoming TBM is disassembled completely. Second, each component is cleaned residue-free. Third, analyses and checks are performed. Forth, remanufacturing is done (see above). Fifth, the component is used in the manufacturing process. Sixth, additional function and quality controls are realized on the newly manufactured TBM.

This technical remanufacturing process is accompanied by internal administrative processes: within the design phases of new TBMs, engineers take existing and available components or subsystems into account. A database collects all relevant information on technical details of the parts or subsystems and also includes prior uses and related performance and stress indicators.

---

[9]https://allaround.herrenknecht.com/en/issue-6.html.

[10]https://allaround.herrenknecht.com/en/issue-6.html.

Herrenknecht's activity follows the "R5-Remanufacture" CE practice in the framework of Reike et al. [37]. The company recirculates subsystems and parts in the manufacturing process. It partially satisfies its energy demand with renewable energy from a shallow geothermal power plant and two rooftop photovoltaic systems.

Drivers/barriers

The origins of the necessary firm resources and capacities for remanufacturing lie close to the traditional business model and the established technical and the aforementioned administrative processes in the company. The remanufacturing activities developed and professionalized slowly over time as the result of an economic necessity which was not directly related to environmental sustainability issues. In parallel, the related firm resources and capacities were built up internally.

Knowledge and people were identified as the most important drivers in this context. As a technology leader, the company had no major difficulties in realizing learning and experimenting processes. These led to an increasing specialization, professionalization and sophistication of people and remanufacturing processes. The development completely took place in-house, i.e. without external knowledge acquisition. Currently, the remanufacturing process at Herrenknecht relies on deep technical knowledge and know-how on parts, subsystems and manufacturing-related processes including testing and quality control as well as engineering and industrial design.

A barrier for remanufacturing is the limited availability of skilled personnel in the German job market (Fachkräftemangel). At times, vacancies cannot be covered with sufficiently skilled personnel. Customer relations are another important barrier. This is due to the abovementioned limited acceptance of partly remanufactured TBMs.

Herrenknecht's excellent reputation and its wide network and personal contacts did not play a decisive driving role in the development of the remanufacturing activities. The company did not report any other resource constraints.

Regulation has had and has a neutral role in the development of remanufacturing activities at Herrenknecht. On the one hand, ITA guidelines have helped to establish industry-wide and comparable denominations. On the other hand, there aren't any EU or national regulations in place favouring sustainability issues in mechanized tunnelling. Rather, the opposite is true: remanufactured components compete on a price basis, yet they need to address additional issues such as guarantees. Nevertheless, the company stated that regulation and policy were neither drivers nor barriers.

Regarding the characteristics of the technologies, from a producer perspective, the remanufacturing activities are largely compatible with established manufacturing-related business processes and business models, addressing the same target market and clientele. Remanufacturing is based on existing technology and knowledge related to traditional manufacturing processes, yet it is much more complex. As such, it is not made up of one, but of many incremental advancements of technology, knowledge and processes related to remanufacturing. While each individual piece of technology, knowledge or process is incrementally increasing complexity, taken together, the management of remanufacturing activities has a rather high complexity. This is due to its high context dependency (state of each component or subsystem, suitability for the new TBM, customer wishes and acceptance, etc.).

The costs of remanufactured and new components are comparable, yet as remanufacturing is more complex, deeper knowledge and more specialized capabilities are needed throughout the company. This includes also seemingly "unrelated" departments, such as accounting or sales, as only available and suitable components can be planned with.

On the other hand, remanufacturing of existing components generally takes less time than the purchase or manufacturing of new components; this is mainly due to the fact that manufacturing processes are complex and therefore slow and because the transportation time of raw material and other subcomponents need to be taken into account.

By remanufacturing large percentages of TBMs, a significant reduction of the environmental footprint in the manufacturing of TBMs can be achieved. Herrenknecht quantifies environmental impacts in the case of a fully remanufactured TBM with up to 80% of avoided energy consumption and up to 99% of avoided raw material consumption. From the customers' side, in principle, a TBM containing large percentages of remanufactured parts is "as new" and could be accepted interchangeably with newly manufactured TBMs. Many clients' reluctance may be based on inaccurate perceptions of what remanufacturing is.[11]

Lessons learnt

Herrenknecht's remanufacturing activities were born as a necessity and later transformed into a virtue. The change did not take place overnight but developed rather slowly with many interlinked and mutually conditioning adaptations and developments. Remanufacturing is clearly a significant contribution to a circular economy, despite its main motivation not being environmental. The company was perfectly capable of developing its solution in-house without major obstacles. The role of customers rejecting more ecological solutions is surprising and needs to be addressed by public policy, i.e. maybe through green procurement laws. The neutral role of regulation is also surprising. A more stringent industrial policy framework which favours remanufacturing in all industrial sectors, especially in those with high environmental impacts such as (underground) construction and manufacturing, would surely help initiatives such as the one carried out by Herrenknecht.

In short, there are several clear managerial and policy takeaways: innovative action in companies without major influence from outside (including, i.e. RD&D policy) leads to solutions towards the circular economy. Once the market stage is

[11]https://allaround.herrenknecht.com/en/issue-6.html.

reached, public policy should stringently favour ecological (circular) solutions over non-circular ones. A combination of prices (taxes) and demand (minimum ecological requirements) of circular versus non-circular alternatives could be useful. Nevertheless, this cannot be effectively done on a case-by-case policy approach but by designing an adequate general policy framework. This, in turn, most likely also directs future innovative company action towards such a stated policy objective.

6.1.5 Case Study 5. German Construction Sector/Kaspar Kraemer[12]

Introduction

Overall, the construction sector is front and centre in many social debates, including the topics of urbanization, demographic change and availability of affordable housing. In most of the European economies, including Germany, the sector is important in terms of GDP weight and employment. In 2015, the construction sector made up around 10% of the German GDP[13] and generated 5.6% of total employment in Germany.[14] On the other hand, it is also a sector with large environmental externalities, including resource, material and energy use. This case study focuses on the sustainability efforts in the German construction sector from an architectural (construction design and planning) perspective.

In Germany, the construction sector is highly regulated. This includes very diverse aspects ranging from fire safety and accessibility for persons with reduced mobility to energy efficiency. All these aspects have to be taken into account in building design. As for energy efficiency regulation, there are strict requirements on energy use for heating, water, ventilation, etc. Additionally, in recent years, the requirements of self-production of renewable energies, such as rooftop photovoltaics or underground heat pumps, are mandatory for almost all types of new constructions and major renovations in both commercial and residential construction. All these measures have to be properly integrated into architectural design and building construction or renovation.

Compared to the above-mentioned aspects, the sustainability aspects of the construction phase of buildings are less regulated. Only some architects rely on the concept of "grey energy" in order to estimate the environmental impact of the building they design. Grey energy includes all energy expenditures of raw material

[12]Based on a telephone interview on July 16th 2020, follow-up interview on September 17th 2020, with Mr. Thomas Gießler, Architect at Kaspar Kraemer Architekten, Cologne, Germany. Duration 1.5 h + 0.45 h.

[13]https://www.bauindustrie.de/zahlen-fakten/statistik-anschaulich/bedeutung-der-bauwirtschaft/anteil-am-bruttoinlandsprodukt/.

[14]https://www.bauindustrie.de/zahlen-fakten/statistik-anschaulich/bedeutung-der-bauwirtschaft/anteil-den-beschaftigten/.

extraction, transformation and transportation to the usage location. It is higher for materials that are sourced and produced far away or require complex and energy-intensive sourcing and production processes.[15] As such, it is a comparative measure aiming at evaluating the levels of sustainability of different materials. Yet, in practice, such indicators do not have a great relevance for design decisions in the building sector by clients, for the simple reason that construction is a very expensive activity. For private clients, building a house is often a once-in-a-lifetime action, and commercial clients sometimes focus on efficient spending, whereas incorporating additional sustainability aspects (beyond the mandatory requirements) can be very costly.

On the other hand, there are strong tendencies in architecture and the construction sector in general to increase the sustainability of construction activities and to move towards more circular business practices. For instance, sustainable architecture and building design is an important aspect that is increasingly incorporated in some architecture courses in German universities. Also, some architectural studios specialize on sustainable or "eco-architecture", including not only new concepts such as wood houses. But only a very small fraction of commercial and private clients is willing to adopt such solutions. Hence, this segment is at present still a market niche, and one that is slowly growing.

This case study tries to shed light on the German construction sector as a whole. It is carried out with Kaspar Kraemer Architekten GmbH, an architectural studio in Cologne, Germany, with a 20-year history. It has won numerous awards and honours, including the Hanns-Schaefer-Preis 2019. The studio was awarded for being actively and productively engaged in urban development through critical analyses, outlining shortcomings and providing solutions that combine both aesthetics and functionality. This case study includes both the experiences of the firm and wider reflections on the sector as provided by the company interviewee.

Circular practices

Material use, reuse and recycling

Architecture and the construction sector face severe technical difficulties to implement completely circular practices and patterns for the reuse of construction materials and components. Individual materials used in buildings deteriorate; i.e., they change their quality significantly over time. For example, certain construction components such as windows or metal pipes deteriorate so much during the use phase that they are either impossible to reuse or extraordinarily expensive to recondition. Modern construction requirements, i.e. regarding insulation or energy efficiency, directly impede reuse. Additionally, most construction materials are used in compounds (bricks are fastened by mortar) making it almost impossible to dismount the individual materials. For example, during the demolition processes of buildings, such compounds of materials are mostly shattered into mixed building waste. At best, such waste could be reused as road-fill. Other materials such as

---

[15]http://www.umweltchemie.ch/wp-content/uploads/Graue_Energie_im_Fokus.pdf.

concrete cannot be directly reused. Also, buildings are non-standardized products, further increasing the difficulties for reuse. Lastly, the tiny fraction of materials or components that could be reused requires immense labour input (demolition, transportation, cleaning, reparation, reconditioning or refurbishment), and this is economically unfeasible. In short, the construction sector struggles to achieve material circularity and, in practice, out of the top five most-used construction materials and components (bricks, mortar, concrete, insulation, steel and wood), the share of circulated materials and components is "close to zero", according to the interviewee.

Compared to reuse, the recycling of demolished construction materials and components is in a more advanced state. In earlier decades, German legislation allowed dumping of unsorted demolition material at normal waste disposal sites. The present regulation requires the separation of materials and recycling through special recycling channels wherever this is technically possible, i.e. for metals, wood or plastics. Some materials are treated in a special way, such as those with high toxicity or carcinogenicity which are found, for instance, in some older insulation materials. Only unrecyclable material is landfilled at disposal sites. Despite the recycling efforts, the majority of demolition material still belongs to this category due to technical constraints.

Energy efficiency and reuse

Although the concept of grey energy for evaluating the energy expenditure of the materials used for construction exists, it is not frequently used yet, as explained above.

On the other hand, energy use during the building's use phase is an essential part of modern architecture and construction. Both commercial and private buildings must comply with the very stringent German efficiency standards of the Energy Savings Ordinance (Energieeinsparverordnung, EnEV). Two aspects stand out: first is the reduction of energy input (i.e. the energy needed to heat a building) and second is the reuse of energy through continuous circulation thereof (i.e. air heat exchange and recovery through closed ventilation systems or wastewater heat recovery, among others). The overall aim of the EnEV was to drastically reduce the energy consumption of buildings. The German legislator has therefore addressed all (major) parts of architectural design and building components. For example, windows and materials for walls and roofs must meet strict insulation requirements. Heating systems must comply with energy efficiency standards. Even "simple" aspects of buildings such as ventilation are regulated with regard to heat exchange, reuse and loss.

The EnEV was originally introduced in 2007 and has since been amended several times, increasing the mandatory efficiency standards each time. Experts agree that the overall achievements of the ordinance are very good in terms of energy efficiency, reaching the originally envisioned drastic drop of energy consumption by buildings, according to the interview with the architect of the company. Also, the sector generally moves towards increasing sustainability. Yet, it is also recognized that there are some unintended side effects that will be described in the following paragraphs.

Trade-offs between different targets

As the Ordinance constantly increases the mandatory efficiency levels of buildings, compliance can no longer be reached by intelligent architectural design and planning only. The sector must increasingly rely on the implementation of new and synthetic construction components, such as insulation or mixed-material ("filled") bricks. Such filled bricks are no longer pure clay bricks with air holes but are filled with synthetic material. Every year, new constructions need a slightly thicker layer of insulation or mixed-material bricks in order to comply with the EnEV. Overall, this leads to an increase in total material use. Also, it is not possible to dismount such mixed materials (see above) at building demolition. Due to its impure nature, their reuse is almost impossible and recycling but also landfilling get increasingly complicated and, as a consequence, costly.

Furthermore, additional problems arise from such high building energy efficiencies. After rain or phases of high humidity, the external walls of older buildings tend to dry relatively quickly because of small heat losses from the inside that evaporate the humidity. Some modern buildings do not dry as easily, as no heat losses from the inside occur and, thus, evaporation takes longer. In extreme cases, greenish algae may grow on such poorly dried external walls. To combat this, chemical substances are added to the plaster. Over time, these wash out, new chemicals need to be sprayed onto the plaster, and the chemicals slowly enter the groundwater.

Regarding the inside of the building, the EnEV established very high technical standards for windows which discourages manual ventilation ("opening windows") in favour of technical solutions (closed ventilation systems). As such, modern buildings are almost hermetically closed and there is a significant risk for mould to grow. To combat this problem, ventilation systems are connected to the outside, discharging wet air and replacing it with fresh dry air. In order not to lose energy, heat exchange systems must be installed.

Drivers and barriers

The German construction sector is in a very advanced state of energy efficiency and energy circular reuse and in very early stages of material circularity.[16] According to the interviewee's view, German policy-makers have achieved very high building energy efficiencies of new constructions at the cost of very complex (and therefore expensive) technical solutions. Some architects believe that reaching predefined levels of energy efficiency could also be managed differently and in a simpler manner. The German EnEV focuses mainly on energy efficiency of individual components (such as walls and windows), instead of overall efficiency. The huge

[16]https://www.bmwi.de/Redaktion/EN/Dossier/energy-efficiency.html.

complexity of the EnEV, that some consider overregulation,[17] arises when all individual measures must be applied simultaneously, leading in some cases to undesired side effects. Also, the EnEV clearly lacks an integrated or global perspective and building energy efficiency and circular use is "traded" at the expense of less recyclability and increased toxicity of construction materials.

The strong policy push for energy efficiency has clear trade-offs and target conflicts with other sustainability and circularity aspects. As such, the overall picture is mixed and the role of public policy is both positive and negative. It has clearly been a strong driver in increasing energy efficiency exponentially. Yet, at the same time, it is a huge barrier to complementary sustainability initiatives. The (over-)regulation leaves architects with very little design choices towards more circular practices in the construction sector and, paired with the physical and material constraints, advances in this direction are currently very slow. As a consequence, almost all innovations in the sector are related to incremental sustainability advancements.

New and innovative trends do exist in the sector, such as eco-architecture and sustainable construction, but they are still the exception rather than the norm. Such trends nourish from young and dynamic teams in special architecture studios and pioneering clientele. High personal motivation and commitment by the architects and clients for "doing good" is the main driver for these outsiders, as the market acceptance of sustainable solutions is still not very high, mainly due to the additional cost. Sustainability-oriented studios acquire a strong sustainability reputation that favours the attraction of likeminded clients. If these are commercial (repeating) buyers, a persistent customer relationship may develop over time.

In the rest of the sector, sustainability and circularity are mainly driven by compliance with the EnEV. As a consequence, improvements in this regard are oriented by the efficiency increases established by the Ordinance. Outperformance in sustainability or circularity criteria is generally not a decisive competitive advantage outside small market niches. Also, radically new innovations are not the norm in the sector, as compliance with the variety of rules and pieces of regulation in the EnEV makes developing such innovations very difficult.

On the other hand, a few German universities transmit a considerable amount of knowledge for sustainable and increasingly also circular construction or eco-architecture. There are some obligatory and numerous voluntary courses in the architecture university career. The knowledge supply towards the sector is relevant.

Many clients reject sustainable and circular solutions if these include additional costs. Environmental awareness does generally exist, but it is sometimes given up in the trade-off between sustainability and building costs. Many clients go for second-best sustainability solutions such as additional energy-certifications beyond the requirements of the EnEV, for example the DGNB certification (Deutsche

---

[17] https://www.bda-bund.de/wp-content/uploads/2020/02/BDA-Standards-im-Wohnungsbau.pdf, https://www.geea.info/fileadmin/Downloads/Positionspapiere/2016/2015_09_03_Positionspapier_EnEV_ueberarbeitet_final.pdf.

Gesellschaft für Nachhaltiges Bauen/German Society for Sustainable Construction), but reject more radical solutions.

Finance is neither a driver nor a barrier towards an increased sustainability and circularity of the sector. Banks take these issues into consideration, yet there are not strong differences in financing conditions of traditional versus sustainable construction. Some clients seek to obtain additional public finance from the KfW financial institute (Kreditanstalt für Wiederaufbau), which provides additional finance at attractive conditions for energy efficiency measures or installing rooftop photovoltaics, for example.

Architecture is an entirely creative profession. As such, aspects such as the development of a "vision" and also the desired character of the building are key to any architectural design. Vision is also a motor of change and innovation. Great architectural visions for sustainable or circular buildings exist but their realization is severely restricted by two main barriers: policy, and related to that, design complexity. According to the perception of the interviewee, it is very difficult to develop a vision beyond the state of the art due to the numerous and interrelated policy regulations. Additionally, and also according to this view, these regulations exponentially increase the technical complexity of building design. At a certain point, it is technically (and economically) no longer feasible to develop innovative designs.

The construction sector seems somehow locked-in in an incremental advancement trajectory of ever-increasing modular efficiency (and doing a good job at that). However, this seems to be a major barrier for the introduction of any major change beyond this trajectory.

Lessons learnt

The architecture profession and the construction sector are located in between strict regulation that encourages energy efficiency and circular energy reuse, on the one hand, and the potential for more radical innovations or different approaches to sustainability and circularity in a broader sense on the other. While the success of the current regulation is undisputable, its focus is also narrow, component-based and on efficiency only. As a result, the interviewee argues that the totality of the current German EnEV regulations increase design and construction complexity to a maximum. As a direct result, it seems difficult to break out of this efficiency-increasing trajectory to comply with the law.

It is also argued that it is time for a new kind of regulation that focuses on overall macro-(building) level sustainability and circularity instead of defining micro (component) level requirements. This would leave more room for radical innovations. Such a next-generation policy-making should also understand sustainability and circularity in broader terms, go beyond the topic of energy efficiency, and explicitly address the trade-offs and negative side effects of the current regulation. In short, it should give architects more room to develop innovative solutions.

This case study has shown that there are incipient tendencies towards sustainability and circularity in the architecture profession and the construction sector. But they struggle to reach a larger market. A policy mission could be to facilitate the growth of these tendencies in niches first and, later, in larger market segments. Such growth support does not mean the provision of financial incentives for more sustainable solutions only, but allows for competition of designs and approaches, which is currently inhibited by strict and efficiency-focused regulation, making sustainability and circularity a core element of competitiveness in the sector instead of simply being an add-on.

On the other hand, another case study (Madaster, see below) provides an additional and complementary viewpoint on CE practices in the construction sector, highlighting that the CE is indeed an important topic in the sector.

6.1.6 Case Study 6. Camper[18]

Introduction

The origins of Camper date back to 1877 when the founder, a Majorcan shoemaker in the town of Inca, had the idea of importing British machinery to Majorca, and, together with a group of local artisans, set up Spain's first shoe factory. The values inculcated by the founder of this family firm have remained solid ever since: a pioneering spirit, love of the profession, honesty, austerity and high-quality products.

The second-generation brought new values with it, such as a concern for overseas expansion, diversification and the urge to compete with the best in the field, all with the overall aim of making the company last into the long term.

A century later, one of the grandchildren of the founder reinvented and updated the company's shoe design and, in 1975, the Camper brand was created. The concept of Camper—which means "countryman" in Majorcan—was inspired by the rural spirit, culture and landscape of the Mediterranean landscape. With its first model (the "Camaleón" or Chameleon), the new brand introduced the casual look into a country (Spain) that was still largely drab and formal at the time. This unusual shoe, based on a 1928 model, was handmade and used leftovers from coach hoods, scraps of leather from shoe manufacturing and soles made from used tyres. The "Camaleón" was the first shoe made by the Spanish shoe-making industry to receive a European eco-label.

In the early 1990s, Camper had 25 shops across Spain. In 1992, coinciding with various events bolstering Spain's image internationally (the Barcelona Olympics and the World's Fair in Seville), Camper decided to launch its products in new markets. Between 1998 and the year 2000, around 30 new stores were opened outside of Spain in locations ranging from New York to Milan. Since its international expansion began, Camper has registered annual sales growth of two digits. The company put on sale around 1200 different products each season, of which 1100 were new. Approximately 70 out of every hundred pairs of shoes were sold

[18]Based on personal interviews in 2005 and 2007 with the company's management team.

outside of Spain. Camper, which at the time employed around 800 people directly and more than 3000 indirectly, had a turnover of around 200 million US dollars from the sale of approximately 3.5 million pairs of shoes all around the world [6].

Within its structure, the areas of product development and communication stand out. The latter is closely linked to the sales department.

There were two clearly separate functions in the product development area: design, closer to aesthetics and the development of collections, and engineering, which was present in practically all the phases of product development. The Camper Innovation Centre, comprising a small group of designers and engineers, was established to meet the needs of special projects. Camper had never manufactured shoes directly; it undertook the design of its various footwear lines, but it subcontracted all production to different workshops. The majority of these workshops worked exclusively for the brand, some of them have done so for over 30 years. Sixty percentage of production was undertaken in Spain. When proposing the designs of its collections, the company dismissed market research in favour of the creativity of its designers, who were encouraged to follow their whims.

Camper's Communications Area heavily relied on the sales department. The Camper shops were conceived not only as points of sale, but as distinctive spaces or territories, strategically located in cities in over 50 countries in the five continents. In these shops, clients participated in the "Camper experience", a carefully crafted image of tradition, imagination, well-being and Mediterranean culture.

The footwear sector, like textiles, is marked by seasonal trends and a strategy of product differentiation. Notwithstanding design development, the productive process of footwear remained labour-intensive and based on discontinuous flows and multiple manufacturing phases. Due to the intensification of worldwide competition in low- and medium-quality footwear, mostly from Asian countries, European manufacturers had concentrated their efforts on offering products of a greater added value and on exploiting the advantages of production dispersion. The trend towards a more labour-intensive and inefficient footwear production led to enormous quantities of waste and used resources and materials unsustainably. The fall in prices drove many producers to look for savings in the use of cheap components, often manufactured with unsustainable materials and processes.

Circular practices

In the year 2000, Camper inaugurated the Wabi project, as a culmination of the most traditional values of the brand and the path to sustainability initiated in 1975 with the Chameleon model. The project counted upon the personal commitment of the Company President and was led by the then Design Director. "Wabi" is a Japanese word which can be translated as "rustic", in the sense of simple, uncontrived, modest, lacking in pretension and inwardly orientated. It was proposed as a design constructed upon merely three elements: a protective mould from a single material and 100% recyclable; an insole, which acted as a cushion and thermal regulator, fabricated from natural and biodegradable materials, and, lastly, an incorporated ecological sock of cotton or wool, which had the dual function of thermal regulator and cushion.

A two-stage approach was followed in the manufacture of the protective mould:

A) *The techno-industrial path* which, in turn, is constructed upon two alternative materials. The first industrial mould, named Llit, consisted of a single piece injected with thermoplastic polyolefin elastomer (TPE), antistatic and with small holes allowing air to pass. The material was very flexible, highly abrasion-resistant, long-lasting, recyclable and easy to maintain. The second industrial mould, called "Jersey", was also fabricated from a single piece of felted knitwear. Its wool absorbs and expels moisture, impeding the formation of fungi and bacteria. It is also an effective thermal insulator. The model possessed a sole injected with TPE which is very thin, light and flexible.
B) *The handicraft path*. The handcrafted protective mould, named Mon, was made from a single piece of intertwined jute, lined with cotton. This model was fabricated in collaboration with a rural community of women in Bangladesh, and natural indigenous fibres were used to manufacture it. It also had a very thin sole, fabricated from antistatic thermoplastic polyurethane (TPU).

With regard to the second element of the Wabi, the insoles, there were also various models which were all totally biodegradable and elaborated upon a base of coconut fibre compacted with latex and covered by a layer of woollen felt, for the absorption of moisture, and another layer of binchotan, a high-quality vegetable charcoal. One of the models covered its surface with a linen weave, while another used (on its surface) a weave of wool and viscose. This is a totally biodegradable material, and toxic substances were not used in its elaboration.

The third and last element of the Wabi was an incorporated ecological sock, of cotton or wool, with the dual function of thermal regulator and cushion. Five types were developed, for different climates, all of them derived from natural materials.

Drivers and barriers

Camper was very demanding with regard to the environmental impact of the materials and processes with which its entire collection was fabricated. However, the Wabi project went considerably further than the rest of Camper's designs. From the beginning, the team in charge of the project had the objective to design and produce a totally biodegradable shoe. Nevertheless, that objective was not easy to satisfy with regard to the protective mould, which was produced (as described above) from a single piece of injected TPE. The material derived from the natural rubber which is commonly used in the footwear industry was difficult to reuse, unless cut and added in small quantities to new rubbers. Through their heat-based shaping for a new end, the thermoplastics, however, allowed reusing 100% of the material employed (in theory), with no loss of their initial properties.

Given these difficulties with materials, the company decided to develop a system of inverse logistics for the recovery of the used Wabi, which would once more produce protective moulds with the same materials, although this initiative was fraught with difficulties. In any case, the team in charge of the Wabi project understood that this was a transitory solution, while work continued in search of totally biodegradable rubbers which could be used in the production of footwear. The main obstacle was that the materials available in the market were developed by large chemical multinationals such as Bayer or Huntsman, who were not at that time concerned about the technical demands of footwear in terms of resistance, durability, etc. To further this search, at the end of the year 2003 Camper contacted Dr. Michael Braungart, founder of EPEA International Umweltforschung GmbH, a German research institute then focused on "the improvement of quality, utility and the environmental performance of products through eco-effectiveness" (https://epea.com/). Despite the notable economic and technical efforts made, Camper continued to struggle to introduce an environmentally superior alternative to TPE into the production of Wabi. Camper was required to technically and financially assist its manufacturers, as the technology involved was very advanced and expensive.

With regard to the communication of the product, beyond its objective characteristics, the need arose to disseminate the complexity of the initiatives inherent in the Wabi project. In line with Camper's general strategy, its shops were the vehicle for such information. Wabi was the first line of the brand to have shops specifically dedicated to its different models, the Wabi Shops, in which the philosophy behind this new footwear was explained to the public via wall drawings and texts. Furthermore, a large proportion of the staff in other shops received specific information regarding the project. Additionally, each pair of shoes was accompanied by a detailed label, which described the Wabi concept, and a card with the direct contact details of an interlocutor in the Camper project.

Elsewhere, the sales of Wabi via the Camper e-shop, the online sales tool of the brand, performed comparatively better than its remaining designs. The characteristics of the product, fundamentally the simplicity and standardisation of its components, appeared very suitable for this type of remote purchase.

However, the project team was conscious that Wabi was not an easy to sell product to new customers, and that its market potential was limited. It was necessary to "understand and believe" in Wabi in order to decide to purchase, something which was unusual in decisions to purchase conventional footwear.

Lessons learnt

It should be underlined that the origin of the Wabi project within Camper was due, both, to more reactive reasons (pressure from environmental regulation competition and consumers) and to Camper's proactivity in terms of environmental and social sustainability (commitment of the company's management, its tradition, its culture and its innovative spirit). Among the organizational features favouring this proactivity, the fact that it is a family firm should be emphasized. The figure of the brand's founder transcends all decision-making areas. In the literature on environmental innovation in companies, management commitment is usually underlined as a fundamental condition for success. The tradition of social and environmental commitment in Camper should also be stressed. This was already shown with the Chameleon model in 1975 which was, in turn, inspired by a model from 1928.

At the same time, great importance should be placed on the innovative attitude of the organisation, rooted in its organisational culture. In operational terms, the absence of self-production gave it considerable flexibility to undertake path-breaking projects. Elsewhere, Camper had consolidated itself as a global trend creator, a status which permitted it to take more innovative and risky gambles than its competitors.

Wabi faced numerous institutional barriers. One of these was the limited size of the market, given the social conventions regarding the appearance a shoe should have. In addition, the competition from footwear imported from Asia, manufactured under environmental and social standards which were less demanding than European shoes, and sold in Europe at much more competitive prices, was deemed a relevant obstacle. Furthermore, Camper's research, development and innovation efforts found no support in the Spanish science and technology system, and thus, it had to recur to a private and foreign research centre (EPEA). The lack of connection between companies and universities and public research centers is often mentioned as a difficulty in the literature. Lastly, although the company did not make information public on the manner in which these efforts were financed, this area of institutional barriers usually emphasises the inadequate availability of risk capital which permits progress from the blackboard to the production line.

Regarding technological barriers, a key difficulty, which in fact impedes the attainment of the Wabi ideal, namely absolute biodegradability, resides in its lack of bargaining power with materials suppliers in accordance with company specifications. Similarly, it should be emphasized that Camper works closely with its manufacturers and helps them to acquire the machinery and technology involved. As a further barrier, it should be noted that the system of collection and recycling of the protective TPE moulds represented significant technical and logistic difficulties.

With respect to the strategies employed by Camper to overcome these barriers, the creation of the Camper Innovation Centre can be underlined. This is in addition to the abovementioned aspects such as management commitment, innovative approach, flexibility through the subcontracting of production and a long-term vision concerning future consumer needs. The Camper Innovation Centre was perhaps the only formal expression of the innovation process within Camper, with the objective of isolating a team of engineers and designers from the market, which were able to satisfy the requirements of these special projects. Another noteworthy strategy is the specific training regarding Wabi provided to the employees of the Camper shops and, more specifically, the creation of the Wabi shops, as ways to overcome the information barriers and social conventions which might have limited Wabi's market size.

It seems obvious that abundant benefits, not strictly financial, resulted from the project, despite lack of data on the company's economic results. On the one hand, it is clear that Wabi was somewhat more than a new product line: it was a learning project, in terms of new capacities, tools and knowledge. On the other hand, the project and its communication helped to consolidate the social reputation of the

Camper brand. This differentiation was essential for the survival of Western brands in a mature sector facing strong competition from Asian imports.

6.1.7 Case Study 7. Rebattery

Introduction

Batteries are a widespread product in our daily lives. They are used for many applications, cell phones, electric cars, computers, etc.... As with any other product, a main issue is what to do with them when they reach the end of their useful life. Indeed, one of the major environmental problems that society faces today is the increasing volume of waste generated by the disposal of secondary or rechargeable batteries [29]. The new Circular Economy Action Plan, recently approved by the European Commission, identifies batteries as one of the seven product value chains in which further efforts to the CE can be made, mitigating the barriers for the development and adoption of circular practices.[19]

Obviously, there are many alternatives in this regard, some of which are more circular than others. Recycling their parts is one circular option. However, an even better solution from a CE point of view is to extend their useful lives by remanufacturing them. This is exactly the aim of Rebattery: the batteries which are sent for recycling are recovered and sent back to the market.

Circular practices

Rebattery was a company set up in 2013 in the Basque country (Spain), with the aim to repair and remanufacture lead/acid batteries which are worn or non-functional and send them back to the market, although some batteries are recycled; i.e., all their materials are recovered and sold in the raw materials markets [29, 39].

Interestingly, according to its CEO, the company started carrying out a technological activity but, then, influenced by their clients, turned to provide a technological service in addition to being a remanufacturer [39].

---

[19]The Commission states that "to progress swiftly on enhancing the sustainability of the emerging battery value chain for electro-mobility and boost the circular potential of all batteries, this year the Commission will propose a new regulatory framework for batteries. This legislative proposal will build on the evaluation of the Batteries Directive and the work of the Batteries Alliance with the consideration of the following elements: (1) rules on recycled content and measures to improve the collection and recycling rates of all batteries, ensure the recovery of valuable materials and provide guidance to consumers; (2) addressing non-rechargeable batteries with a view to progressively phasing out their use where alternatives exists; (3) sustainability and transparency requirements for batteries taking account of, for instance, the carbon footprint of battery manufacturing, ethical sourcing of raw materials and security of supply, and facilitating reuse, repurposing and recycling" [20, p. 11].

The firm, which was founded by four people in 2013, had an initial capital of 800,000 euros, clients inside and outside Spain, a sales volume of 1.2 annual million euros (2018) and a staff of 14 employees [4, 39]. The firm offers a warranty,[20] 50–70% cost savings for the customer and a 75% life extension for batteries [29].

Regarding its environmental impacts, a life cycle analysis carried out with the support of Ihobe, the public firm for environmental management owned by the Basque government, led the firm to conclude that the remanufacturing of the batteries reduces CO_2 emissions and energy consumption compared to the manufacturing of a new battery [10, 39].

Drivers and barriers

Drivers

Four main factors seem to have driven this initiative: the personal motivation of the founders, the existence of a market niche for remanufactured batteries, technological developments as a result of R&D and public support.

Apparently, the environmental awareness of its CEO was a crucial driver in starting this initiative. According to an interview with him, he decided to found Rebattery when he was working for another company at the time. "I started to question myself if what I was doing was what I dreamt to do when I was a child. The answer was clear and easy: no. Then, I decided that coherence required me to take a more uncertain path, searching for a business opportunity which positively impacted the environment" [39].

The founders initially detected a market opportunity, e.g. a stable and mature market niche in the segment of battery service [10], given the boom of sustainable mobility and strong expectations about its future evolution. "There are more and more batteries for different applications, including cleaning robots, mobile phones, lap tops, hybrid and electric vehicles and a lot of technological support will be needed to serve these markets" [34, p. 26]. The wide range of potential clients increased the business opportunities of the initiative and provided a potentially important client base, as argued by its CEO [39].

This initiative seemed to be attractive for potential customers, given its attractive economic features in terms of cost savings and the provision of an improved product as well as a customized service.

On the one hand, in an interview with its CEO, he claims that "the cost of our service for an industrial battery is paid with the savings the client achieves in his electricity bill, recharging it after our intervention" [39]. According to one of the founders of the firm, remanufacturing may involve savings of between 30 and 35% with respect to its replacement with a new one [5], although Innoenergy [29] increases the cost savings for customers up to 50–70%. Martínez [34, p. 27] argues that "the cost of remanufacturing is between 20 and 40% lower than buying a new

[20]The length of such guarantee is not clear, however. Whereas it is between 2 and 5 years for Innoenergy [29], it is 1 to 2 years for Eco-Circular [15].

one, and repairing may be between 35 and 60% cheaper, although the process takes days, whereas remanufacturing only takes hours". According to the CEO, "we could not compete with the Asian market. If we wanted to compete, then the only way would be to reduce our raw material, energy and water costs and, in this way, the battery remanufactured would cost half a new one" [2]. This cost saving is quite relevant especially for expensive batteries, as the ones in vehicles, trucks or forklift trucks, which cost more than 20,000 euros [10]. In addition, the cost driver seems to have been even more important in a time of economic crisis [44].

On the other hand, the company offers the service of a remanufactured battery with the same guarantee and performance of a new battery [5, 39]. But the company also offers an integral, customized service.

Related to the previous point, capturing this market niche requires that a new product/service is developed, which, in turn, requires technological developments as a result of R&D. Desulphating the batteries required a five-year technological development process, according to the CEO [34]. Technological efforts are directed at two consecutive stages: first, the batteries of hybrid vehicles and, then, those of electric vehicles [34, p. 26]. The firm has its own patented technology [15] and was the first European company to develop its own technology for the remanufacturing of batteries [39]. According to its CEO, "the weight of R&D in the project is very important" [39]. These R&D efforts do not take place in a vacuum, but benefit from a supportive R&D environment (regional innovation system) made up of regional R&D support, technological centres and universities.

Finally, the regional (Basque) public administration acted as an important driver in at least two senses: it promoted the project through support for technological development and R&D [34], and provided visibility to the initiative by putting it as an example and asking the firm to give presentations on it [44].

Barriers

Two main barriers seem to have played a negative role in this project: sluggish demand for the products and limited financial resources.

Apparently, the company had problems to commercialize its products and services. This is pointed out as the main reason why the firm ceased operations and went bankrupt [10, 13]. On the one hand, it was mentioned that potential customers may have been reluctant to repair the battery compared to buying a new one because there might be doubts on the performance of the repaired batteries compared to new ones. This also occurs in the case of Revov (see below). This disbelief about something which is unknown and the doubts of the client about how long this remanufactured battery was going to last was pointed out by the CEO in a presentation [44]. On the other hand, the CEO mentioned that they did not notice an increase in the demand for their products and services because "sustainability concerns only a very small set of the population" [39].

An interview with the CEO of the firm also revealed that "the only limitation was, obviously, the available economic resources" [39]. According to Cluster Energía [10] and Bernal [4], after four years of growth, the firm searched for funds in order to initiate its national expansion. It was estimated that the firm would need around 3 million euros in order to finance its expansion. However, this money never arrived.

Initially, the start-up had a very limited geographical presence: two towns in the Basque Country and a joint venture in California. It then became a priority for the managers of the firm to expand nationally and internationally [4]. The national expansion focused on the opening of their own technological nodes as well as their "Rebattery points", which are delivery points where the batteries could be deposited [4]. Regarding the international expansion, the firm operated in Colombia, El Salvador, USA (Los Angeles, California) and France (Toulouse) [5, 34].

Lessons learnt

This case shows that remanufacturing can be a good circular option. It is high in the circular economy hierarchy and can result in considerable reductions of environmental impacts. In addition, it can lead to substantial cost savings for their users, which suggests that there is an economic case, i.e. a business opportunity for remanufacturing.

Furthermore, this case shows that not only economic savings can be achieved with this practice, but also an improvement of the product/service. Rebattery goes beyond improving a product, but provides an integral customized service, encouraging customer loyalty.

However, this option requires considerable economic resources, and particularly high upfront investments as well as a large technological development effort. The availability of funds seems to have been a considerable challenge, particularly when upscaling it.

In addition, although the service provided seems to be attractive for potential customers, given the cost savings and the better performance of the remanufactured product compared not only to substitutes, but to the original battery, problems to commercialize the product and service seems to have scuttled this experience. This suggests that a big effort should be made to advertise it widely and inform potential customers about this circular practice and indicates that there is a role for the public administration to be played in this context.

6.1.8 Case Study 8. Upcycling the Oceans (ECOALF)

Introduction

Pollution of the sea due to plastic wastes has become a serious environmental problem worldwide. Annually, 8 million tons of plastic are discarded to the sea and 75% of this plastic ends up in the seabed [38], with severe consequences for marine ecosystems.

In order to mitigate this problem ECOALF, a Spanish firm in the fashion industry set up in 2009, committed to remove sea wastes with the help of fishermen through its flagship project: Upcycling the Oceans. Implemented in 2015 in the Spanish Mediterranean coast, this initiative focused on recovering wastes from the sea and convert them into high-quality thread to make clothes. The goal was to create the first generation of recycled products with the same quality, design and technical properties as the best non-recycled products [3]. According to the company's webpage, the aim was three-fold: "to remove wastes from the sea, to use those residues as input in production processes through recycling, thereby contributing to the CE and to raise awareness on the huge global problem of sea wastes" [16].

Circular practices

This project has mainly two stages: recovering the material from the sea and recycling it into high-quality thread. It would enter the category of "repair, reuse, refurbish" [19], or R2, R3 and R4 according to the taxonomy of Reike et al. [37].

According to Calvo-Porral [8, p. 275], the Ecoalf project is made up of eight steps: (1) fishermen recover waste from the sea bed; (2) marine waste is deposited in containers at the ports; (3) polyethylene terephthalate (PET) is separated from the rest of the resources; (4) PET is recycled into flakes; (5) flakes are converted into pellets; (6) yarn is produced from pellets; (7) fabric is weaved using yarn, which is 100% recycled from marine and terrestrial PET; (8) garments and accessories are designed.

Once the sea wastes have been recovered, they are classified and stored in order to recycle them. According to the European Commission [19], the bottles made up of PET plastic are converted into flake and pellets by using sophisticated technological processes (polymerization). The bales of PET are taken to a recycler that cleans and transforms them into pellets. The pellets that are obtained are between 3 and 6 mm in size, and they are prepared for the next step in the extrusion process. Hundred percentage recycled polyester filament is obtained through the extrusion and spinning of the pellets and this is used to make thread and, thus, clothes [16]. The project started in 2015 with a few harbours (9), fishermen (165) and boats (743) involved, but those numbers have substantially increased overtime to 40 harbours, 550 fishermen and 2602 boats in 2019.

Recently, the experience has been exported to other parts of the world and, particularly, to Thailand, "in partnership with the Ministry of Tourism of Thailand and the company PTT Global Chemical Public. The three-year project focused on education and awareness raising first, but has already begun collecting, segregating and transforming waste on Thailand's beaches" [19].

According to the company, the project has led to considerable environmental benefits over time, in terms of the sea garbage removed from the sea (from 23 tonnes in 2015 to 152 tonnes in 2019) and the percentage of PET (from 6% in 2015 to 9% in 2019) [16].

Drivers/barriers

The analysis of the drivers and barriers in the Ecoalf case has been exclusively based on secondary sources: news published in the general press and interviews with the founder of the project included in those sources [3, 7, 9, 12, 16, 19, 22, 31, 35, 36, 38, 41].

This case study shows that the adoption of circular practices is often hindered by a wide array of barriers of a different nature, including technical, economic and managerial. However, it also shows that drivers and barriers to such adoption coexist, each pushing in an opposite direction and, at least in this case, with the balance tilting towards success in implementation.

Regarding the barriers/challenges, the following are worth mentioning, together with some actions taken by the firm to mitigate their impact.

- *Technical.* The low quality of the residues obtained from the sea has been a concern since the start of the pilot project. The technical complexity of the project has required considerable investments in R&D [7]. These investments have also been crucial to develop environmentally improved products which nonetheless have similar product attributes in terms of quality to competing products [3, 12], taking into account that some consumers may be willing to pay more for environmentally friendly products but high-quality products, but that few would be willing to do so if the product has a poor quality. The challenge for the firm was to develop the first generation of recycled products with the same quality features as those of non-recycled ones [3, 31, 36].
- *Involvement of actors upstream the value chain.* In particular, getting the collaboration of fishermen to take the residues from the sea and bring them to the harbour was recognized as a main challenge from the start [3, 41]. Obviously, there is not an inherent economic incentive for fishermen to take the wastes from the sea. Rather, the opposite is true: the incentive is to send the wastes back to the sea. At least initially, some fishermen were reluctant because they did not see an economic benefit [3]. However, many seem to have been convinced by the founder of the project on “moral persuasion” terms.
- *Upscaling from a pilot project into a widespread practice.* The project started with a few fishermen in one harbour and the challenge was to extend this practice to other harbours and involve many fishermen. This improved over time and, certainly, one of the objectives of the project (raising awareness on ocean pollution) has been achieved. However, despite the current involvement of many harbours and fishermen, the project obviously makes a limited contribution to the very complex problem of mitigating sea pollution and, particularly, removing the wastes from the sea, and should diffuse to other geographical locations.
- *Economic barriers: High price of the products and high initial costs.* As mentioned above, some consumers may be willing to pay an additional price for environmentally improved products compared to competing products without such environmentally benign attributes, although many may not and a higher price may be an important barrier in this regard. However, the fact that the sales of the firm have increased overtime suggests that a market niche has been captured in which

this higher price is really a limited obstacle for certain types of environmentally aware consumers. On the other hand, the high initial investment cost of circular practices is usually mentioned in the literature as one main barrier to their uptake. In this case, transporting, managing and recycling of marine debris are considered to be expensive [18].

– *Managerial/product inertia.* In general, firms have resources, competencies and dynamic capabilities which have accumulated over time and which lead to some inertia in the way things are done at the company level. In addition, if the sales of the existing products are as successful as expected, then changing to a different design is always a risk, although one that possibly pays in the long term. There is a high level of uncertainty in the adoption of innovative practices. In this case, it has been mentioned that an initial difficult decision was to stop doing profitable but not sustainable products [41]. As mentioned by the founder of the project himself, it was difficult to convince other actors in the value chain on the existence of a market niche. "When I started in 2009, many people did not understand what I wanted to do and, perhaps, many people was not prepared to buy recycled products" [35].

On the other hand, some factors have played an enabling role, sometimes offsetting the influence of the aforementioned barriers. The drivers are also multifaceted and include:

– *Collaboration: Involvement of large players.* Over time, other large actors have supported the project, such as Ecoembes or Generalli [16]. Ecoembes, a company whose objective is to recycle packaging waste, has played a particularly relevant role in this regard, by providing the infrastructure. Ecoembes was involved in the project one year after it started, helping to widen it to many places along the Spanish coast and facilitating the management of the wastes being recovered. Ecoembes has installed specific containers on ships and harbours to collect trash. Since 2017, Ecoalf is owned by a Luxembourg fund specialized in renewable energy sources (Treïs Group, 66% of shares) [41]. Ecoalf has collaborated with big players such as Apple, Barneys, CoolHunting, Ekocycle, Goop, Swatch, Starbucks or RC Deportivo football club [36]. It has partnered with the textile firm Sanyo in a joint venture in Japan [41]. A philanthropist (Henry Pincus) supported investments on containers in harbours [3]. The involvement of other players has allowed ECOALF to upscale the initiative, i.e. being present in more harbours and even exporting it to other countries (Thailand).

– *Top management commitment.* This initiative seems to have been impossible without the leading role played by his founder (Javier Goyeneche), who showed since its start a high degree of commitment with the project, putting a lot of effort into it. His environmental motivation seems to have been a crucial factor driving this project.

– *Accumulated knowledge and R&D investments.* As mentioned above, this circular practice is a high-technology one. R&D was needed in order to develop and innovative product which, according to his founder, would capture a market niche (a design of clothes made up of recycled material) [35, 41]. This required knowledge, which has been accessed or created through strong R&D investments and through knowledge searched and captured by his founder when travelling all over the world [7, 35]. According to European Commission [19], "the Ecoalf Foundation has managed to involve Spanish companies that are leaders in their respective areas (from waste management companies, technological centres and recyclers, to thread and fabric manufacturers) that will collaborate in this project and share their experience in recycling different types of debris (PET bottles, fishing nets, used tires, etc.) and the R&D accumulated through their international alliances with specialized technological recycling specialists".

– *Perception of a business opportunity: Capturing a market niche*. This case study suggests that there is clearly a market niche of green products, which Ecoalf has benefited from. At least some consumers are willing to pay a higher price than for similar products without environmental attributes [35].

– *International recognition*. The efforts made by the firm in developing circular practices have been rewarded with the B Corp certificate, which is awarded to those firms which have shown a particular commitment to environmental protection [3, 41]. This does not only recognize previous activities, but it is also important to engage other actors in the project for its future upscaling. In other words, being awarded with such certificate may make it easier for the firm to penetrate other markets or to have a better image from institutional actors, which facilitates the implementation of the circular practice of the firm.

– *Abundant raw material*. There are a lot of wastes in the sea, so availability of raw material is not a hindering factor. However, collecting and processing such waste is not for free; i.e., it entails considerable costs, although the first are (partly) borne by a third party (fishermen).

– *Incentives for fishermen to collaborate*. The involvement of fishermen is a sine-qua-non condition for the success of this project, and the data shows that the number of fishermen being involved has increased substantially overtime. Pure economic reasoning would suggest that fishermen, who are not paid for collecting the garbage from the sea and bringing it to the harbour, would not have any incentive to support the project based on economic motives alone and, therefore, would not actively participate. However, the evidence seems to indicate that exactly the opposite has occurred. No in-depth research on these motives has been carried out and, thus, it is very difficult to know the reasons behind the involvement of fishermen. There is anecdotal evidence that they may have done so to improve their environmental image. They might have thought this would be a good idea to show their best practices when fishing [3]. The environmental proactivity of fishermen, above and beyond any other consideration, may have played an important role (i.e. "morally committed" fishermen).

Lessons learnt

This case study shows that the barriers and drivers to the development and adoption of CE practices are multifaceted and that they may reinforce each other. A critical driver is top management commitment, fuelled by a high degree of environmental awareness and ability to perceive a niche market for innovative green products.

However, this study also shows that collaboration is a main driver of circular practices, which mitigates relevant barriers. Interestingly, collaboration has many aspects and takes place at different levels in the supply chain: R&D collaboration is critical, but also collaboration upstream the supply chain to ensure the availability of the raw material, and downstream the supply chain to ensure the sales of the product. It is both important for setting up the project (fishermen) and for upscaling it. The collaboration of other actors in the implementation of circular practices is needed at different levels, suggesting that different players take a relevant role along the process.

One critical aspect of collaboration is the need for R&D. This case study suggests that technological changes for circularity are sometimes radical; i.e., they entail breakthrough innovations. For this, R&D investments, whether in-house or accessed through cooperation with other actors, are strongly needed.

Finally, an interesting finding is that pure economic motives cannot explain the engagement of actors upstream the value chain in the adoption of circular practices. In this study, fishermen did not have any direct economic incentive for getting involved in this project. But, in spite of this, they were willing to take the wastes from the sea and bring them to the harbours. However, the extent to which we may rely on this "environmental awareness" driver in the absence of economic incentives for the implementation of the CE is debatable.

6.1.9 Case Study 9. Madaster Platform

Introduction

The construction industry is responsible for about 60 per cent of the raw materials extracted from the lithosphere. Within this €2 trillion annual revenue industry, recycling and reuse are still in their infancy. For example, in the demolition of a building, the building material is often seen just as waste.

New approaches are developed, however. When buildings are deconstructed, they can become a mine of materials; demolition materials need no longer be turned into waste and therefore wasted. In 2017, Thomas Rau, a German advisor in circular architecture and Pablo van den Bosch, a Dutch expert in business modelling and IT solutions, together with several other experts, founded the Madaster Foundation to develop a digital platform to disrupt the costs associated with management, construction and deconstruction of property [33]. Their business issues so-called material passports for buildings, where each construction material and component is given an identity, thus creating a financial value to the materials. Ideally, if every building was assigned a material passport, it would give an overview of the materials which would be available in certain areas, which could then be taken into account while planning new construction projects.

The independent Madaster platform provides easily accessible information for everyone (from private individuals to companies, governments and scientific organizations) on the materials and how a building is built. In turn, this provides useful information on how easily the material can be extracted. This can lead to a completely different ways to design buildings—with deconstruction in mind.

Circular practices

Madaster has developed an online cloud platform providing a one-stop access point for real estate owners to leverage their property data. Together with an ecosystem of partners, they can meet and exceed environmental-, regulatory-, health- and financial-driven ambitions across the full life cycle of a construction object.

In a nutshell, the Madaster platform is a materials registry. It creates transparency about material assets in the built environment. In the platform, the users can store, enrich, share and manage product and material data. The Madaster platform is designed as a public, online library of materials in the built environment. It links the identities of materials to their locations and registers these in a materials passport [14]. There are now over 2.5 m square metres of building matter logged in the Madaster database, and the company is currently working with the city of Amsterdam to provide a catalogue of the components of every public building in the city [49]. Madaster does not only issue material passports but also provides a systemic overview of the data and applications of the data, such as a circular indicator and the economic value, which are discussed below.

Material passport

A material passport is a compact but detailed view of a building information as registered on the Madaster platform. Like a regular passport, it gives identity to a building, including all its separate materials, components and products. A material passport is a PDF document that is added to a building dossier each time it is generated and can, subsequently, be printed or downloaded. Additionally, the material passport contains information on the quality and quantity of materials, their locations in the building, and their monetary and circular value. This way, it becomes a lot easier to reuse materials, minimize waste and reduce the cost of material consumption.

Building data

In the Madaster online platform, the material passports of buildings can be gathered and connected to their location. The platform displays (based on active source files) the materials, components and products which exist in the various building layers (e.g. structure, skin and services), including their totals (in volume, weight and percentages). The data about the building are structured in a table with a vertical division in building layers and horizontal disaggregation into material families. The platform also allows property owners to search for the location of a specific type of material in a building. It divides a building into six layers: site, structure, skin, services, space plan and stuff. The division of the layers is made based on their different lifespans. The building data made available in Madaster can also be displayed in a 3D model viewer.

Building process

The building process data indicate the five phases of a renovation cycle:

1. The current situation: the materials in the existing building.
2. Deconstruction: the materials that are removed from the building during deconstruction.
3. Casco: the remaining hull.
4. Virgin materials: new or recycled materials.
5. The final situation after renovations..

For each phase, Madaster clarifies which materials are used and their quantities (volume, weight and as a percentage of the whole). The data about the building are structured in a table with a vertical and a horizontal division in construction phases and material families, respectively.

Circularity indicator

The Madaster circularity calculation gives insight into the circular value of a building. The Madaster circularity indicator is based on the Material Circularity Indicator of the Ellen MacArthur Foundation [17]. A building can score in between 0 and 100%. A building that scores 100% has a higher-than-average lifespan and can be disassembled easily at the end of its life cycle. Besides the total indication of circularity on the building level, Madaster also gives insight on the level of circularity for each phase of the life cycle of a building (which can then be displayed for the whole building but also for the different building layers).

Economic value

In the platform, the residual value of a building at the end of the different lifespans of the products is expressed in the material value. Besides this, Madaster shows the actual material value and the predicted development in the future. To make an accurate prediction of the end values of a building, the material values are corrected with the deconstruction costs, handling feedstock costs, a correction for the size of the raw material flow and transportation cost per kilo of the material.

The residual value of the different building layers on the various functional lifespans is calculated with the net present value of material in a building layer. This is the net present value of the residual value based on the expected functional lifespan of the materials. The functional lifespan is the expected lifespan of a building layer and differs per building layer. The end value can result in a more positive business case when making an investment decision during construction or when purchasing a building. In this way, the circular goal of Madaster is connected to the residual value of a building and, therefore, to money.

Business model

The business model of the Madaster platform is based on a yearly subscription fee that users pay to register, maintain and download data through a data web service. The price depends on the number of users and the total gross square metres of construction being registered. Madaster facilitates also the registration of multiple buildings per single subscription [33].

Customers

The initially targeted users of the Madaster platform include designers (architects, installation and construction engineers), construction companies, real estate owners and construction product suppliers. Once the platform has gained coverage and momentum of these initial users, new services are developed to attract also accountancy firms, insurance companies, real estate controllers and marketplace-like creators that enable the buying and selling of materials. Madaster is also part of the initiative with "Rijkswaterstaat", "ProRail" and "Alliander" to adapt the platform for infrastructure activities in the Netherlands. The shipping industry (and other industries) will also be addressed [46].

Drivers/barriers

The reuse, remanufacture and recycling industry is vastly growing in Europe as it is supplying ever-increasing value when compared to raw material production. One of the main aspects of the construction industry is its massive investments and revenues, with over €2 trillion annually [33]. For banks, investors and other real estate owners, it is important to determine the end value of their buildings. Firstly, it is important for them because knowledge of a building decreases the risk factor for demolition-related debits. Secondly, the material value of a building can be representative of the end value of a building.

In general, the construction sector (and many other industries) is greatly affected by the uprising of the circular economy. This can be due to government policies as well as to intrinsic consumer choices. In this context, the construction sector is strongly impacted by the EU Waste Directive (2008/98/EC). This strongly incentivizes firms and government agencies to take action in order to implement circular business models in the construction sector.

Material reclamations, like the Materials Passport, are beginning to take off in Denmark, Belgium and the Netherlands, perhaps because these countries have less restrictive building regulations. In the UK, the challenge is to find a way to incorporate these circular economy principles when building with very tight budgets and time constraints [50]. The Dutch government has now introduced tax incentives for developers who register material passports for their buildings, and it is considering making this a mandatory requirement for all new projects, in line with its ambition to achieve a circular economy by 2050. As the construction process is increasingly digitized, with the rise of Building Information Modeling (BIM), the material passport is merely another layer of data that can be easily incorporated and tracked throughout a building's life [49].

Initial interest on the adoption of the materials passport has already been shown by firms and government agencies in Belgium, Switzerland, Portugal, Canada, Dubai, China and Singapore. Parties that have already showed interest in the materials passports include major players like Mitsubishi, ING, Volker Wessels, TBI, Schiphol Group, Redevco, ABN Amro and Rabobank [46].

Competition

Despite the obvious advantages of the creation and use of the materials passport, there are only several materials passport initiatives throughout Europe. Apart form the Madaster platform, for instance, the BAMB project is focused on the use of BIM-files as a standard within the European construction sector in order to gain experience with specific pilot projects around Europe. Also, various local business initiatives have started to gather data about construction and building information that can lead to the creation of materials passports. With the support of the existing network, the Madaster platform is well positioned in the commercialization of the material passports for the construction sector taking advantage of its first-mover advantage and the network of important construction sector players.

Internal factors

The promising start of the platform is based on several internal factors of the business. In particular, its shareholders involved offer access to a broad range of skills, an extensive network and a proven track record in starting and building successful companies. A network of over 30 parties and representatives from various sectors has made substantive contributions to the Madaster platform. As mentioned above, the platform has obtained funding also from the EU Horizon 2020 research and innovation programme but also debt capital through crowdfunding.

Supervision is organized through a non-profit foundation while the provision of the solution is based on a business model that ensures financial stability. Thus, such a unique governance model balances the wide public interest, as promoted by Madaster Foundation, and the commercial and entrepreneurial interest, as promoted by Madaster Services BV [33]:

- The Madaster Foundation, a Dutch non-profit foundation with a public interest status (ANBI) was founded in 2017. The Madaster Foundation is governed by a Board of Directors that supervises Madaster services.
- Madaster Services B.V. is the implementing organization, to which the foundation has outsourced the development and management of the Madaster platform. Madaster Services provides the platform and its development, operational processes, communication and training toolkits.

A partner model with strategic service partners also strengthens and expands the Madaster user functionality and reliability of building data. These partners are representing several industries, including public, construction, real estate, banking and software engineering. The partner model allows the users to leverage the knowledge and services of the partners and use the functionality of integrated solutions, for instance, the use of marketplaces to monetise the residual value of materials and products.

As in other business platforms, the first-mover advantage is important for market share and establishing standards. Madaster claims to be the first market-ready ICT platform that can generate widespread materials passports for constructions and has a wide coverage of constructions in the database. It is also interoperable, which facilitates coupling to other ICT systems and allows the integration of information from various sources.

Lessons learnt

The development of a standardized approach for improved insight into the use of materials will stimulate the circular economy and will lead to better design solutions. With the help of the material passport, materials get an identity, which means that they do not disappear in anonymity as waste. Once gathered to the digital platform, the recorded material data of buildings and other constructions offer immense opportunities to reutilize the materials and close loops. The database can be used by other related businesses like finance and insurance.

The government can also play a relevant role. For instance, it can offer a sufficiently flexible regulatory environment that allows innovating in new approaches. More specifically, it can promote the application of tax incentives, in this case for material reclamations (passports).

Both this case study and the one on the German construction sector described above provide insights on the need for increased sustainability of constructions in general. Firms within the sector show promising new approaches to the CE, yet policy support is crucial, especially with regard to providing flexible and adequate framework conditions so that new, innovative circular solutions can be developed by firms and introduced into the market and sector.

6.1.10 Case Study 10. REVOV

Introduction

Worldwide sales of electric vehicles (EVs) reached 2.1 million units in 2019. Although this figure hardly represented 2.6% of worldwide sales of all types of automobiles, it meant an increase of 40% compared to the previous year. Some analyses hold that, by 2040, EVs could account for approximately two-thirds of worldwide sales of new automobiles, although these will still be a third of all the cars in circulation [21].

The lithium-ion batteries used in EVs lose their capacity for electrical charging in the successive cycles of charging and discharging. The majority of manufacturers guarantee their batteries for a period of between 5 and 8 years, although it is estimated that their average useful life may be between 10 and 20 years. After being for some time in an EV (between 8 and 12 years), these batteries conserve more than two-thirds of their original storage capacity. If they show minimum wear and have no defects, some can be restored and reused directly as a spare part for the same model of vehicle. Automobile manufacturers such as Nissan or Tesla offer these services to their clients. The remaining batteries, depending on their condition, may be useful for an additional 5–8 years in a secondary application which is different from EVs. That is to say, they can be the subject of the circular practice termed repurposing, described in Chap. 4 of this book.

Given the increasing market for EVs, second-life batteries may also represent an attractive market for low-cost storage for both utilities and electricity consumers. Various studies suggest a range of between 112 and 275 GWh annually for the second-life batteries available towards 2030 [1]. The reuse of these batteries in the form of cheaper stationary storage can encourage a greater diffusion of solar energy, in both the urban on-grid field and the rural off-grid area, from small to large clients.

The REVOV Company defined itself as "a Revolution in Energy Reliability". It was founded in 2016 in South Africa by Lance Dickerson (CEO) and Felix Von Bormann (Technical Director), with the aim of providing energy storage systems based on second-life batteries to residential, commercial and industrial sectors in the African continent. The instability in energy supply and the growth in demand in many countries in the region suggested the existence of a buoyant market for these accessible and guaranteed storage stations.

In 2018, the company imported the first container of batteries from China. These batteries came from buses and other EVs, at 80% of its original load capacity. By 2020, REVOV had sold storage stations equivalent to over 60 MWh and had more than 200 installers associated with its brand. In addition to sales in South Africa, it had exported their stations to Namibia, Botswana, Zimbabwe, Mozambique, Swaziland and Lesotho.

Circular practices

As explained in earlier chapters of this book, repurposing is a circular practice in which obsolete products, or parts of such products, are given new applications, distinct from their previous uses, recapturing their partial or total value. REVOV chose carefully from among the considerable supply of rejected batteries from EVs, for their testing, balancing and integration in an energy storage station, for domestic or commercial use. In this way, they contributed to reduce the pressure on natural resources (lithium) and the waste from batteries and to develop renewable energies such as solar and wind energy, facilitating their storage. This contributed to environmental sustainability through a circular strategy of repurposing and, at the same time, it enabled a profitable business model, supported by an abundant and cheap supply of raw materials with a high residual value.

The list of REVOV products included the following proposals:

- 10.2 kWh 2nd Life battery pack.
- 11.2 kWh 1st Life battery pack with cells from CATL (the Chinese leader in the development and manufacturing of lithium-ion batteries).
- 5.1 kWh battery pack.

According to the company sources, total sales were distributed between approximately 80% from 2nd Life and 20% from 1st Life [32]. This was believed to represent an expression of client confidence in their 2nd Life supply. Both types of products offered the same guarantee, 10 years, and the first was more accessible for purchasers. In addition, the 2nd Life supply offered a higher performance than the 1st Life. The batteries designed for use in EVs must respond to demanding conditions of vibrations, temperatures and loading cycles. This means that the quality of 2nd Life battery cells was greater than that of batteries designed directly for storage.

In the words of Lance Dickerson, CEO of Revov, "By using 2nd Life, we are encouraging our customers to think green, by not putting extra pressure on global commodities and resources by using recycled EV batteries. Lithium ferrophosphate (LFP) batteries have the added environmental benefit of being free from cobalt, the mining of which has a massive and negative environmental and social impact. The operating performance of EV LFP batteries is of the highest standard and compared to storage grade LFP batteries are actually manufactured to international standards and are therefore of a much higher quality and have more predictable lengths of life which we can rely upon for second life" [32].

Drivers and barriers

Drivers

One of the main advantages of this business model based on repurposing is its economic logic: it is profitable for all the parties concerned. A study by the MIT showed that, under certain assumptions, and using a hypothetical solar farm of 2.5 MW in California as a model, adding a new lithium-ion storage battery would be more expensive than using repurposed batteries from EVs, given that they could cost 60% or less of their original value [40]. Also, in economic terms, behind-the-meter storage batteries help consumers to reduce their electricity bills, through a better management of demand [30].

In conclusion, in this example of repurposing, the user receives a market proposal (2nd Life) whose purchase and use is clearly profitable, in addition to equivalent in terms of guarantee and even superior in technical terms to a newly manufactured product (1st Life).

In addition to the economic argument, the adoption of this circular practice may be facilitated by the environmental arguments mentioned above with regard to the reduction of the pressure on the natural resources used in batteries, as well as in the waste derived from them. Additionally, it would contribute to store electricity generated from renewable energy sources such as solar and wind power and, thus, encourage them. These environmental arguments could reinforce demand from those users, individual or corporate, which are more environmentally conscious.

Similarly, in this case, the social argument should be mentioned as a driver. REVOV allows citizens and businesses in countries with great instability of their electricity grid to have affordable and independent access to energy.

Both arguments, environmental and social, could justify the provision of public subsidies to the business promoters. Political support can play an important role in this context, encouraging these practices but, above all, reducing the regulatory barriers that they face, as detailed below.

Barriers

According to the researchers from the abovementioned MIT study, "there are many issues on a technical level. How do you screen batteries when you take them out of the car to make sure they're good enough to reuse? How do you pack together batteries from different cars in a way that you know that they'll work well together, and you won't have one battery that's much poorer than the others and will drag the performance of the system down?" [40]. These and other technical aspects could be a technical barrier to the adoption of this circular practice, if the company does not have the necessary in-house knowledge, although REVOV seems to have such knowledge.

However, the difficulties are not only technological, but also commercial and administrative. Faced with a well-established sales and maintenance model for newly manufactured products, with availability of spare parts and guarantees on the part of the makes of storage stations, REVOV needed to confront the difficulty of offering an equivalent after-sales service to its clients. In the words of its CEO, Lance Dickerson, "We have realized that with considerable sales, we need to back that up with quality after-sales support. We have grown our team and have cut down on time taken to resolve customer concerns dramatically". [32].

Definitively, the distrust of consumers is a barrier which could be faced by this type of products.

Although the advantage of this proposal in economic terms was argued above, it is true that, in order to be employed as storage stations, used batteries must undergo numerous costly and time-intensive processes (transport, testing, discharge, reconfiguration, assembly, etc.) [1]. Only those companies which are capable of efficiently undertaking these processes can have competitive costs of repurposing, compared to those in the business of new storage stations. This appears to be the case of REVOV.

A difficulty of repurposing, which is common to other circular practices based on the exploitation of products at the end of their useful life, such as reuse or recycling, is the need for reliable and appropriate information regarding their characteristics. In the case of used batteries, it is essential to know the data regarding their history of use and their technical conditions. The Global Battery Alliance (GBA) was founded in 2017 as the result of the collaboration of public and private organizations.[21] Its aim was to establish a sustainable chain of value in batteries, including recycling and repurposing. The information barrier mentioned above was combated by the development of a "Battery Passport", with the aim of standardizing battery data and making it more transparent.

Nevertheless, beyond the aforementioned technological, administrative or productive barriers, the principal obstacle in this case, at the margin of their circular character, is the regulatory barrier. The behind-the-meter energy storage stations, whether new batteries or reused batteries for this purpose, and the distributed

[21]https://www.weforum.org/global-battery-alliance/home.

energy systems are usually faced with legal and fiscal difficulties in numerous countries.

Lessons learnt

This case study illustrates the case of a circular economy practice (repurposing) as a circular strategy which combines reuse and recycling. It is the only circular practice in which obsolete products, or parts of these products, are oriented to new applications, which are distinct from previous uses and recapture their partial or total value.

The case study shows that, despite the costs this practice may involve in logistic and productive terms, it can provide products which are competitive in comparison with new alternatives in the market. Thus, in the case of REVOV, the user receives a market proposal (2nd Life) whose purchase and use are clearly profitable, in addition to equivalent in terms of guarantee and even superior in technical terms to a newly manufactured product (1st Life). These advantages appear to surmount, in this case, the possible distrust of consumers concerning newly manufactured products.

Beyond the economic arguments, the environmental and (at times) the social advantages, could justify access to public subsidies on the part of the promoter of this practice. As in other circular strategies, political support can play an important role, incentivizing these practices and reducing the regulatory barriers they face. In the specific case of repurposing, as it also occurs in reuse and recycling, the subproducts and secondary raw materials are confronted by a series of challenges in their competition with raw materials, not only for reasons linked to their safety, but also related to their performance, availability and cost. Policies here can entail incentives to companies, or direct requirements for reused content. However, this would not be effective if an efficient market had not been established earlier, as well as agile procedures for the consideration of subproducts and the finalization of the condition of waste.

Lastly, in the circular practice of repurposing, as it also occurs with reuse and recycling, there is a clear need to have available reliable, accurate and timely information on the characteristics of subproducts and raw materials. Consequently, the collaboration between public and private organizations interested in the development of digital technologies and procedures which permit their traceability becomes necessary, as we have seen in this case study with the Global Battery Alliance.

6.2 Synthesis and Main Conclusions from the Case Studies

The following table summarizes the results of the case studies. It identifies the circular practices covered by them, the addressed Rs, their main drivers and barriers and the lessons learnt (Table 6.1).

Table 6.1 Summary of the case studies

Firm name	Sector	Circular practices	Addressed Rs	Main drivers	Main barriers	Lessons learnt
Too Good To Go	Food waste	Providing leftover food so that it does not become waste through a digital platform	Reuse, repurpose, reduction of waste, sharing	Social awareness of huge amounts of food waste, strong top management vision and commitment, direct and focused targeting through the app, engagement with households, businesses and policy-makers	Public policy partially prohibits or increases the difficulty of reusing or redistributing "waste"	Software helps to address a societal problem and offers an innovative solution. Digital services are easy to scale. All participants are empowered to act in their environmental and societal interest
Rubicon Global	Recycling	Provision of a digital platform for waste management and recycling	Recycling, recovery of energy, remining of resources	Top management commitment, environmental-friendly culture and attitude, reputation, networking and fund-raising capabilities and partnerships, consumer awareness, digitalization and IT platform acceptance	High cost and lack of adequate infrastructure for recycling	New entrants may disrupt established sectors and markets with innovative and circular solutions. The CE has inherent environmental but at the same time economic benefits (waste as resources). The political and social context is very favourable for innovative, digital and transparent recycling practices in the context of the CE
IKEA	Furniture	Making furniture use circular	Recovery of products, recycling of products, repair	Experimentation, inspiration from circular practices in the	Unclear and incomplete regulations (i.e.	Demand from society and stakeholders make the company offer a

(continued)

Table 6.1 (continued)

Firm name	Sector	Circular practices	Addressed Rs	Main drivers	Main barriers	Lessons learnt
			and maintenance, remanufacturing, reuse, reduction of waste, product-as-a-service	textile sector, price sensitivity of the Spanish furniture market (which creates demand), already existing strong second-hand culture for furniture, clear strategic outline from top management, environmental commitment by customers and stakeholder pressure	regulations on waste, inverse logistics, taxation, unregulated second-hand market), operational difficulties, new client channels needed (online), high infrastructure investments	circular approach to furniture. Clear customer segmentation (new vs. second-hand) helps to prevent cannibalization. Learning from competitors and peers is key. Upscaling works once operational know-how is created. Clear environmental and economic objectives help to frame the development of such new circular solutions
Herrenknecht	Tunnel boring machines (TBMs)	Take-back of TBMs after original use, extensive reconditioning to "as new" quality	Remanufacturing, refurbishment, reuse of parts and components, repair and maintenance, extension of product life cycle, reduction of raw material input	Knowledge and technology available in the company, engineering and industrial design capabilities, learning and experimenting	Low availability of skilled personnel in the German labour market, low customer acceptance of "used" TBMs	The remanufacturing process was developed slowly and initially out of an economic necessity (instead of motivated by environmental concerns). It was relatively easy to adapt existing technology, know-how and processes to develop new remanufacturing

(continued)

Table 6.1 (continued)

Firm name	Sector	Circular practices	Addressed Rs	Main drivers	Main barriers	Lessons learnt
						practices. The role of regulation is neutral. For it to be a driver, a more stringent policy framework is needed including green public procurement of underground infrastructure
Kaspar Kraemer	Architecture	Identification of grey energy as starting point, energy-efficient building design, eco-architecture, usage of new or different construction material	Recycling of construction demolition material, reduction of energy consumption, reuse of energy (circulation), reuse of some materials	Public policy with regard to energy efficiency, personal motivation and top management commitment, reputation	Public policy with regard to wider sustainability or circularity (lock-in produced by regulation), extremely high costs for reuse of building material (mostly compound materials), very high cost of sustainable construction in general	Policy has achieved tremendous energy efficiency gains at the cost of worsening other sustainability criteria. As the sector is highly regulated, it is locked-in in current practices and radical innovation cannot take place. On the other hand, the sector is open and there are opportunities for eco-innovations that need to be facilitated (legalized) by regulators

(continued)

Table 6.1 (continued)

Firm name	Sector	Circular practices	Addressed Rs	Main drivers	Main barriers	Lessons learnt
Camper	Shoes, fashion	Design and manufacture	Recycling of materials, replacement of materials with renewable alternatives, reduction of material and energy consumption in simplified production processes	Clear environmental objectives regarding materials and final products, experimentation processes and R&D, information dissemination through store staff, internal labelling, employee training, effects on brand image	Difficulties in processing materials, limited availability of renewable materials on the market, large financial requirements for R&D, complex processes, low bargaining power with suppliers, limited market potential and logistical shortcomings (reverse logistics)	Premium footwear has a place besides low-cost competition mainly from Asia. For many customers, premium includes environmental and social aspects of sustainability. Both pressure from stakeholders as well as proper environmental motivations and top management commitment led the company to develop a more circular solution. Innovation capabilities and organizational flexibility embedded in a long-term vision were success factors
Rebattery	Batteries	Remanufacturing electrical batteries to reuse them and to avoid e-waste	Remanufacturing batteries to "like new" or "better as new", recovery of components	Technological progress, personal motivation, perception of a business opportunity and market niche, abundant availability of batteries as input, high demand	Rather low demand for remanufactured batteries, high need for financial resources, difficulties for	Environmental benefit and cost savings of remanufactured products with the same quality as new ones provide a solid business opportunity. Awareness must be created among

(continued)

Table 6.1 (continued)

Firm name	Sector	Circular practices	Addressed Rs	Main drivers	Main barriers	Lessons learnt
				for batteries, cost advantages over new batteries, product guarantees, support by policy-makers	upscaling and geographic expansion	potential customers and the quality guarantees are essential for that. Support (especially financial) is needed
Upcycling the Oceans (ECOALF)	Textile industry	Removing ocean plastic waste to manufacture high-quality threat for clothes	Recovery, recycling, reuse	Collaboration with larger players for the provision of infrastructure and finance, personal commitment by top management, environmental awareness of customers, pursue of R&D and knowledge leadership, perception of a business opportunity, image and recognition, abundance of plastic waste as input	The plastic waste being recollected is of low quality, need for high R&D investments, price competition by traditional threat, actor involvement (i.e. to get fishermen to recollect plastic waste), inertia of clients to change their supply sources and operational processes, high costs	The project would have been impossible without strong top management commitment and a high environmental awareness that creates a specific market niche. Collaboration was also key to success, i.e. regarding complex R&D processes as well as with fishermen (upstream) and potential clients (downstream)

(continued)

Table 6.1 (continued)

Firm name	Sector	Circular practices	Addressed Rs	Main drivers	Main barriers	Lessons learnt
Madaster	Reuse of building materials	To register building materials digitally	Refurbishment and repurpose of buildings as well as recycling and remining of materials	Revaluing the building materials, increasing the value of the building, tax incentives, first-mover advantage to build a standard, flexible regulation allowing innovation, top management commitment, networks for financial support and piloting	Lack of supporting regulation, lack of standard practices (causing wait and see behaviour), inertia in the sector	The development of a materials registry could be perceived as a public sector task, but this case shows that the private sector can indeed realize such a task and combine a specific aim (information-provision) with a functioning business model. Also, the private sector can be a driver for standard-setting in this regard, especially in the digital platform economy where it may have advantages over the public sector
Revov	Energy storage	To provide energy storage systems based on second-life batteries	Repurpose of electric vehicle (EV) batteries after their original use for energy storage	Lower cost compared to new batteries, high quality (sometimes higher than batteries directly designed for storage only), long guarantee time, profitability for value chain, environmentally	Different highly complex technical challenges related to repurpose of batteries, high knowledge requirements, restricted supply	"Obsolete" products can have a second life. With a clear market proposal (market niche, business model, operations), repurposing of EV batteries can be profitable. Policy plays an important direct and indirect role for the

(continued)

Table 6.1 (continued)

Firm name	Sector	Circular practices	Addressed Rs	Main drivers	Main barriers	Lessons learnt
				positive image for clients	of parts and establishment of a supply chain, high cost of operational processes, legal, fiscal and administrative difficulties related to sales and after-sales	update of such solutions. Collaboration between numerous actors in or along the value chain is also very important

Source: Own elaboration

6.2.1 Main Drivers

Despite the large differences between the different circular practices, economic sectors and firm characteristics in the case studies, a surprisingly clear picture of drivers and barriers emerges. Regarding the drivers for more circular solutions, firms are generally well prepared and state that their internal firm capabilities, some highly specialized in their respective sectors, allowed for successful development or implementation of such circular solutions. Within these capabilities, two major ones stand out: learning and experimenting were frequently highlighted as a strong driver, as were networking capabilities. The latter refers to the creation of new networks of firms along value chains or within sectors or the exploitation of existing ones, because circular practices are mostly contingent on "common adoption". Another strong diver is a committed top management that provides clear strategic guidance on environmental, social and economic targets. Knowledge and technology also drive the development of circular solutions, as they facilitate new or improved products, services and processes. The perception of new circular business opportunities is also highlighted as a major driver, and goes in the same direction as high and rising customer awareness for sustainability issues in general and CE solutions specifically. Lastly, firms also engage in circular solutions because they expect a strong positive impact on their brands or firm name (Fig. 6.1).

6.2.2 Main Barriers

Conversely, the role of barriers is much less diverse. Two major barriers can be highlighted: those related to cost and investment, on the one hand, and those which refer to public policy and regulation on the other. Most firms state that high costs compared to traditional or linear solutions make pursuing circular solutions a difficult task. This is mainly due to the very high upfront investment needed in infrastructure and processes (note that R&D or technology acquisition is not mentioned as a major cost barrier) and the low initial efficiency resulting in higher product or process cost, paired with large difficulties for upscaling and creating economies of scale to overcome this issue. Some firms feel literally "trapped" at low and thus inefficient production numbers. Lastly, the role of public policy is often perceived as a barrier, specifically because some regulations lead to lock-ins in existing solutions and make it very difficult or impossible to introduce radically new or different circular solutions. Also, overregulation is mentioned as problematic in this regard. For some cases, unclear, partially incoherent or simply inexistent regulatory requirements do not provide a solid and reliable legal framework in which firms may operate and innovate safely in CE practices (Fig. 6.2).

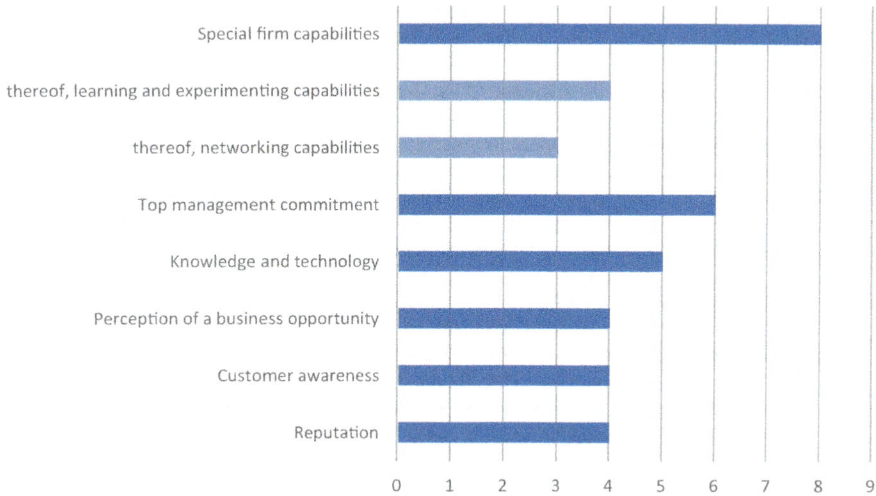

Fig. 6.1 Main drivers in the selected case studies. *Source:* own elaboration. *Note* the number refers to how many times a specific factor has been identified as a driver in the case studies

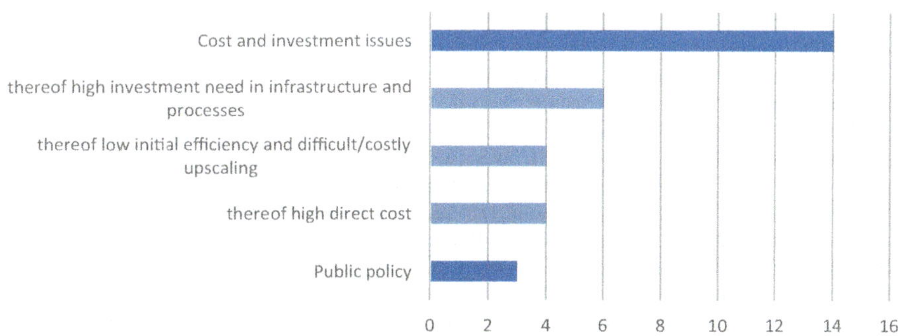

Fig. 6.2 Main barriers in the selected case studies. *Source:* own elaboration. *Note* the number refers to how many times a specific factor has been identified as a barrier in the case studies

References

1. Ambrose H (2020) The second-life of used EV batteries. Retrieved from https://blog.ucsusa.org/hanjiro-ambrose/the-second-life-of-used-ev-batteries
2. Ballesteros B (2016) Intervención de Benjamín Ballesteros de la empresa Rebattery. Retrieved from https://www.youtube.com/watch?v=MEjVv37Y9sQ
3. Barroso M (2018) Ecoalf, la empresa de Javier Goyeneche que fabrica ropa con basura de los océanos. Retrieved from https://www.expansion.com/fueradeserie/cultura/2018/06/29/5b320e32268e3e23088b45ce.html#: ~ :text=Desde%202015%20ECOALF%20lidera%20un,en%20tejido%20para%20sus%20prendas.&text=Restos%20de%20botellas%20y%20otros,capturada%20con%20redes%20de%20arrastre

4. Bernal I (2017) De reestreno continuo. Retrieved from b-venture.com/2017/09/20/de-reestreno-continuo/
5. Bernal I (2019) A tope de energía. Retrieved from https://www.elcorreo.com/economia/tu-economia/tope-energia-20190131145651-nt.html#: ~ :text=La%20firma%20de%20Eibar%20Rebattery,bater%C3%ADas%20de%20sus%20coches%20h%C3%ADbridos&text=Y%20eso%20es%20justo%20lo,sus%20modelos%20de%20dos%20motorizaciones
6. Business Week (2005) One step ahead—and running hard: hip Spanish shoemaker Camper can feel Nike breathing down its neck. Retrieved from https://www.bloomberg.com/news/articles/2005-04-17/camper-one-step-ahead-and-running-hard
7. Calero J (2019) Upcycling the oceans. Superhéroes pescadores que limpian las aguas de mares y océanos. Retrieved from https://www.innovaspain.com/anuario2019/comunidad-valenciana-upcycling-the-oceans/
8. Calvo-Porral C (2019) The role of marketing in reducing climate change: an approach to the sustainable marketing orientation. In: Climate change and global development. Springer, pp 261–283
9. Cirino E (2017) Can upcycling really help the oceans? Retrieved from https://www.greenbiz.com/article/can-upcycling-really-help-oceans
10. Cluster Energía (2017) Rebattery prepara su expansión nacional. Retrieved from http://www.clusterenergia.com/bazkideen-berriak-2/rebattery-prepara-su-expansion-nacional-2
11. Cole Market Research (2020) Commercial waste management market 2020 size global industry analysis, segments, top key players, drivers and trends to 2025—cole of duty. Retrieved from https://coleofduty.com/military-news/2020/07/18/commercial-waste-management-market-2020-size-global-industry-analysis-segments-top-key-players-drivers-and-trends-to-2025/
12. Comunidad #PorElClima (2020) Ecoalf se suma a la Comunidad #PorElClima. Retrieved from https://porelclima.es/javier#: ~ :text=ecoalf%20se%20compromete%20a%20reducir,de%20la%20acci%C3%B3n%20contra%20el
13. Del Moral J (2019) Quiebra el fabricante vasco de baterías Rebattery. Retrieved from https://ganzania.com/quiebra-el-fabricante-vasco-de-baterias-rebattery
14. Druijff B (2019) BIM-based material passport in Madaster during the operational and maintenance phase of a building. University of Twente
15. Eco-Circular (2017) Economía Circular, proyecto de éxito: Rebattery. Retrieved from https://eco-circular.com/2017/04/12/economia-circular-proyecto-de-exito-rebattery/
16. ECOALF (2020) Upcycling the oceans. Retrieved from https://ecoalf.com/es/p/upcycling-the-oceans-15
17. Ellen MacArthur Foundation (2020) Material circularity indicator. Retrieved from https://www.ellenmacarthurfoundation.org/resources/apply/material-circularity-indicator
18. European Commission (2017a) Upcycling the oceans by ECOALF. Retrieved from http://www.circulary.eu/project/upcycling-oceans-ecoalf/
19. European Commission (2017b) Upcycling the oceans collects marine trash and turns it into quality yarn. Retrieved from https://circulareconomy.europa.eu/platform/fr/node/1005
20. European Commission (2020) Circular economy action plan. For a cleaner and more competitive Europe. https://ec.europa.eu/environment/circular-economy/pdf/new_circular_economy_action_plan.pdf
21. Forbes (2020) Will The Internal Combustion Engine Really Take A Back Seat To EVs? Retrieved from https://www.forbes.com/sites/peterlyon/2020/09/27/will-the-internal-combustion-engine-really-take-a-back-seat-to-evs/?sh=2fb456e653d5
22. Huffpost (2016) Upcycling the oceans—with style! Retrieved from https://www.huffpost.com/entry/upcycling-the-oceans–wit_b_12027178?guccounter=1&guce_referrer=aHR0cHM6Ly93d3cuZ29vZ2xlLmNvbS8&guce_referrer_sig=AQAAAAEy2mWD2Doid8VuDuxgD5kFZswCu8aisuTVsrBrYomtLv95Qn7dmek8H_YyeVdVdl-umUjZKEcVJJ_TZwDq5QANAahqFSpFWqwbEPt12SEtYIvNiTwOe9OEUZjJNsdacv_kznLLz2LEHLA9sTN9HSgA7jn-8sDV-QWwnBgfSQHY

23. Huidobro Giménez C (2019) Normalizing sustainable consumption: how marketing is used to fight food waste. A case study with Too Good To Go, the movement that fights food waste across Europe, IIIEE Master Thesis
24. IKEA (2018a) IKEA sustainability report FY18. Retrieved from https://newsroom.inter.ikea.com/publications/all/ikea-sustainability-report-fy18/s/409b1d78-7d7b-4f48-a63d-368d5fb69c2d
25. IKEA (2018b) IKEA sustainability strategy—people & planet positive 2018. Retrieved from https://preview.thenewsmarket.com/Previews/IKEA/DocumentAssets/511938.pdf
26. IKEA (2019a) Circular product design guide 2019. Retrieved from https://newsroom.inter.ikea.com/gallery/image/ikea-circular-product-design-guide-2019/a/567266c8-96ed-4024-8d71-a881446ce9af
27. IKEA (2019b) Highlights 2019. Retrieved from https://about.ikea.com/en/organisation/ikea-facts-and-figures/ikea-highlights-2019
28. IKEA (2019c) Inter IKEA group FY19 financial performance. Retrieved from https://newsroom.inter.ikea.com/publications/all/inter-ikea-group-fy19-financial-performance/s/1abb101d-c91e-4a41-9d6a-4575dcc16570
29. Innoenergy (2019) Batteries. Retrieved from https://www.innoenergy.com/discover-innovative-solutions/sustainable-products-services/energy-consumption-end-user/transport-mobility/batteries/
30. IRENA (2019) Innovation landscape brief: behind-the-meter batteries. Retrieved from https://irena.org/-/media/Files/IRENA/Agency/Publication/2019/Sep/IRENA_BTM_Batteries_2019.pdf?la=en&hash=86DF5CFBEDB71EB9A00A5E3680D72D6E346BD23A
31. itfashion (2015) Upcycling the oceans, by ECOALF. Retrieved from https://www.itfashion.com/moda/eco-eco/upcycling-the-oceans-by-ecoalf/
32. Kuhudzai RJ (2020) Revov south africa goes big on second-life batteries for stationary storage applications. Retrieved from https://cleantechnica.com/2020/10/21/revov-south-africa-goes-big-on-second-life-batteries-for-stationary-storage-applications/
33. Madaster (2020) Home Corporate: Madaster. Retrieved from https://www.madaster.com/en
34. Martínez M (2018) Europa elige la FP vasca como modelo de excelencia.
35. Mercer E (2019) Javier Goyeneche, de Ecoalf: La moda debe respetar el planeta. Retrieved from https://www.ultimahora.es/noticias/sociedad/2019/08/22/1101933/ecoalf-javier-goyeneche-moda-debe-respetar-planeta.html
36. Mollejo V (2018) Ecoalf, moda española hecha con desechos marinos. Retrieved from https://www.redbull.com/es-es/tecnologia-ecoalf-moda-espanola-desechos-marinos
37. Reike D, Vermeulen WJV, Witjes S (2018) The circular economy: new or refurbished as CE 3.0?—Exploring controversies in the conceptualization of the circular economy through a focus on history and resource value retention options. Resour Conserv Recycl 135:246–264. https://doi.org/10.1016/j.resconrec.2017.08.027
38. Residuos Profesional (2019) El proyecto upcycling the oceans recuperó 140 toneladas de residuos marinos en 2018. Retrieved from https://www.residuosprofesional.com/upcycling-the-oceans-reciclaje-2018/
39. REV (2017) Rebattery, una segunda vida útil para las baterías. Retrieved from https://www.redemprendeverde.es/pg/entrevistas/admin/read/66229/rebattery-una-segunda-vida-til-para-las-bateras
40. REVOV (2020) MIT study says using retired EV batteries for grid-scale energy storage could be profitable. Retrieved from https://revov.co.za/news/mit-study-says-using-retired-ev-batteries-for-grid-scale-energy-storage-could-be-profitable/
41. Rodríguez JC (2020) Javier Goyeneche, fundador de Ecoalf, el defensor de la moda eco. Retrieved from https://www.expansion.com/fueradeserie/personajes/2020/01/16/5e0f1cf3468aeb0b278b4593.html
42. Rubicon Global (2020) Rubicon|Software company offering smart waste and recycling solutions. Retrieved from https://www.rubicon.com/
43. Sahlman WA, Ashmore H (2015) Rubicon Global. Retrieved from http://www.hbs.edu/faculty/Pages/item.aspx?num=50206
44. SER (2019) Recargando baterías en Euskadi: el ejemplo de Rebattery. Retrieved from https://cadenaser.com/emisora/2019/10/17/radio_coruna/1571305671_286701.html

45. Smart Cities World (2020) Smart waste and global science company team to promote circularity. Retrieved from https://www.smartcitiesworld.net/news/news/smart-waste-and-global-science-company-team-to-promote-circularity-5406
46. Symbid (2019) Madaster—material matters! Crowdfunding. Retrieved from https://www.symbid.com/ideas/8376-madaster-material-matters?locale=en&action=show&controller=ideas&id=8376-madaster-material-matters
47. Too Good Too Go (2020) Too Good To Go. Retrieved from https://toogoodtogo.com/en-us
48. van der Haar S, Zeinstra GG (2019) The impact of Too Good To Go on food waste reduction at the consumer household level: an explorative study. Wageningen Food & Biobased Research
49. Wainwright O (2020) The case for ... never demolishing another building. Retrieved from https://www.theguardian.com/cities/2020/jan/13/the-case-for-never-demolishing-another-building
50. Williams F (2020) Virtuous circles: can reusing building materials in new projects go mainstream? Retrieved from https://www.architectsjournal.co.uk/news/virtuous-circles-can-reusing-building-materials-in-new-projects-go-mainstream

Chapter 7
Managerial and Public Policy Implications

The aim of this chapter is to discuss some of the managerial and policy implications deriving from the analysis of the CE at the micro-level. The former refers to measures private decision makers in firms can take in order to facilitate the uptake of circular practices in-house. The latter includes framework conditions and specific policies that public policy-makers can implement in order to encourage such uptake, by either activating the drivers or mitigating the barriers to their development or adoption.

7.1 Managerial Implications

Companies are increasingly looking for *win-win* solutions which simultaneously contribute to business competitiveness and better environmental results. This search is leading to innovative responses beyond waste or emissions management that, far from being an impediment, can create new circular opportunities. It has long been sensed and is now corroborated that environmental sustainability and firm competitiveness can be achieved simultaneously through innovations leading to lower environmental impacts of production or consumption activities (i.e. [1, 3, 10]). Today's boards of directors are increasingly exposed to strategic decisions related to the environment. It is the change in value chains and business models that ultimately lead to the transformation of the market towards a more sustainable path.

The general business response to these challenges has been to improve management controls through the implementation of environmental management systems (EMS). Beyond official certifications, EMS has become the dominant practice in environmental management globally. EMS-based incremental environmental management approaches now account for 70–90% of environmental technology expenditures and have focused primarily on waste management, energy expenditure and water consumption [3]. Procedures for the analysis of the life cycle

P. del Río et al., *The Circular Economy*, Green Energy and Technology,
https://doi.org/10.1007/978-3-030-74792-3_7

environmental impacts of products (*Life Cycle Analysis, LCA*) have gradually gained ground as an important part of environmental management standards, such as ISO 14000. However, the LCA often focuses on the environmental assessment of existing products. The results of these efforts towards the CE are significant efficiency gains in the short term, but in the long term, they may be less profitable and may lead to limited improvements in environmental performance [20].

Unlike these incremental LCA improvements, far-reaching environmental improvements can be achieved through more circular and strategic actions, aimed at supporting innovation in the early stages of a product development process, for example, in connection with the management of innovation (see UNE 166000 and CEN/TS 16555).

Beyond the above, the application of the principles of the CE implies the change of value chains and business models, which makes the transformation of the entire economy towards a new paradigm of a more sustainable system possible [19]. In all places and sectors, companies are beginning to incorporate CE principles into their processes.

The case studies presented in Chap. 6 provide some examples of how companies have materialized circular business opportunities and also offer an opportunity to reflect on how other companies can take forward their circular agenda and the drivers and barriers they are likely to face in so doing. Therefore, in the following paragraphs, we relate the lessons learnt from the case studies to the internal factors of the firm and, particularly, the resources, capabilities and competences (RCCs) introduced in Chap. 5 in order to infer some implications for company managers.

In-house knowledge and human resources

As mentioned in Chap. 5, firms with a strong knowledge base and R&D competences can help address circularity challenges but also possibly suffer inertia for change, especially when radical changes are needed. The greater the level of change is, the greater and more different the required skills of employees should be, but also the needed capacity for stakeholder integration (see below). The diversity of case studies shows that, indeed, existing in-house competences are valuable. For example, in the case of Herrenknecht and ECOALF, knowledge leadership is sought for. In case of start-ups like Rubicon, Too Good To Go and Madaster, the needed competences are acquired and suggest the importance of the ability of firms to attract talent. From the case studies, it is also clear that the knowledge base is not static but can be enhanced overtime. Herrenknecht, Ikea, Camper and Revov built the development of their circular solutions on organizational learning and experimentation to specifically acquire a sufficient knowledge base and experience which would allow them to refine the circular solution before scaling up the production. In the case of Herrenknecht, training their staff was relevant, because of a low availability of skilled personnel in the German labour market. The case of

Camper suggests that both innovation capabilities and organizational flexibility are key in developing circular business lines.

Financial resources

Both the financially healthy situation of the company as well as its capacity to acquire financing and attract new investors are often crucial for ensuring sufficient financial resources to develop and scale up the circular solutions. Again, greater changes also require larger capital outlays. Camper had to face large financial burdens of R&D and complexity of new production processes. Ikea, in turn, had to plan carefully before investing in new infrastructure. In the cases of Rebattery and Revov, the high need for financial resources was evident, especially since, despite cost advantages over new batteries, the clients require product guarantees. The growth path of Rubicon Global was largely facilitated by the top management contact networks and capacity to raise sufficient funding when entering in the markets with a potentially highly disruptive approach. The investors were attracted partly by the expected positive environmental impact but even more by the high growth expectations related to the scalable digital platform and business model. Similar dynamics are visible in the Madaster case. Therefore, both cases are strongly linked to the investor expectations on high growth.

Physical resources

The existence of an installed base can be a strong starting point, but also may turn out to be difficult to change. Hence, it is an important barrier to the adoption of CE innovations (see [17] for an in-depth analysis). Physical resources play a major role because an existing installed base can help address circularity challenges but may also act as a deterrent to systemic change. In the cases of Herrenknecht, Ikea and ECOALF, existing physical resources offered a baseline to develop the solutions, whereas start-ups like Rubicon, Too Good To Go, Revov and Madaster have been in the position to build from scratch and have come to the market with a radically different approach, without the risk of cannibalizing other business lines.

Reputation

It is well known that reputation takes years to build but days to lose. In the sphere of sustainability, firms are, in general, increasingly aware of the risks of greenwashing possibly turning against their business one day. Hence, they are rather cautious in their communication. Our case studies seem to validate this view. While firms like Camper, Ikea and ECOALF are aware of the positive link between circular practices and reputation, this is the result of constant efforts across the organization rather than a singular service or product. For instance, Kaspar Kraemer believes that its work on eco-architecture benefits its overall reputation in the architecture sector.

As a start-up, Rubicon Global is actively pursuing to position itself in the market as a sustainability leader and acquiring sustainability certificates as well as other third-party validation of their responsible practices. This indicates the strategic importance of building an excellent reputation. The Revov case shows that, in the specific case of repurposing, as it also occurs with reuse and recycling, a barrier faced by this type of products is the distrust of consumers, which also suggests the importance of building up a reputation.

Motivation and attitude (top management commitment)

The environmentally proactive attitude of managers in the firm is likely to facilitate the adoption of CE-related innovations. This is most visible in the case of start-ups launched with the mission to contribute to the CE. The founders working day to day in company operations transmit their commitment and values to other personnel and, thus, gradually create a favourable culture. For example, in the case of Rubicon Global, the top management commitment and environmental-friendly culture and attitude created the basis to align the company with investors and other stakeholders. The cases of ECOALF, Ikea, Too Good To Go and Madaster, for instance, emphasize the role of personal commitment and vision of the top management for the success of circular business. In Ikea and Camper, clear environmental and economic objectives have helped to frame the development of new circular solutions. It is increasingly understood that there is a positive relation between sustainability efforts and financial performance. When aligned with the company culture, the managers who explicitly commit to broad sustainability targets can gain broad support to their agenda. Beyond commitment, pushing forward the circular practices came up also in the case of Rebattery as a motivational factor for the personnel, who truly believe that they are making a difference. Revov was founded to capture part of an attractive market but also to encourage their customers to think green, according to its founders.

Networking (cooperation)

Cooperation with stakeholders encourages development and adoption of environmental innovations, including CE-related innovations. Substantial changes usually lead firms to collaborate with other stakeholders in the supply chain and emphasize the important role of networking and the capacity for stakeholder integration. The digital platforms like Rubicon, Too Good To Go and Madaster are specifically built to facilitate cooperation in their respective fields of application. In fact, without engaged stakeholders (users), such platforms are worthless. In the cases of Rubicon and Madister, in particular, the contacts of the management in the sector and investment community played a crucial role in establishing partnerships and a broad user ecosystem around the platforms.

In ECOALF, the collaboration with larger players for the provision of infrastructure and finance allowed the company to scale up operations. It is worth noting, however, that broad actor involvement, especially regarding recollection of plastic waste by fishermen, was a major barrier initially due to a lack of (economic) incentives. To establish a beneficial cooperation, Camper also had to overcome its low bargaining power with suppliers, limited market potential and logistical shortcomings (reverse logistics).

Lastly, the Revov case shows that in the circular practice of repurposing, as it also occurs with reuse and recycling, collaboration between public and private organizations becomes necessary in the development of technologies and procedures that allow for the exploitation of products at the end of their useful life.

Conclusions

The response of business to the challenges and opportunities of the CE requires a combination of changes in the management of firms. Therefore, the greatest challenge for managers is to develop a holistic strategic approach involving the different stakeholders, proactively managing their commitment to development in a way that creates synergies and avoids unpleasant surprises, for example, regarding the lack of user acceptance or institutional support. This holistic approach relates to the overall corporate environmental, social and governance (ESG) agenda. This invites us to reflect on how the role of the company and its processes, products and services are defined in line with the ambition of the CE.

Hence, dual management approaches to ensure positive incremental improvement and results, as well as more radical systemic changes for the long term are worth exploring. This requires a reasonable balance between standardization enabling cost reduction through economies of scale and maintaining a certain degree of diversity, which can be cheaper in a long-term ecological transition perspective, but maybe costlier in the short run.

The circular approaches offer invaluable guidance for companies to move beyond incremental improvements towards more radical sustainability solutions. To capture the major opportunities the CE offers for business, managers need to reimagine and redesign their operations, products and services and, overall, their relationship with other actors in society. The case studies in Chap. 5 suggest that the CE is actionable. Management can start with a single product line or even take CE as a guiding principle to build the whole business. In both cases, the market opportunities exist to pilot and test the developed solutions. When the response is positive, the managers should turn their focus to scale up the operations with a wider impact on their bottom line and the environment.

The CE calls for companies to modify their production and operation models and consider eco-design and the recovery of products that have reached the end of their useful life early on. It requires closing the cycle and designing a reverse logistics system to recover products which reached the end of their useful life. It may also offer opportunities for more substantial changes in their business models and even for the dematerialization of value creation. Unlike incremental improvements, far-reaching environmental enhancements can be achieved through more fundamental and strategic actions. With this, it would be possible to transform business models and related organizations. To really take advantage of this opportunity, the CE should be based more on a system change, which requires a more radical transformation, rather than on incremental improvements from the current situation.

7.2 Public Policy Implications

There is a widespread agreement that public policies remain crucial in driving countries towards a full CE implementation [2, 11, 23]. Policy-makers play a particularly relevant role in creating the enabling conditions for the CE [7].

The CE has undeniably reached a top place in the agenda of many governments around the world. For example, the European Union and its Member States have engaged in the CE with the aim of achieving and maintaining industrial and economic leadership and recognizing opportunities for growth by overcoming the traditional dichotomy between economic growth and environmental protection. The EU's CE Package of 2015, which includes the European Commission Action Plan on the Circular Economy [9], emphasizes the core goals for the continent with regards to economic functioning (durability, reparability and recyclability of products) and has several priority areas (plastics, food waste, critical raw materials, construction and demolition, biomass and bio-based products). As such, the EU's perspective is to redesign production and consumption processes in order to increase circularity and sustainability. The CE Package was regarded as part of the vision of the European Commission to make the CE a key cornerstone of future EU industrial policy and for "developing Europe's future economic model", with the ambition to make Europe a "world leader in CE and clean technologies" [26]. On the other hand, China adopted a CE Plan in 2008 [22, 29]. The CE policy strategy followed by China seems to be less economically oriented and is focused on mitigating direct health and environmental threats to its population. A new Circular Economy Action Plan has recently been adopted in the EU, which includes legislative and non-legislative measures to promote circular initiatives along the entire life cycle of products [8].

The CE is evidently on the policy-makers' table and closing cycles as well as encouraging its uptake at different levels (macro/meso/micro) is a considerable challenge in this regard. This would require designing policies which take into account the different barriers to the CE. In turn, this would lead to the implementation of a combination of policies. The question is no longer whether policies and policy mixes should be designed for a CE, but *how* to effectively and efficiently do so.

In the following, we propose a set of specific guidelines to orient CE policies in a coherent manner, leading to an effective and efficient policy mix for the CE. These guidelines are sought to be adjustable to individual policy-maker's situations and objectives.

The starting assumption is that appropriate policies in almost any realm, but certainly in the area of the CE as well, include several blocks of decisions or policy components: an appropriate policy approach, adequate framework conditions, specific instruments and the design elements within these instruments. These blocks need to be consistent, coherent and aligned to the policy goals and the context where they are implemented. Each represents a sine-qua-non condition, i.e. a missing block would simply lead to a failure to implement an effective and efficient CE policy.

A comprehensive, systemic and holistic policy approach

First of all, and before any policy measures are implemented, an appropriate vision for the CE needs to be adopted by policy-makers. This should be a systemic, holistic and comprehensive one. Thorough policy-making needs to understand the underlying premises of the problem and target its relevant aspects.

In particular, it should be taken into account that, as stressed in Chap. 5, the drivers and barriers to the uptake of CE practices are not isolated from each other, but interact sometimes in complex ways, leading to synergies, complementarities and conflicts. Policy-makers should take into account these interactions.

Generally, the recognition that there are several drivers and barriers suggests the adoption of different types of policy interventions (i.e. a policy mix) which activate the drivers or mitigate the barriers. Such a systemic, holistic perspective has been followed at both policy-making and academic levels. Regarding the former, the 2015 Action Plan envisages a mix of policy futures across all stages of the product life cycle, with the aim of ensuring resource efficiency in a holistic manner [28]. At an academic level, Hartley et al. [15, p. 3] argue that "a mix of complementary policies with a systemic perspective can generate collective efforts towards systemic transformation".

Policy style: A cooperative policy approach

As in other policy areas, cooperation between different actors is crucial for the successful implementation of policy measures. This cooperation refers to collaboration between policy-makers and other stakeholders (most importantly, firms and consumers) and also between different government departments.

On the one hand, stakeholders on multiple levels, both public and private, should be engaged [27]. This can be done through constant consultations. Hartley et al. [15, p. 3] find out that the stakeholders interviewed in his study supported a collaborative and bottom-up approach to set standards.

On the other hand, policy-makers in different policy areas should cooperate "so that no new unintended policy barriers are created and—like the business solution—the policy response is designed to maximise system effectiveness" [7, p. 14]. This could be done by setting groups across governments or government departments [27].

Policy framework conditions for the CE

Policy should provide an enabling regulatory framework that encourages innovation and adoption of CE practices. Beyond specific instruments, there are two crucial conditions for the success of policies which aim to promote the CE: the existence of targets and the stability of the policy.

Tangible and quantifiable targets on circular practices should be set [27]. This is true in any policy-induced sector and even more in those capital-intensive sectors which, in addition, require high up-front investments which take time to pay off. Setting short-term, medium-term and long-term targets provides the necessary signal for potential investors to encourage long-term circular investments in all the stages of the value chain.

On the other hand, policy stability is often cited as a critical enabler of investments in eco-innovations in general [3, 5] and low-carbon technologies such as renewable energy technologies [4] in particular. A country where policies are constantly changing, especially retroactively or retrospectively, is unattractive to invest in CE innovations. However, stability should not mean policy rigidity, i.e. that some changes in certain design elements cannot be modified in response to changing circumstances or to detected drawbacks of the policies (policy learning). Thus, some degree of policy flexibility should be allowed, but no sudden "change in direction" should be imposed [24].

Policy instruments

Within a wider set of a well-defined framework, objectives and plans, individual policy instruments can be implemented to achieve specific targets effectively and efficiently. Different types of instruments may be useful in this context. They include collaboration platforms, internalization of environmental externalities (through the fiscal system), public procurement, information provision and RD&D support, among others.

Instruments can be designed to activate certain drivers towards the CE or mitigate certain barriers. Instruments are implemented in a certain context and level, such as an industrial sector, a type of CE activity (e.g., the Rs) or a product or process level. Instruments translate, for each specific case, the objectives into specific steps to be taken by economic actors. As such, they encourage firms and consumers to adjust their behaviour accordingly.

The literature provides different broad categories of instruments (demand-pull vs. supply-push, command-and-control (CAC) vs. market-based instruments). However, whereas those instruments are helpful to address some of the problems to the uptake of the CE, the range of the potentially useful policy interventions to encourage the CE is much broader, given the existence of several drivers and barriers to the CE. The following paragraphs provide a brief description of these instruments and discuss how they tackle specific barriers.

- *Command-and-control (CAC) regulations: regulations and standards.*
  Although CAC regulation is usually not very popular among environmental economists, governments could pass product, process and waste regulations. The former would include requirements for longer product lifetimes and an easier repair and recyclability of products, whereas process regulations would refer to requirements to continuously increase energy and material efficiency in production processes [16, p. 9]. Waste regulations would encompass collection

and treatment standards and targets, the definition of waste, extended producer responsibility and take-back systems [7, p. 47].

- *Information to consumers and managers.*
  Measures tackling the supply-side of the CE (firms) needs to be complemented with measures to address the demand-side, e.g. encourage consumers and citizens to demand and follow circular products and practices. As argued by Horbach and Rammer [16, p. 9], demand needs to acknowledge circular innovations "through a higher propensity to buy or a higher willingness to pay for CE-based products". However, policies need to combat the inertia of consumers, who have a tendency to stick to the products they know and may have difficulties to shift to new, more circular products. Several instruments may address this driver/barrier. Eco-labels and information campaigns to raise awareness of the economic, environmental and social benefits of a transition towards the CE may be useful to change behaviours (of citizens and consumers) towards circularity. Education is also a powerful driver of behavioural changes in the long term, and thus, CE thinking should be integrated into school and university curricula [7, 21].
  In addition, the case studies in Chap. 6 of this book suggest that top-level commitment is a key driver of the uptake of CE practices. Acceptance of this new model requires changing the mentality of companies with regards to their involvement in CE activities [11]. Thus, managers of firms should be aware of the potential benefits that the implementation of the CE in their company may bring and could be the target of information policies. For example, policy-makers can "emphasize that 'it pays to be circular' by stressing the economic benefits that a more circular business model can provide" [14, p. 324].
- *Public provision.*
  Governments can generate a significant demand-pull for CE products and processes through their purchases of goods and services with particular specifications (contributions to environmental sustainability, closing of cycles, etc. …). This is broadly referred to as "sustainable public procurement" [15, p. 2]. In addition, they can support the CE through their investments in infrastructure [7]. Reike et al. [25, p. 259] stress that the state can act as a role model and, through its public procurement, "should be first in going beyond low hanging fruits and incur more efforts to seriously measure the sustainability impacts to demonstrate viability, increase legitimacy and thereby scalability of CE". Ghisellini et al. [12, p. 19] highlight the importance of public procurement (accounting for 1/5 of EU27 GDP in 2009) in stimulating the uptake of more environmentally friendly products and services. They also stress the institutional barriers to this instrument worldwide and the need for a coherent international set of agreed indicators to monitor and evaluate green public procurement activities.
- *Use of the price system through fiscal measures.*
  Traditional market-based instruments of environmental policy (taxes or cap-and-trade systems) will continue to be useful to internalize environmental externalities but also to change relative prices (e.g. of products using secondary

and virgin materials), making circular practices more attractive with respect to linear ones. More direct, targeted interventions through the fiscal system are recommendable to accelerate the uptake of the CE. Some EU Member States already use taxation as a steering mechanism towards the CE, i.e. by applying tax reductions for desirable circular activities such as reparation. In this context, several authors advocate the use of value-added tax (VAT) to favour (more) circular products and discourage (more) linear ones. For example, Hartley et al. [15, p. 3] propose a higher VAT for linear-based products and a lower one for reused products and those having a certain percentage of recycled content. Similarly, the Ellen MacArthur Foundation [7, p. 47] puts forward a VAT or excise duty reductions for circular products and services and suggests that taxes should be shifted from labour to resources (e.g. in the framework of an ecological tax reform). Kirchherr et al. [18] also propose a reduced VAT for reparation and, simultaneously, the reduction of subsidies that favour linear products. The World Business Council for Sustainable Development (WBCSD) [27, p. 9] provides an interesting case from China, where VAT policy creates tax incentives for multiple sectors (e.g. paper, tyres, cement and food). China VAT policy stipulates tax refund opportunities for products containing recycled content. This has led to behavioural changes, for example, in the use of waste tires in the Chinese automotive industry [27].

- *Promotion of networking.*
  Involvement in networks is often considered in the literature on innovation and eco-innovation as an important tool to access new knowledge developed by others and, thus, for innovation. Thus, networks for innovation and knowledge exchange between universities, research centres, civil society, firms and governments could be created, as these networks favour the exchange of circular experiences, knowledge and techniques [21, 27]. This can be done by promoting public–private partnerships with companies and voluntary industry collaboration platforms, encouraging value chain and cross-sectoral initiatives and information sharing [7, p. 47]. The WBCSD [27, p. 18] proposes to establish centres for knowledge-sharing, which facilitate exchanges among traditionally unrelated sectors and promote "knowledge transfer from potential expert experience to nascent circular policy-building. The sharing of knowledge and coalitions formed will lead to new ideas and innovative solutions that connect stakeholders and accelerate effective strategy and implementation".
- *Development of circular trading platforms.*
  Virtual platforms which connect post-production, pre-consumer and post-consumer excess materials to reuse and recycling markets, as it is the case of The Netherlands' Circle Market, could be implemented through fund-matching schemes and tax breaks for new and existing platforms and VAT exemption for products and resources sold through such platforms [15, pp. 4–5].
- *Support for R&D investments.*
  Directly supporting R&D with grants and tax relief measures to research centres and companies can also make an important contribution to the CE. Public R&D

is a main source of innovation and an important complement to private R&D. Public policies for R&D with a focus on the CE should be designed and implemented, since the CE requires technological innovation which allows closing loops through new materials, more efficient processes based on artificial intelligence and the use of clean energy, among others [21, p. 36].

- *Direct financial and technical support for companies.*
  Financial or technical support to companies for the development or adoption of CE innovations can be justified, particularly in the case of SMEs. This could include direct subsidies, provision of capital, financial guarantees (financial support) or advisory and training and demonstration of best practices to business (technical support) [7]. The role of finance in the CE has been researched by Ghisetti and Montresor [13]. The authors warn policy-makers to take into consideration that traditional finance is not a decisive barrier to the CE, that both internal (equity) and external (debt) financing are significant drivers, that public funding is also relevant and that alternative (new) forms of financing are even a barrier to the CE. They recommend policy-makers to adjust their funding schemes for the CE among SMEs and to promote external (debt), public and internal (equity) financing (in that order) [13].
- *Removal of administrative hurdles.*
  Administrative barriers are often considered an important obstacle to the CE, particularly for SMEs. As argued by García-Quevedo et al. [11, p. 11], "the transition towards the CE implies a complex set of administrative and legal procedures stemming from environmental legislation that frequently requires SMEs to dedicate excessive financial and time resources to addressing them". Many authors have proposed to address this hurdle by simplifying compliance/implementation approaches [27], streamlining administrative procedures and permits [24] and implementing less strict and simpler legislative frameworks, particularly for SMEs [11].
- *Specific instruments for SMEs.*
  Overall, governments must address the specificities of SMEs and the concrete policy-related barriers they encounter in their efforts to implement the CE. SMEs are a highly relevant part of the economic fabric everywhere, but several barriers impact them in an stronger manner than it is the case of their larger counterparts: lack of access to finance, low technological competencies to introduce and absorb eco-innovations, low priority assigned to environmental matters, not viewing environmental actions within their responsibility, not perceiving clear benefits to eco-innovation, the lack of support from demand and supply networks, lack of financial resources and know-how and administrative burden [6, p. 1610] are often cited by the eco-innovation and CE literatures as stronger barriers for SMEs to carry out CE activities. For those actors, mitigating often-complex administrative procedures (as mentioned before) and providing a solid and stable legal framework may be among the policy priorities. Stimulation of demand for circular solutions by the government, either directly

through public procurement or public–private partnerships, or indirectly, can potentiate the efforts undertaken by SMEs.

The findings of Demirel and Danisman [6] on the uptake of eco-innovations in SMEs emphasize the importance of eco-design as the sole circular EI that produces significant growth returns for SMEs, and thus, they indicate that there is a need to raise the eco-design capabilities of SMEs. This is in line with prior literature that suggests SMEs are more likely to focus on and benefit from product innovations as opposed to process innovations. Their findings suggest that the "current grant funding strategies of European governments are not working efficiently for the CE and require rethinking to ensure that governments can provide the right amounts of funding through visionary strategies to boost green entrepreneurship" [6, p. 1615].

Design elements for instruments

Regarding the specifications of each policy instrument and, thus, of policy mixes, different design choices are available to policy-makers in order to achieve the specific aims of the instrument. Design elements represent the lowest level of granularity in policy measures, and following the traditional dictum that "the devil lies in the details", the success of particular instruments depends on the choice of design elements. Design elements fall into different categories, and usually, for each category, there are different alternatives. For example, there might be ten categories of design elements, for category 1, a given instrument can be designed with either a design element A or B, in category 2, the choice is between design elements C, D or E and so on and so forth. Therefore, the design elements for the CE should follow the consistency and congruence that is required for instruments, although some changes in those design elements should be allowed in order to facilitate flexibility in policy-making. In fact, the requirement for stability of the policy should be relaxed as we move to lower levels of the policy hierarchy: long-term stability of the overall policy framework (including targets) should be required, but a bit more flexibility for changes in instruments and even more for design elements should be allowed.

Challenges, tensions and conflicts in the policy mix

The simultaneous application of the aforementioned instruments would lead to a policy mix. As stressed by the Ellen MacArthur Foundation [7, p. 3], "within each sector, effective CE policymaking requires the combination of many policy interventions, and does not rely on a 'silver bullet' or blanket solutions". When several individual policy instruments are in place, or a specific policy subject is covered by different policy instruments, close attention must be paid to avoid conflicting signals. Policy mixes must be carefully designed so that each instrument is complementary or even synergistic to the others. However, the policy-maker must be aware that there might not only be synergies and complementarities between the instruments, but also conflicts. In particular, they must take into account that trade-offs between instruments may exist and they should try to mitigate those conflicts.

Conclusions

The discussion above suggests a set of recommendations to orient CE policies per level (micro, meso and macro).

At the *micro-level*, economic actors (firms) and consumers are highly innovative when enough room for experimentation is given under a stable legal framework. In most sectors, policy focus should therefore be on providing adequate conditions instead of external policy micro-management. In other words, policies should focus on the framework, general goals and targets and not only on the details of products and processes (e.g. micro-management), since firms are better equipped to take the decision on the development and adoption of innovations (see, e.g., the construction sector case study). Specific initiatives should promote eco-design, cleaner production, resource and energy efficiency with specific instruments. Monitoring and reporting should be supported and fiscal incentives for circular practices (and disincentives for linear ones) should be provided.

At the *meso-level*, coordination of involved actors seems crucial. Independently of how circular eco-innovations are developed (individual firms, groups or networks), they need to be diffused into the market to be successful and have a meaningful impact with regards to the CE. This wider diffusion is very difficult for some economic agents, especially for smaller ones. Public policy may play a key enabling role in this context by scaling up initiatives, coordinating functions in regional clusters or networks or providing local or regional public procurement. Also, a solid legal framework for secondary materials is needed.

Finally, at the *macro* and national economy levels, it should be taken into account that circular eco-innovations take place in a wider institutional context. Here, financing for eco-innovation development or adoption is crucial. Policy-makers could definitively assure a constant and stable supply of finance for those eco-innovative activities through, e.g., soft loans. Taxation can contribute to shift economic activity away from linear and to circular economic activities. Funding of large-scale RD&D programmes (such as the EU's Horizon Europe) and public procurement at the national level also have an important role to play. Data on national economy levels for all mayor activities and sectors should be collected. The development of indicators allows checking for progress made with respect to the specific targets.

Overall complementary recommendations can also be provided. First, at the level of framework conditions, aims should be connected with strategic plans and policy action, leading to a policy package that is coherent as a whole. Second, at the level of instruments, it is important to use prices to encourage the uptake of circular practices, both by producers and consumers. Consistent and stable price signals can spur innovation by all stakeholders and economic agents. Third, a constant monitoring and measurement of status and progress is required. Finally, adjustments should be made where necessary within a stable and foreseeable legal framework.

References

1. Boons F, McMeekin A (2019) Handbook of sustainable innovation. Edward Elgar, Cheltenham, UK
2. Cainelli G, D'Amato A, Mazzanti M (2020) Resource efficient eco-innovations for a circular economy: evidence from EU firms. Res Policy 49(1):1–11. https://doi.org/10.1016/j.respol.2019.103827
3. Carrillo-Hermosilla J, del Río P, Könnölä T (2009) Eco-innovation: when sustainability and competitiveness shake hands. Palgrave Macmillan, Hampshire
4. del Río P, Ragwitz M, Steinhilber S, Resch G, Busch S, Klessmann C et al (2012) Key policy approaches for a harmonisation of RES(-E) support in Europe—main options and design elements. A report compiled within the European research project beyond2020 (work package 2). Supported by Intelligent Energy—Europe, ALTENER (Grant Agreement no. IEE/10/437/SI2.589880). Retrieved from www.res-policy-beyond2020.eu
5. del Río P, Carrillo-Hermosilla J, Totti K (2010) Policy strategies to promote an integrated framework. An integrated framework. J Ind Ecol 14:541–557. https://doi.org/10.1111/j.1530-9290.2010.00259.x
6. Demirel P, Danisman GO (2019) Eco-innovation and firm growth in the circular economy: Evidence from European small- and medium-sized enterprises. Bus Strategy Environ. https://doi.org/10.1002/bse.2336
7. Ellen MacArthur Foundation (2015) Delivering the circular economy: a toolkit for policymakers. Delivering the circular economy: a toolkit for policymakers, vol 177. https://doi.org/10.1038/531435a
8. European Commission (2020) EU Circular Economy Action Plan. A new Circular Economy Action Plan for a Cleaner and More Competitive Europe. https://ec.europa.eu/environment/circular-economy/
9. European Commission (2015) Closing the loop—an EU action plan for the circular economy. Retrieved from Brussels: https://ec.europa.eu/environment/circular-economy/index_en.htm
10. Fussler C, James P (1996) A breakthrough discipline for innovation and sustainability. Pitman Publishing, London
11. García-Quevedo J, Jové-Llopis E, Martínez-Ros E (2020) Barriers to the circular economy in European small and medium-sized firms. Bus Strategy Environ. https://doi.org/10.1002/bse.2513
12. Ghisellini P, Cialani C, Ulgiati S (2016) A review on circular economy: the expected transition to a balanced interplay of environmental and economic systems. J Clean Prod 114:11–32. https://doi.org/10.1016/j.jclepro.2015.09.007
13. Ghisetti C, Montresor S (2020) On the adoption of circular economy practices by small and medium-size enterprises (SMEs): does "financing-as-usual" still matter? J Evol Econ 30(2): 559–586. https://doi.org/10.1007/s00191-019-00651-w
14. Gusmerotti NM, Testa F, Corsini F, Pretner G, Iraldo F (2019) Drivers and approaches to the circular economy in manufacturing firms. J Clean Prod 230:314–327. https://doi.org/10.1016/j.jclepro.2019.05.044
15. Hartley K, van Santen R, Kirchherr J (2020) Policies for transitioning towards a circular economy: expectations from the European Union (EU). Resour Conserv Recycl 155:104634. https://doi.org/10.1016/j.resconrec.2019.104634
16. Horbach J, Rammer C (2019) Circular economy innovations, growth and employment at the firm level: empirical evidence from Germany. J Ind Ecol 24(3):615–625. https://doi.org/10.1111/jiec.12977
17. Kiefer CP, Río P, Carrillo-Hermosilla J (2021) On the contribution of eco-innovation features to a circular economy: a microlevel quantitative approach. Bus Strategy Environ:1–17. https://doi.org/10.1002/bse.2688

18. Kirchherr J, Piscicelli L, Bour R, Kostense-Smit E, Muller J, Huibrechtse-Truijens A, Hekkert M (2018) Barriers to the circular economy: evidence from the European Union (EU). Ecol Econ 150:264–272. https://doi.org/10.1016/j.ecolecon.2018.04.028
19. Kirchherr J, Reike D, Hekkert M (2017) Conceptualizing the circular economy: an analysis of 114 definitions. Resour Conserv Recycl 127:221–232. https://doi.org/10.1016/j.resconrec.2017.09.005
20. Könnölä T, Mulet J, Aguirre M, Corcho O, Davara F, Egea E et al (2020) Hacia la economía circular inteligente—El papel de la digitalización. Retrieved from http://espanadigital.org/hacia-la-economia-circular-inteligente-el-papel-de-la-digitalizacion/
21. Martínez Cerna L, Henríquez Aravena H, Freire Castello N, Rodríguez Urrutia R (2019) Economía circular y políticas públicas. Estado del arte y desafíos para la construcción de un marco político de promoción de economía circular en América Latina. Centro de Innovación y Economía Circular (CIEC) y Programa Regional Seguridad Energética y Cambio Climático en América Latina (EKLA). Lima (Peru)
22. Mathews JA, Tan H (2011) Progress toward a circular economy in China. J Ind Ecol 15(3): 435–457. https://doi.org/10.1111/j.1530-9290.2011.00332.x
23. Moktadir MA, Rahman T, Rahman MH, Ali SM, Paul SK (2018) Drivers to sustainable manufacturing practices and circular economy: a perspective of leather industries in Bangladesh. J Clean Prod 174:1366–1380. https://doi.org/10.1016/j.jclepro.2017.11.063
24. Reichardt K, Rogge KS, Negro SO (2017) Unpacking policy processes for addressing systemic problems in technological innovation systems: the case of offshore wind in Germany. Renew Sustain Energy Rev 80:1217–1226. https://doi.org/10.1016/j.rser.2017.05.280
25. Reike D, Vermeulen WJV, Witjes S (2018) The circular economy: new or refurbished as CE 3.0?—exploring controversies in the conceptualization of the circular economy through a focus on history and resource value retention options. Resour Conserv Recycl 135:246–264. https://doi.org/10.1016/j.resconrec.2017.08.027
26. Rizos V, Behrens A, van der Gaast W, Hofman E, Ioannou A, Kafyeke T, Topi C (2016) Implementation of circular economy business models by small and medium-sized enterprises (SMEs): barriers and enablers. Sustainability 8(11):1–18. https://doi.org/10.3390/su8111212
27. WBCSD (2019) Policy enablers to accelerate the circular economy. Scaling up actions across regions and stakeholders. Retrieved from https://www.wbcsd.org/Programs/Circular-Economy/Factor-10/Resources/Policy-enablers-to-accelerate-the-circular-economy
28. Whicher A, Harris C, Beverley K, Swiatek P (2018) Design for circular economy: developing an action plan for Scotland. J Clean Prod 172:3237–3248. https://doi.org/10.1016/j.jclepro.2017.11.009
29. Yuan Z, Bi J, Moriguichi Y (2006) The circular economy: a new development strategy in China. J Ind Ecol 10:4–8

Chapter 8
Conclusions

Sustainability and competitiveness have long been the subject of debate, and it has become clear by now that they can be achieved at the same time, creating a win-win situation for businesses and the environment. In this context, the circular economy (CE) draws a desirable future end state of an economic system that is fully circular, sustainable and also competitive. It stands thus in the tradition of related earlier sustainability concepts. Many academic, policy and private debates recognize that the current way of living is not sustainable. Since the eighties of the past century, science has addressed the issue of "(un-)sustainability".

Sustainable development highlights the need to understand the interrelatedness of the economic, social and ecological dimensions of sustainability, which need to be balanced. This basic idea of sustainability has created awareness in society and influenced both the public policy and private business practices around the globe at an increasing pace. This has built the ground for the wider buy-in for operative approaches to develop win-win solutions towards greater sustainability. A decade ago, in our book on eco-innovation [1] we, in parallel to several other scholars and practitioners, already pinpointed the importance of innovation for change and specifically for redirecting existing production and consumption patterns to reduce their negative environmental impacts.

More recently, with the rhetoric of redesigning the economy in an innovative way, the concept of CE has attracted the interest of decision-makers from both business and policy. The CE outlines the basic functioning of an ideal economic system that respects the fundamentals of sustainable development and generates, as a consequence, a harmonic state between social, ecological and economic systems. As the concept promises simultaneous benefits in all these systems, it is indeed desirable to achieve the CE. Also, the CE has been able to create a positive outlook for economic development and societal momentum.

In this book, we focus on the actors at the micro-level (firms and other organizations) as the motors of change through innovation and assess the drivers and barriers for circular practices of firms as well as their implications for business

P. del Río et al., *The Circular Economy*, Green Energy and Technology,
https://doi.org/10.1007/978-3-030-74792-3_8

leaders and public policy-makers. Furthermore, we propose a policy framework with instruments which encourage the uptake of CE practices.

The book provides a broad view of the CE, contextualizing it in the wider discussion on sustainability. It assumes that the CE is a construct of several components and it is instrumental in facilitating a transition towards sustainability. While both the aims of the CE, its hierarchical levels and the associated general CE-related actions are relatively well-defined, most CE theorizing is silent on specific tools for involved actors (producers and consumers as economic actors, and policy-makers as transition-encompassing and guiding actors). Many suggested guidelines towards CE identify concrete actions or tools, but it is often not clear what involved actors can do in practice. Some authors address this issue and "connect" CE to other concepts such as business models, firm strategy and eco-innovation. They make use of other concepts and their tools to operationalize the CE for economic actors.

Thus, this book relates the CE to a range of other concepts in the realm of sustainability and provides an integrated analysis of the CE in the wider context of sustainability transitions. Among all related concepts, we have argued that the CE is included in the broader concept of eco-innovation. The latter offers a more overarching approach for policy by connecting with the ecological, social and economic dimensions of sustainable development. From a firm perspective, eco-innovation offers specific and action-oriented implications that can be realized within innovation-related toolsets in firms.

Our focus on eco-innovations does not intend to downplay the importance of the CE concept. On the contrary, it is our aim to help firms and policy-makers address the CE and to translate rather general discussions about sustainability and basic economic principles into actionable firm strategy and projects. In this way, we intended to put the CE into the reach of firms, so that these can pursue CE projects with their resources and competences and generate benefit for the users of their products and services, and also for the environment and society. That is, in short, the aim is to address simultaneously the economic, environmental and social systems.

The book contextualizes the concept of CE within eco-innovation by connecting them to systemic thinking developed around industrial ecology and several other concepts. Eco-innovation focuses on individual projects, i.e. business models, processes, products and services. It also helps to consider how different activities, even in different sectors, can establish symbiosis in emerging industrial parks of interrelated businesses and resource, material, water and energy flows. The concepts of cradle-to-cradle and regenerative design, among others, contribute to discussions on how sustainability can move forward from only reducing the negative impacts to maximizing positive impacts and exploring new ways to regenerate and restore the livelihood and service performance of ecosystems.

After exploring the diverse definitions, taxonomies and classifications on the CE, we conclude that it is a two-sided concept: it is inspired by sustainable development, insofar as the CE is a **vision** of how an economic system can be ideally sustainable, practically based on closed cycles of physical resource and energy flows at different hierarchical levels and by different actors, in which after each original use, subsequent use maintains or enhances the resource-based economic value and creates or enhances environmental and social value. The CE vision of clos*ed* cycles and retain*ed* value is connected to being an **instrument** which contributes to sustainable development and which involves a rupture with the current state of the linear economy. The instrumental part of the CE is embedded in the eco-innovation concept and refers to the subset of practices which are related to closing cycles and retaining value.

Furthermore, the CE is a multi-level **systemic** approach, which can be applied at the micro-level (products, companies, consumers), meso-level (inter-firm networks, symbiosis association, (eco)-industrial parks, green supply chain management) and macro-level (city, province, region, nation and beyond). Also, different **hierarchies** of circular practices have been proposed. The most simple, popular and easy to remember hierarchy is the 3Rs (reduction, reusing and recycling). Other hierarchies are more detailed, such as the 9Rs or the 10Rs. The systemic and hierarchical approaches are not isolated from each other.

The focus of this book is on the micro-level of the CE, i.e. on the companies and their efforts to improve processes and develop eco-innovations to "close the loop". Several types of CE practices (or circular eco-innovations) can be implemented in firms, including eco-design and cleaner production strategies, resource efficiency initiatives and sustainable production and consumption methods.

Towards this end, we elaborate a conceptual framework on the drivers and barriers to CE practices to be applied in the case analyses at the micro-level. In addition to the internal and external drivers, determinants of adoption are included to take into account the specificities of circular eco-innovations. Our case studies across different firms, sectors and countries highlight that different drivers and barriers exist and, in some cases, they illustrate how these interact with each other.

The response of business to the challenges and opportunities of the CE requires a combination of changes in firms comprising existing and new resources and competences embedded in adequate business models and management set-ups. The firms under study have developed both incremental and radical circular eco-innovations. Incremental circular eco-innovations are more compatible with the linear way of doing business and can more easily be embedded in existing firm infrastructure and business, whereas radical circular eco-innovations require and are based on much more fundamental changes in the firm. They have a much higher inherent risk, most prominently of financial nature, but have the potential to contribute much more to the goals of sustainable development and the CE. In the case studies analysed in this book, the firms have introduced a significant amount of such innovations, highlighting that companies are indeed a significant motor of change.

While firms are generally capable to develop new technology, products, business models or networks that allow them to successfully realize circular eco-innovations, the motivation and commitment of managers and the staff are key factors for success. Existing knowledge and technology bases as well as customer awareness allow the firms to identify and exploit new business opportunities. However, most firms struggle with cost and investment issues, especially in early market stages and in attempts of upscaling towards larger markets. Public policy may be a driver, but also a significant barrier, as shown in some of our case studies, when policies for the CE are either non-existent or only partially or incoherently addressing CE-related issues. Some firms state that they are even affected by non-CE-policies that have "side effects" on circular eco-innovations. This understanding of drivers and barriers, as well as the fact that some barriers are out of reach for firms, has allowed us to derive managerial and policy implications in order to better adapt the CE at the micro-level.

Public policy-makers play a particularly relevant role in creating the enabling conditions for the CE. At the *micro-level*, policies should focus on the provision of suitable framework conditions to meet general goals and targets, rather than defining the details of products and processes (e.g. micro-management), since firms are better equipped to decide on the development and adoption of innovations. At the *meso-level*, the coordination of involved actors is critical. Public policy may also play an enabling role in scaling up initiatives in regional clusters or networks. Finally, at the *macro-* and national economy levels, financing and taxation, among other measures, can drive economic activity away from linear to circular economic activities. Those levels are related, and the aforementioned measures at the macro- and meso-levels have impacts on the incentives of firms to develop or adopt CE practices. This book has developed a policy framework with instruments which encourage the uptake of CE practices and suggests a set of recommendations to orient CE policies per level (micro, meso and macro).

The CE is a useful concept to address sustainability and competitiveness, being able to create and maintain widespread public interest and action, particularly among businesses and policy-makers. With this book, we aspire to contribute to the CE by embedding it in the academically strong concepts of sustainable development (vision) and, especially, eco-innovation (instrument). As we wrote in the introduction about our journey on exploring win-win solutions, we firmly continue to believe in the role of firms as the motors of change in production and consumption systems towards environmental, economic and social progress.

To conclude, we welcome further engagement of humanities and social sciences to seek interconnections between the CE and other related concepts, and jointly elaborate more nuanced and inclusive guidance for action. In a similar vein, major opportunities lie in the intersections of different areas, technologies and business sectors that invite practitioners to bravely cross any frontiers for a more circular, innovative and sustainable future.

Reference

1. Carrillo-Hermosilla J, del Río González P, Könnölä T (2009) Eco-innovation: When sustainability and competitiveness shake hands. In Eco-Innovation: When Sustainability and Competitiveness Shake Hands. https://doi.org/10.1057/9780230244856

Made in United States
Orlando, FL
25 June 2026

83334177R10109